essential

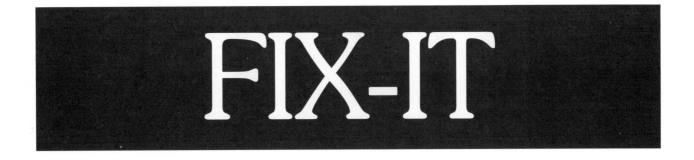

FIX-IT

essential

FIX-IT

Everything You Need to Make
Repairs Around the House

Yvonne Jeffery

Adams Media
Avon, Massachusetts

To my parents, who always knew I could

Published by Adams Media, an F+W Publications Company
57 Littlefield Street, Avon, MA 02322 U.S.A.
www.adamsmedia.com

ISBN: 1-59869-074-4
Printed by KHL Printing Co Pte Ltd, in Singapore

J I H G F E D C B A

This publication is designed to provide accurate and authoritative information with regard to the subject matter covered. It is sold with the understanding that the publisher is not engaged in rendering legal, accounting, or other professional advice. If legal advice or other expert assistance is required, the services of a competent professional person should be sought.
—From a *Declaration of Principles* jointly adopted by a Committee of the American Bar Association and a Committee of Publishers and Associations

Many of the designations used by manufacturers and sellers to distinguish their products are claimed as trademarks. Where those designations appear in this book and Adams Media was aware of a trademark claim, the designations have been printed with initial capital letters.

Important Safety Notice

Readers are urged to take all appropriate precautions when undertaking any fix-it task. Always read and follow instructions and safety warnings for all tools and materials, and call in a professional if the repair stretches your abilities too far. Although every effort has been made to provide the best possible information in this book, neither the publisher nor the author are responsible for accidents, injuries, or damage incurred as a result of repairs undertaken by readers. This book is not a substitute for professional repair services.

Previously published as The Everything® Fix-it book
Copyright ©2004, F+W Publications, Inc.

Contents

Acknowledgments

There are many people who helped make this book possible, and I appreciate this opportunity to thank them. First, Dad, for reading every word . . . and Mum and Dad, my sister Lorraine, and my British cheerleading contingent, for your unwavering support, love, and understanding.

I also owe a great deal to my writer colleagues and truly wonderful friends, Judith, Katharine, Laura, and Linda, who have laughed and cried (but mostly laughed) with me almost daily—and who have put me back together more times than I can count.

For technical advice, my gratitude goes to Rocco and Dan, along with Don and Walter, in Calgary, for sharing both power tools and expertise.

On the publishing side, many thanks to my agent Barb and all the folks at Adams Media, including my editor Eric, for your guidance, enthusiasm, and encouragement.

Top Ten Reasons
to Fix It Yourself

1. Fixing it yourself means not paying to have it fixed for you.

2. Safety, as an important part of your regular maintenance schedule, protects both your home and your family.

3. Your friends and family will be impressed with your new skills (they may even let you borrow their tools!).

4. There's nothing like the feeling of satisfaction when you realize that—because of your efforts—your leaky faucet isn't leaking any more.

5. Maintaining a safe and efficient home protects your most valuable investment.

6. You'll soon be exchanging helpful hints with the friendly people you'll meet at your local home improvement store.

7. Fixing small problems yourself helps to prevent them from becoming large problems that will require expert—and expensive—solutions.

8. Knowing the ins and outs of home repair will help you recognize when you need professional help and how much it should cost.

9. Easy fix-it tasks such as weatherproofing and insulating can make a big difference to your energy consumption.

10. Having good fix-it skills will help you overcome the anxiety of home ownership.

Introduction

▶HOME REPAIR doesn't have to be difficult. That's this book is all about: easy ways to keep your home in tip-top condition. In fact, you might think of it as your fix-it coach—cheering you on while providing the play-by-play instructions to ensure success.

This book guides you through your entire house, using a how-to, problem-solving approach to help you understand how your house works. From the foundation up to the roof, and through the inner workings of plumbing, electrical, heating, and cooling systems, this is your guide to the tips, tools, and techniques to keep everything working smoothly. After all, whether your home is a funky downtown apartment or a rambling country farmhouse, it's likely the single biggest financial investment you'll make. Home fix-it is about protecting that investment—making it safe and energy-efficient, extending the life of its systems, and ultimately increasing its value. And if you rent or lease, tackling fix-it tasks yourself means not having to rely on a landlord or building manager's availability.

This book can also help you to save both time and money. Identifying and fixing small problems right away means that you can often avoid large—and expensive—repairs in the future. And there's nothing like the sense of satisfaction that comes with doing the job yourself, from fixing a leaky faucet to insulating your attic. You'll also find advice that's valuable no matter where you live, whether you're dealing with rainfall or snow loads, high humidity or searing winds, squirrels or termites. This book covers a broad range of common climate- and environment-related problems, as well as focusing on energy conservation and healthy home issues.

This book also provides a guideline to the complexity and time requirement for house maintenance and repair projects, and suggests where expert assistance is called for rather than home handiwork. It's no secret that we lead busy lives these days, so it pays to know when to call in a professional. It also pays to understand the system that the pro is about to tackle. You'll know how to explain the problem clearly, describe the job requirements more accurately, and work with the experts—plumbers, electricians, or building contractors—more easily. You'll also be able to recognize when a contractor isn't being straightforward with you or when someone's attempting to overcharge or carry out a repair that isn't necessary.

Most of all, however, this book aims to remove the intimidation factor from home fix-it projects—the overwhelming feeling you get when you're standing in the plumbing aisle of your local building store wondering which of the myriad pieces is the exact fit for your task. Instead, this book can help you turn intimidation into adventure and fear into fun.

You'll be able to set up a regular maintenance and inspection schedule that will catch problems at their earliest (and most easily solved) stage. You'll learn how to keep the house interior as comfortable as possible, in summer and in winter. You'll keep your heating, ventilating, and cooling appliances, your furniture, and even your floors in good condition, for longer. Most importantly, you'll look at your house and see a mosaic of systems and structures, all working together—not a mystery.

What will it take? Just a little time, a little patience, and a little energy. Oh, and a willingness to get a little dirty won't hurt, either. But the end result will be a home that you know intimately, inside and out—one that rewards you by sheltering your family and your financial investment. It's worth it. (E)

Chapter 1

Getting Ready for Home Repair

The key to protecting your home's long and happy life cycle is regular and ongoing maintenance. This sounds time consuming and even intimidating, but it doesn't have to be—you just need a place to start. To make that start, ask yourself how well you know your home. Consider not only the physical structure of your home and its systems, but also the comfort and ease that it offers to family members, and the cost of running it.

Aim for Energy Efficiency

Older houses have a well-deserved reputation for high energy costs. Depending on the age of your home, it might contain little or no modern insulation, windows that radiate both winter ice and summer heat, and attics that aren't much more than energy evaporators. Not only does this reduce your comfort level and increase utility bills, but it also places a strain on house components such as furnaces, which must work harder to heat or cool the house.

To find out whether your home needs an energy-efficiency boost, consider an energy audit. Many utility companies offer excellent programs that evaluate where your house is "leaking" energy and advise you on how to improve it. But you can also check potential problem areas yourself (see Chapter 6). Evaluating your trouble spots will allow you to target them more accurately, giving you the best possible return on your fix-it investment.

The result will be a more comfortable house, reduced utility bills, better indoor air quality, and longer-lasting heating and cooling systems. Of course, there's an additional benefit, and that's to the environment. Every time you reduce your energy consumption, you also reduce the greenhouse gases produced when fossil fuels such as coal, oil, and gas are burned to produce heat and electricity. So, take a look at your home's energy efficiency, do what you can to improve it, and then head to your local park . . . the trees will thank you.

Why You Need a Home Inspection

It's not just potential homebuyers who can benefit from having their house inspected by a qualified professional home inspector. A home inspection can identify the condition of the physical structure and systems of your home, letting you know about problems that might be safety issues and about where and when potential repairs might be necessary.

Think of it as a checkup for your house's health—and an excellent way to start learning about your house.

As the home inspector progresses through the house (which typically takes two to three hours), you'll have a chance to see what he or she is looking at, become familiar with signs of potential problems, and ask questions. Many inspectors are happy to provide tips on maintenance during the process and in their written reports. You can use those reports to plan preventive maintenance, find problems before they find you, determine the extent of a problem that you already know about and choose ways to solve it, and help you guide future renovations.

It might be tempting to think that since you live in the house, you know it best. But a good home inspector arrives at your house armed with years of experience and technical knowledge. The inspector understands how the house was put together and what's likely to go wrong, so a home inspection is a sound investment in your home's future.

FACT

The cost of a home inspection varies depending on the size of your house, its age and construction, and any specialized testing that you need—but expect to pay between $300 and $500 for an average home's inspection.

To find a qualified home inspector, ask for recommendations from friends, business colleagues, or real estate agents. You can also check local telephone directories under such headings as "Home Inspection Services." While some areas of the country do license home inspectors, many don't. Look for one who belongs to a professional group such as the American Society of Home Inspectors—membership indicates that the inspector follows a code of practice and ethics.

Ask about the inspector's background. How much experience does he or she have in residential home inspection, and what kind of education or training does he or she have in construction, architecture, or building science? Does the inspector carry valid errors and omissions insurance? Does the inspector encourage your participation in the home inspection and provide you with a written report?

Home Inspection Tips You Can Use

While you should start with a professional home inspection, you also need to inspect your home yourself on a regular basis—at least annually.

Work out a systematic approach so that you include everything from the foundation up to the roof, including exteriors, interiors, and house systems such as plumbing and heating. As you go through the house, take notes and photos, making sure that you date them. You'll then have a record from year to year of key problem areas (such as the roof, or specific foundation cracks) that will show how things are changing or aging over time.

As you inspect your home, look for problems such as water stains and for changes that are taking place. In this process, you're focusing on identifying the symptoms. Once you've done that, you can investigate later to find the underlying causes (water in the basement could be coming from condensation, or from a leak).

The most common problems are related to moisture. Look out for water damage wherever connections are made in the house's construction: around windows, at foundation corners, and where two different materials meet (such as metal flashing around a brick chimney). To check for rot in wood surfaces, bang the wood with the handle of a screwdriver or awl. If the sound is soft, rather than hard, jab the sharp end into the wood. If it goes in easily, the wood is likely rotten.

ALERT!

Be aware that home inspectors shouldn't offer you construction services or recommend particular companies. If they've identified a repair that's needed, it's a serious conflict of interest for them to also offer to solve it for you.

Start Outside

It helps to work from the big picture to the small details. Start your inspection outside, about half a block away from your house, or anywhere that allows you a good overall view of it. Look at the roof (using binoculars if necessary, which is safer than clambering around on ladders). Is the roofline level? Or does it sag anywhere, possibly indicating a problem with the structure? Check the condition of the roof coverings, chimneys, vents, and flashings. Curling, damaged or missing shingles, gaps in flashings, rust on metal chimneys, or crumbling mortar in brick chimneys indicate repairs that are needed to prevent moisture from penetrating the roof. Also check that overhead power, phone, and cable lines are well clear of outbuildings and trees.

As you move closer to your house, examine the condition of walls, window and door frames, decks, fences, the garage, driveways, sidewalks, and ground slopes (which should direct water away from the house). Gutters and downspouts should run freely, not overflow or leak anywhere. Plants should clear the house exterior by 6 to 8 inches. Look for insect trouble signs as well, such as piles of wood powder along the foundation. All roof or wall vents should be free of debris and screened to prevent animals such as squirrels from paying you unauthorized visits.

Note any loose or missing siding or trim pieces. Siding forms a seal around the house, which when damaged can allow wind to drive rain behind it. If you have brick on the house, ensure that drainage (weep) holes aren't blocked. Crumbling mortar is also a problem. Mortar seals the masonry, protecting it from moisture that can be especially damaging to brickwork if temperatures drop below freezing. On window and door frames, look for rotting wood, flaking paint, damaged caulking or weather stripping, broken glass, or chipped putty.

Wall cracks may be an entirely normal sign that the house is settling, which all houses do. It can signal a larger problem, though, if it's changing over time—getting bigger or shifting direction. If it's not, sealing it will prevent water from seeping through it.

Head Inside

On the inside, start with the structure of the house, in the basement, crawlspace, or ground floor. Check that exposed framing or supports aren't twisted, sagging, or rotting, particularly at their bases. Cracks in concrete basement floors aren't usually a structural concern but can allow moisture to seep in. Water staining, damp spots, crumbling concrete, or a white powdery substance (called efflorescence) are all signs of moisture. Watch for signs of insects and mold as well.

As you continue through the house, check for sloping floors, and ill-fitting doors and windows. Do all doors and windows open easily? Do locks and handles operate properly? Are stair rails and carpeting secure?

Check ceramic tiles. If they "give" when you press against them, the wall behind them is probably water damaged. Discolored, cracked, or missing grout means that it's time to regrout the tiles.

Also look for condensation, particularly in winter. If it's excessive, consider reducing the humidity in your home or increasing the ventilation. Examine areas where air circulation is reduced, such as behind curtains and inside closets, for mold or mildew.

In the attic, are there signs of water damage? Check that insulation is dry and that vents are clear. When temperatures drop below freezing, ice damming (a buildup of ice on the edges of the roof) can signal inadequate ventilation.

As a rough guide, attics should have at least 1 square unit of passive ventilation for every 300 square units of floor space if there's a vapor barrier in place. So, if you have 1,000 square feet of attic floor space, you should have about 3.3 square feet of venting. (Power- or wind-assisted vents will reduce the ventilation square footage needed; lack of vapor barrier will increase it.)

The Systems

Once you've checked the house's structure, turn your attention to its systems: heating, electrical, and plumbing services. To check water pressure, run the sink, tub, and toilet located in the highest part of the house at the same time. If a significant drop in pressure results, there's a problem with either the service coming into the house or the distribution within the house (ask neighbors if they have similar problems to help narrow it down). Other water problems include dripping faucets and rust stains or water damage under sinks and pipes or around toilet bases. Do all faucets, toilets, and drains work properly?

Check electrical outlets and switches for safe operation (see Chapter 19). Are all electrical cords and plugs in good condition? Exposed electrical wires, arcing, frequent blown fuses, flickering or dimming lights, damaged wires, and scorch marks around electric heating registers can mean that your electrical system isn't up to standard. Call your local utility or a licensed electrician to further diagnose and solve the problem.

Also examine the maintenance record for systems such as furnaces, boilers, hot-water tanks, and air conditioners, which should be professionally serviced every year. If you have a fireplace, when was the last time the chimney was cleaned? Also ensure that furnace and boiler rooms are free of anything that's flammable, from paint cans to cardboard boxes.

Your home inspection is a good time to test all smoke and carbon monoxide detectors, and ground fault circuit interrupters (GFCIs, which are electrical outlets in potentially wet areas that protect you against accidental shocks).

Every Homeowner's Basic Tool Kit

As you assess your home, you'll find many fix-it jobs that you can tackle yourself . . . but you'll need tools. Look for the best quality that you can afford. A lifetime guarantee on a tool indicates a good standard. (There's nothing worse than having a cheap tool break halfway through a repair job.) Along with your tools, an all-purpose glue and a sanding block with different grades of sandpaper will come in handy. And, of course, you'll need a tool tote or box to keep everything easily at hand.

- **Screwdriver set.** A multibit screwdriver is definitely the most useful tool in any homeowner's drawer. Most carry a selection of bits, including flat-bladed (slotted) ends, Phillips (cross) ends, and some-times Robertson (square) ends, in their handle—which means that when you're standing on top of a ladder, you need only one tool.
- **Claw hammer.** This is your standard hammer, with one end for pounding nails and one for removing them. Look for a drop-forged steel shank and a comfortable grip, in a 16-ounce hammer.
- **Measuring tape.** Look for a good-quality, retractable, 1-inch-wide, 25-foot-long measure.
- **Power drill.** Look for variable speed, with forward and reverse, a $3/8$-inch chuck, and a good set of drill and screwdriver bits.

- **Handsaws.** For general use, look for a crosscut saw (which cuts across the grain of the wood and can also be used to cut with the grain, especially on plywood) about 26 inches long (which most people find easy to manage). For cutting metal, you'll need a hacksaw, which features replaceable blades in a variety of point measures designed for different metals.

A saw's point measure refers to the number of points, or teeth, per inch. The larger the point number, the more teeth per inch, and the smoother the cut. A 10-point saw is good for general use. For cutting metals, generally speaking, the thinner the material you're cutting, the more teeth per inch you need for a smooth cut.

- **Utility knife.** Look for a retractable, replaceable blade and good-quality construction.
- **Putty knife.** This tool comes in a variety of widths, including a versatile 4-inch metal blade that's often called a wall scraper or tape knife.
- **Pliers.** Pliers are designed to grip and will also cut material such as wires. Long-nose pliers (also called needle-nose) are great for working with small items such as faucet seals and for cutting thin wire. Groove-joint (channel-type) pliers are adjustable and good for gripping all kinds of nuts and bolts.
- **Wrenches.** You'll find 4-inch and 10-inch adjustable (crescent) wrenches useful to tighten, loosen, and grip a wide variety of items around the house.
- **Level.** This is handy for installing anything from shelves to washing machines. Look for a 2-foot level, which will fit most spaces easily. It should have at least two bubbles, to measure both horizontal and vertical surfaces.

When You Need a Building Permit

You'll likely only need a building permit if your home fix-it is a major structural or systems undertaking, such as remodeling a basement, plumbing or electrical work, or building a garage or fence. If you're in doubt, always check with your county or municipal office to find out what the requirements are. For a fence, you'll usually need to submit a design sketch and a site plan for approval, especially if you live in a historic preservation area. Find out what's permitted—and what isn't—before you start planning.

Also check the time requirements. The permit approval process may take several weeks, so plan ahead. It's not worth proceeding without a proper permit, because the municipality can order you to undo whatever you've done—at your own expense.

The permit process can seem an extra hassle, but it's actually there to protect you (and your neighbors). If you're rewiring the basement electrical system, for example, the permit will probably require a building inspector's visit, to ensure that the wiring conforms to building codes. The inspector isn't there to hassle you, so approach the process with an open attitude. The fault that the inspector catches may be the one that prevents a major electrical fire.

Don't overlook the inspector as a source of expert information. It's his or her job to be on top of the latest code changes and new materials and techniques, so a friendly five-minute chat can save you both time and money in the long run. Ⓔ

Chapter 2
Safety First

The most important reason to get to know your home and its systems is safety—because knowing how to handle emergency situations can keep you and your family alive. But safety involves much more than simply reacting to emergencies; it's also about preventing them. This means seeing your house through the eyes of all of its occupants and visitors—from children and pets to guests and repair personnel.

Identifying Utility Shutoffs

In an emergency, you may need to shut off utilities: the water, gas, oil, or electricity supplies. Do you know where the shutoffs are? Are they clearly labeled or identified by bright paint? (You may not be in the house when they're needed; if they're labeled, it allows repair technicians or emergency services personnel to find them quickly.) Here's where to look for utility supplies, when to shut them off, and how.

Water

Knowing how to shut off your water is essential. You'll need to stop the water supply if there's any chance that pipes could be broken (either in an impending storm, such as a hurricane, or after a tornado or earthquake), and also to handle a leaking or burst pipe or faucet, or an overflowing appliance.

When dealing with an isolated problem, such as a broken faucet or overflowing toilet, check for a shutoff valve nearby—under the sink or on the water supply pipe to the toilet tank. (For a toilet, you can temporarily stop the flow of water by lifting the lid off the tank and holding up the float ball or cup.) Otherwise, shut off the water supply to the entire house.

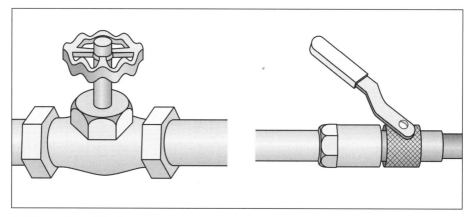

▲ Water shutoff valves

Look for the shutoff valve close to where the main water pipe enters the house. In warmer, southern climates, it could be located on the exterior. In colder areas, it's most likely inside the house, in the basement, crawlspace, or utility room. (If you have a water meter, it could be close by.) You're looking for a valve that has either a wheel-like handle or a lever. Turning it should shut off the water.

Check the operation of the valve at least annually, because it can seize up. If it's difficult to turn, try using penetrating oil and leaving it for 24 hours. If you need a wrench to turn the handle, keep the wrench next to the shutoff, clearly labeled, so that it's always there when you need it. If you can't turn the valve off, call your utility provider.

Natural Gas

The natural gas supply to your home (often used for cooking or heating) needs to be shut off if there's any risk that the pipes could break or are already broken (in case of a disaster such as an earthquake, tornado, hurricane, or brushfire), or if there's a fire or gas leak.

Shutting off the gas supply is a routine task if done as a preventive measure. If gas is already leaking, however, consider your safety. A gas shutoff on the house exterior may be safer to turn off than one in the basement, but if you have any doubts—don't. Evacuate the house, and notify emergency personnel.

ALERT!

If you can smell gas, do not use any electrical switches (even to turn them off) or phones, and do not light any flame. Electrical switches, phones, and flames all present an explosion risk if natural gas is leaking.

To find the shutoff, look for your gas meter on the outside of the house or in basements, crawlspaces, or utility rooms. The shutoff valve is usually on the pipe leading to the meter and will be a handle or knob that, when turned so that it's perpendicular to the pipe, closes the supply. You may need a wrench to operate the valve; if so, keep the wrench nearby and labeled. If you have any doubts about the shutoff location or operation, call your gas utility.

Most newer gas furnaces also have an electrical switch that is likely located on the wall near the furnace. Label the switch in case you need to turn off just the furnace (when you're replacing the filter, for example). You should also buy a red switch plate cover for it.

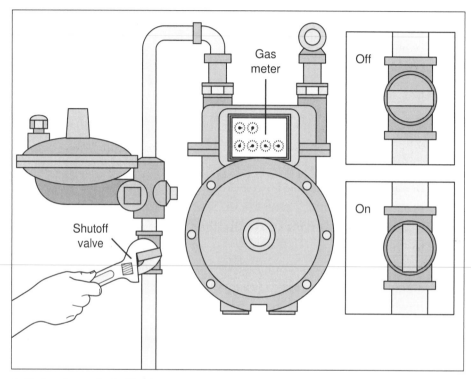

▲ Natural gas shutoff valve

Oil and Propane Tanks

Oil or propane supplies should be shut off under the same circumstances as natural gas. For propane systems, there may be a shutoff near the heater and another on the storage tank. For oil systems there will be a valve on or near the tank. Contact your oil or propane supplier for specific details about your situation.

Propane is heavier than air, so it can sink into low-lying areas such as basements in toxic quantities. If you smell propane, don't try to shut off valves located in the basement or crawlspace—call emergency personnel.

Electricity

The electrical supply to the house should be shut off any time that wiring could be damaged (such as in a hurricane or fire), if a severe electrical storm is forecast (lightning creates powerful electrical surges that can damage circuits and appliances), and if there's a flood risk (water can become electrically charged if it touches electrical outlets). You'll also need to shut off the electricity when repairing switches or outlets.

Find the main electrical panel or box for the house. It is usually located in the basement or utility room, close to where the electrical wires enter the house. You'll find one of four main types. If you find a row or rows of individual switches, you have circuit breakers. There may be one or two large switches on the box or panel. To shut off the electricity, switch the large switches to the "off" position. If you don't have the large switches, switch all the individual circuit breaker switches to "off."

If you find rows of round "heads" or tubes on the panel, you have fuses. There may be a lever on the box. To shut off the power supply, move it to the "off" position. If the fuses are in cartridge boxes, you'll need to use the handles to pull the boxes out of the panel.

ESSENTIAL

Never touch the electrical panel if you're standing in water or if it's smoking or arcing. If the house is flooding, wear rubber boots and gloves to ensure that no part of you touches water, and use a piece of wood to switch the breaker or lever off. If in doubt, evacuate, and notify emergency personnel.

To protect against electrical shocks, use only one hand when operating switches, levers, or cartridge boxes on an electrical panel; keep your other hand by your side, and don't lean against anything metal such as appliances or pipes. Standing on a rubber mat or wearing rubber-soled shoes will also help. Ladders or step stools must be plastic or wood, *not* metal.

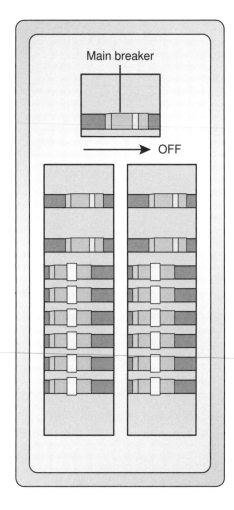

Main breaker

OFF

◀ Circuit breakers with a main switch

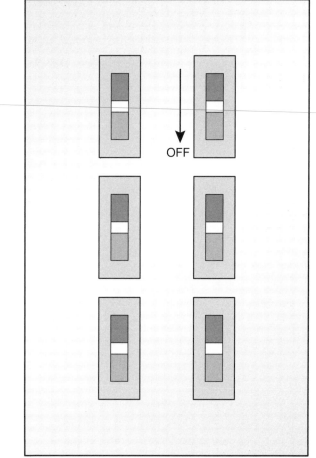

OFF

Circuit breakers without a main switch ▶

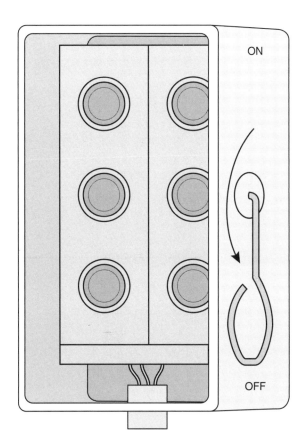

◀ Fuse box with a shut-off lever

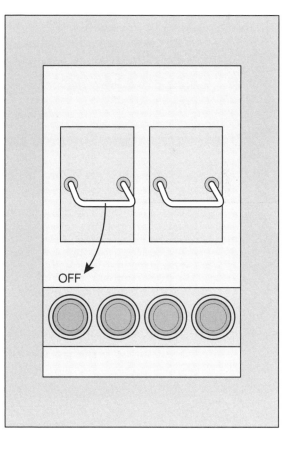

Cartridge-type fuse box ▶

Sewer Lines

While the system that drains wastewater into the septic system or municipal sewer isn't exactly a utility supply, it's useful to know how to access it. There should be at least one 4-inch main drain access, or clean-out, and there may be other 3- or 4-inch clean-outs as well. Look for them in the basement or lowest floor, close to bathrooms or kitchens, or in utility rooms. If the sewer backs up, all of these are potential leak sites. In addition, plumbers may find one of the clean-outs to be more convenient than the others, so let them know where all are located.

Smoke and Carbon Monoxide Detectors

Smoke and carbon monoxide detectors are key home safety elements. While newer homes have smoke detectors that are wired into the house's electrical system, check that these contain a battery backup; ff they don't, install several battery-operated detectors, or replace the detectors with models that have battery backups. Fires don't happen only when the power's on.

Understanding Smoke Detectors

You'll find two types of smoke detectors: ionization and photoelectric. Ionization detectors recognize quickly spreading fires, such as a stovetop grease fire. Photoelectric detectors are better at recognizing when a slow-burning fire is smoldering, such as a couch cushion set on fire by a cigarette. Many cheaper smoke detectors have only ionization technology. Spend a few dollars more, and choose one with both technologies instead. Ensure that the detector is approved by the Underwriters Laboratories (UL) and meets local building code requirements.

You need a smoke detector on every level of your house, especially outside sleeping areas. Avoid locations that will cause frequent false alarms, such as kitchens, steamy bathrooms, and garages. If a smoke alarm goes off frequently, don't remove the battery; clear the air by waving a towel under the detector, and then move the detector to a better location. Install detectors on the ceiling or on the wall 6 to 12 inches below the ceiling. Avoid areas with too little or too much air circulation (such as above forced-air registers).

Test smoke detectors monthly using the test button, and test them yearly using a candle that's just been blown out. Hold the candlewick close to the detector. If the alarm doesn't sound, replace the battery. If the alarm is still silent, replace the detector. Keep in mind that detectors don't last forever. They should be replaced at least every ten years. To remind yourself or a subsequent owner of the house, write the purchase date on the inside of the detector, and enter a reminder in your house records for the year that it needs replacing.

Make a habit of replacing the batteries at least once a year. The spring or fall time change or your birthday make ideal reminders. Use brand-new, nonrechargeable (alkaline) batteries.

Understanding Carbon Monoxide Detectors

Carbon monoxide is an odorless, colorless gas produced when carbon-containing fuels such as oil, natural gas, wood, or coal are burned. Inadequately maintained gas or oil appliances or fireplaces, faulty venting systems, and cars running in garages (even with the garage door open) can allow carbon monoxide to seep into your home's air—which has the potential to kill, because carbon monoxide starves the body of oxygen.

To prevent this, keep all fresh-air vents and intakes unobstructed, and have fuel-burning appliances and their venting systems serviced annually by qualified technicians. All removable furnace panels should be kept in place. Never attempt to heat your home with gas ovens, clothes dryers, or any unvented space heater. Items such as charcoal or gas barbecues and camping heaters should never be used inside. Kerosene heaters should be used inside only if they're rated for indoor use.

FACT

While carbon monoxide detector technology is not considered as advanced as smoke detector technology, it is improving. Some detectors now feature a digital readout of carbon monoxide levels, and new models incorporating a battery backup can be wired into home electrical systems.

You'll need a UL-approved detector on every level of your home, especially near sleeping areas. Additional detectors can be placed near potential carbon monoxide sources, such as gas furnaces. Test detectors at least monthly using the test button, and replace the batteries at least once a year.

If the carbon monoxide detector sounds an alarm, and no one in the house is experiencing symptoms, turn off all potential sources of carbon monoxide, open doors and windows, leave the house, and have a qualified technician check all the systems. If symptoms are present (which include sleepiness, headaches, nausea, confusion and dizziness—sometimes similar to the flu or food poisoning), immediately open the windows and doors to vent the area, and evacuate the house. If you're well enough, turn off all appliances, such as furnaces, that could be emitting carbon monoxide; if you're ill, however, simply leave the house. Phone emergency personnel, and seek medical attention right away. Have a qualified technician identify and repair the carbon monoxide source.

Installing and Cleaning Detectors

Smoke and carbon monoxide detectors are installed in similar ways. Most have two screws that hold the detector to the wall or ceiling. You may be able to hold the detector in position and mark the screw positions using a pencil. If not, measure the distance between the holes and transfer the measurement to the desired wall or ceiling position.

Predrill the screw holes. If there's no stud for the screws to attach to, insert screw anchors into the holes. Drive the screws three-quarters of the way into the anchors or holes. Seat the detector over the screws. Insert the required battery, close the cover, and test the detector.

To clean detectors, check their operating instructions. Generally, you wipe the exterior cover with a damp cloth and carefully vacuum the interior. Test the alarm once you're finished to ensure that none of the circuitry has been jarred loose. A chirping or intermittent beeping from your detector probably means that the battery needs replacing. If you replace the battery and the beeping continues, replace the detector.

Fire Extinguishers

Your home should have a fire extinguisher in the kitchen, garage, workshop, and utility room. The most versatile home-use extinguisher is rated A-B-C and is effective against many small, contained house fires. (The rating system is A, for fires based on ordinary sources such as paper and wood; B, for flammable liquids such as oil and grease; and C, for electrical fires.) If the extinguisher has a pressure gauge, check it monthly; if the pressure is too low, either have it recharged or replace it.

Fire extinguishers should be mounted on a wall where they're easily accessible and away from potential hazards such as the stove (so that you don't have to reach over a stove fire, for example, to grab the extinguisher). Many come with a wall-mounting bracket. To install, find a stud in the wall near the desired location. Using the bracket as a guide, mark the holes for the screws with a pencil. Drill pilot holes, and insert the screws through the bracket. Place the fire extinguisher in the bracket and snap the fastener closed.

All responsible individuals in the house should know how to use the extinguisher. The recommended technique is PASS: Pull the pin in the handle; Aim the nozzle at the base of the flames; Squeeze the trigger; and Sweep the extinguisher or nozzle from side to side, moving toward the fire. Once an extinguisher has been used, either recharge or replace it.

ALERT!

Use a fire extinguisher only if the fire is small, you have a clear exit in case the flames cannot be doused, everyone else is out of the house, and the fire department has been called. Never let the flames come between you and your escape route.

Automatic-Stop Garage Door Closers

Automatic garage doors are a serious safety hazard if they're not installed or maintained properly—especially if they were installed before 1993, when safety standards were improved. Since then, automatic garage doors are required to have an external entrapment protection system (an electric eye, a door edge sensor, or any other device that senses when it comes into contact with something, and immediately reverses the door), or a constant contact control button, which requires you to hold the open/close button all the time that the door is in motion.

If your older garage door does not have an automatic-reverse function, replace it, or retrofit it with a new opener that will reverse. Garage doors are heavy enough that they can seriously injure or even kill a child who gets caught under them.

Even newer garage doors need monthly checks to ensure that their safety measures are working properly. The first check is that the door is balanced—that it will stay in place wherever it's stopped. First, detach the garage door opener from the closed door (there should be a quick-release lever). Open and close the door manually. It should move smoothly, without binding or sticking, and should stay open if you let go of it about 3 to 4 feet above the ground.

If your garage door fails any of these tests, even after being adjusted, immediately stop operating the door in automatic mode (detach the door opener from the closed door if you haven't already done so), and switch to manual operation. Call a qualified technician to repair the door.

To check that the door will automatically reverse, place a 2" × 4" on the ground below the open door and use the automatic controls to close the door. The door should reverse as soon as it touches the 2" × 4". If it doesn't, look for an automatic reversal knob or screw on the power unit, and adjust it until the door reverses properly (check the instruction manual for the exact location and operation).

To test the door's force, hold the bottom of the door as it automatically closes. Again, the door should immediately reverse. If it doesn't, there should be a force adjustment control knob or screw on the power unit (again, check the instruction manual). You'll probably need to open and close the garage door again before retesting it.

Additional safety precautions include warning children to stay clear of garage doors, keeping remote controls away from children, and locating the garage door switch 5 feet off the ground (out of their reach). You should also examine the door's mechanisms, including springs and cables, to check for signs of wear or aging (these items are under high tension, so be careful, and call a qualified professional for repairs). Your garage door instruction manual should also include safety measures. If you need a copy of the manual, call the door's manufacturer or installation company (the model number should be on the power unit).

Ladder Safety

Ladders can be dangerous tools. Ensure that they're sturdy and are sitting securely on dry, level ground. When leaning a ladder against a wall, stand in front of the ladder. Adjust the ladder angle until you can comfortably touch the ladder rungs with your hands outstretched at shoulder height.

Beware if you're wearing kneepads; they can get caught in the ladder rungs as you're climbing. Haul tools up with a rope and bucket or carry them in a tool belt to leave your hands free. Stay centered—avoid any reaching maneuver that moves your hips beyond the ladder's side rails. Don't step on the ladder's top two rungs or on the top of a stepladder.

Improving safety in and around your home will help you respond quickly and appropriately in an emergency. Better yet, it can help you prevent emergencies completely, and it often takes just minutes of your time. In Chapter 3, you'll discover a selection of other fix-it tasks around the house that are both quick and easy.

Chapter 3

Quick Fixes for Common Problems

Quick and easy solutions can be found for a home's most common problems, from leaky pipes to sticking doors. As a rule, start with the easiest possible repair, advancing to more difficult fixes as needed. If you're unsure at any point, or if a problem remains stubbornly unsolved, don't be afraid to call in an expert . . . but do watch how the expert solves the problem. There's nothing like learning from the best.

Keeping Showerheads and Faucets Running Free

If you're dancing around under your showerhead in order to get wet, or your faucets are sputtering rather than flowing, there may be an easy fix. Over time, minerals and particles in your water supply can form deposits on showerheads, faucets, and sink sprayers, eventually obstructing the water flow. Eliminate the buildup (usually visible as a white or grayish deposit), and you can enjoy free-running water again.

You may not even have to remove the showerhead. Fill a plastic bag with white vinegar, and seal the bag over the showerhead so that it's soaking in the solution. Let it sit overnight, and then brush off the deposits with an old toothbrush. If some of the spray holes are still clogged, carefully insert a thin needle or toothpick through the holes. (This can also work for faucets and sink sprayer nozzles—the latter can be dipped into a bowl containing the vinegar.)

If this doesn't work, remove the showerhead. Use one adjustable wrench on the showerhead to unscrew it (counterclockwise) and one wrench on the shower arm (the pipe that the showerhead attaches to) to steady it so that it doesn't twist (potentially breaking the piping inside the wall). Wrapping the wrenches with masking or duct tape will prevent them from gouging the pipes. If the joint still won't budge, try a shot of penetrating oil, and leave it for twenty-four hours.

Once the showerhead is off, wash it well in hot water with some dish detergent to dislodge any loose deposits. Soak the showerhead overnight in vinegar, then try the toothbrush and toothpick tricks again. When you replace the showerhead, wrap the threads on the shower arm with three layers of Teflon (or plumber's) tape first, to ensure a tight seal.

FACT

Always wrap Teflon or plumber's tape in the direction that you'll be tightening—most of the time, this is clockwise. Otherwise, the threads can tear the tape, which clogs the threads instead of sealing them. In this case, the showerhead will screw on clockwise, so the tape should be wrapped clockwise as well.

For stubbornly sputtering faucets or sink sprayers, try removing the aerator (the assembly at the very end of the faucet). If it won't unscrew by hand, use an adjustable wrench or groove-joint pliers on it. (Sink sprayers will often have a screw at the nozzle end that you have to remove to get at the aerator assembly.) Try the faucet or nozzle. If the water now runs fine, your aerator is definitely blocked. Although some newer aerator models won't come apart (in which case you'll need to replace them), most will. You'll find some combination of one or more wire mesh screens, a nylon disk, washer(s), and an O-ring.

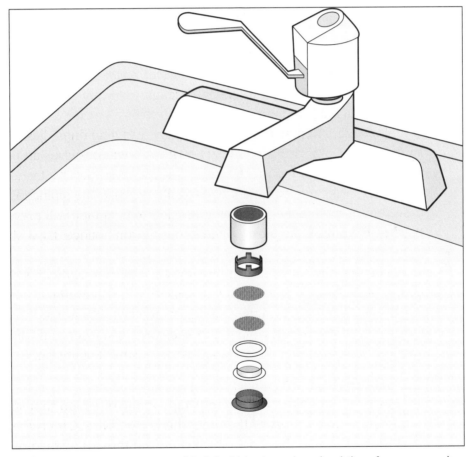

▲ The aerator's components add air bubbles to reduce (and therefore conserve) the water flowing out of the faucet without impairing the effectiveness of the flow.

Soak the pieces in vinegar; then loosen deposits with a toothbrush. Rinse each piece, and put everything back together. If you can't remove the buildup or corrosion, replace the aerator.

When fixing faucets or showerheads, block the sink or tub drain with the plug or a clean rag. If you drop a fiddly faucet part, you won't lose it down the drain. Also, place a piece of cardboard or a paper towel nearby, and lay out the components in the order you disassembled them. This makes reassembling much easier.

First Aid for Leaky Pipes

Leaking pipes signal themselves in a variety of ways—drips, stains, puddles, the sound of running water, a water meter showing usage when no water is being used, or an unusually high water bill (these last three symptoms can also indicate problems with toilets, so check these, too). Your first task is to find the leak, usually by following drips, stains, or sounds to the nearest pipe. If it isn't obvious, try systematically following your pipes as far as you can.

Clearly, leaks mean that a piece of pipe needs to be replaced. But in case you—or a plumber—can't get to the job right away, there are first-aid options. For pinhole leaks, try one or more of the following:

- Insert a wooden pencil point into the hole as far as it will go, then snap off the pencil.
- Wrap the pipe with several layers of electrician's tape, being sure to overlap the tape edges and extending the tape about 4 inches on both sides of the leak.
- Wrap the pipe in a piece of rubber, such as a bicycle inner tube or repair patch, and secure it tightly with a hose clamp.

For larger leaks, wrap a piece of rubber around the pipe, and secure it tightly with a sleeve clamp that's the same diameter as the pipe. If the leak is at a joint (where clamps won't work), dry the surface as much as possible. Use a putty knife to spread epoxy putty over the area of the leak. Applying several thin layers of putty, observing the product's directions for drying time, will be more effective than applying one thick layer.

Silencing Noisy Pipes

A banging noise in pipes can be caused by insufficient supports for the pipes, especially over longer runs in basements. You should have some sort of strapping holding the pipes to the underside of the joists about every 4 feet. Gently wiggle the pipe. If it's loose, add additional supports. Perforated metal strapping that will cradle the pipe is easily secured to the joists with screws.

A banging noise when you turn off a faucet means that the air chambers located close to the faucets (which reduce the effect of sudden faucet shutoffs) have filled with water. To fix this, first shut off the water supply to your toilets (if they have individual shutoffs), and then shut off the house's main water supply. Turn on the cold faucets at the highest and lowest points in the house. When water no longer drains out of them, close the faucets and turn on the house's water supply and the individual water supplies to the toilets.

ALERT!

If this process doesn't work, your system might not have air chambers installed in the pipes. Call a plumber to check out the plumbing and install air chambers, or "water hammer arresters," if necessary.

Fast and Easy Toilet Fixes

Toilets can be trouble—not just because problems with them range from irritating and wasteful (running water) to disastrous (overflowing toilet bowls), but also because they look complicated. To start figuring them out, break the parts down into two groups: the inlet assembly, which allows water into the toilet tank; and the flush assembly, which allows water out of the toilet tank.

Just for fun, take off the tank lid and watch what happens when you flush. When the handle goes down, it lifts up a chain or wire that's attached to a flapper, or stopper, in the bottom of the tank. When this flapper is open, gravity takes the water in the tank into the toilet bowl, which triggers the drain system to siphon the water out of the bowl.

In the toilet tank, the flapper flops back down once the tank empties itself, sealing the tank. At the same time, the float ball or cup that's attached to the inlet assembly has dropped along with the water level, thus opening the inlet valve to let water refill the tank through the refill tube. When the water floats the ball or cup back to the right level, it closes the inlet valve, and the water stops filling the tank.

A broken, leaking, phantomly flushing, or constantly running toilet can be fixed if you take a systematic approach. Try the following fast and easy fixes before calling a plumber or tackling the bigger fixes in Chapter 18.

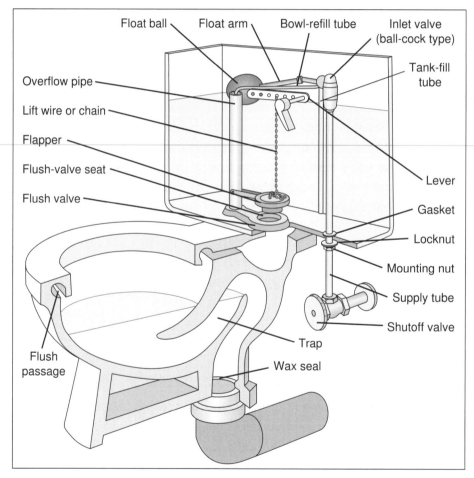

▲ Fixing toilets is much easier when you understand how everything goes together.

Changing the Toilet Seat

Comfort and cleanliness occasionally demand a new toilet seat. This means removing the two bolts that hold the seat to the toilet bowl. They may be hiding under plastic caps, which can be pried up with a flat-bladed screwdriver masked with tape to avoid scratching the surface. Once the bolts are out, lift off the old seat and replace it with the new one, which should come with replacement bolts.

Your biggest problem will be loosening the bolts, which often seize up. Use penetrating oil and leave them overnight if necessary. Two adjustable wrenches or groove-joint pliers (one to turn the nut and one to prevent the bolt from turning) will help. As a last resort, cut through the nut and/or bolt using a hacksaw.

Getting a Handle on the Problem

A loose handle on the toilet tank can interfere with the flapper's operation, not lifting it up properly or causing it to flop down too soon. To tighten the handle, first check that the nut on the inside of the tank is tight; if it's not, snug it up. Do not apply a lot of force to tighten the nut, because this could crack the toilet tank.

Another handle-related problem can be the arm (called a trip lever) that extends from the handle and suspends a chain or wire to the flapper. Try shortening or lengthening the chain or changing the position of the chain/wire on the trip lever to correct the flapper's operation.

If the handle is broken, remove the chain/wire from the trip lever, then loosen or remove the nut on the toilet handle so that you can remove the trip lever and the handle. Check that your replacement trip lever is the same length as the old one, cutting it if necessary. Follow the new handle's instructions to insert the new handle through the tank wall, loosely tightening the nut. Reconnect the chain/wire to the trip lever and snug up the nut. Flush the toilet to ensure that the chain/wire is operating the flapper properly.

Losing Leaks

To test for leaks, add food coloring to the water in the tank (not the bowl), and see where it ends up. If colored water leaks out at a washer or a bolt, replace the washer or gently tighten the bolt (never overtighten bolts, which can crack or break the toilet).

FACT

Condensation on the toilet tank is a common problem, which is caused when the water inside the tank is colder than the air outside the tank. To fix this, drain the toilet tank, clean and dry it, and install foam insulation panels (available at home centers) on the tank's inside walls, ensuring that they don't interfere with the toilet's operation.

If the food coloring shows up in the bowl, it means that water could be leaking past the flapper—either the flapper isn't operating properly, or it's no longer sealing well. (This can also result in the sound of constantly running water, and phantom flushing, when the toilet periodically flushes of its own accord.) Examine the flapper's operation when you flush the toilet. Check to see if the chain connecting the flapper to the trip lever is the problem (see the previous section on toilet handles).

If the flapper opens and closes as it should, press down on it. If that stops the flow of water into the bowl, the flapper isn't sealing properly. The flapper and the edges of the hole (or valve seat) in which it sits can be cleaned. Drain the tank and use fine steel wool on porcelain enamel or a stiff brush on plastic to remove any deposits; then restore the water supply and test the flush mechanism.

If this doesn't work, replace the flapper. Drain the tank, remove the chain/wire from the trip lever, and lift or unsnap the flapper from its anchor point. (Choose a replacement flapper with a chain attachment to the trip lever, rather than wires, to reduce flapper-positioning problems.) Depending on your flapper type, snap it back onto its anchor point or slide it down over the overflow tube and into position. Attach the chain to the trip lever, restore the water supply to the toilet, and test the flush mechanism.

For leaks near the toilet bowl base, you may need to replace the wax seal that connects the toilet base to the plumbing pipes. If the food coloring shows a hairline crack in the tank, you'll need to replace the tank. Leaks can also occur on the water supply line (the riser tube), at the shutoff, for example, or at the connection to the toilet tank. If tightening the nuts doesn't help, you may need to replace the component that's leaking. For these tasks, see Chapter 18.

To drain the toilet tank, close the shutoff valve that should be located on the pipe leading to the toilet tank. If there's no valve, close the water shutoff for the house. Once the water is off, flush the toilet to empty the tank, and sponge up any remaining water.

Continuously Running Water

If water is continuously flowing into the bowl, it could be running through the overflow tube, rather than leaking through the flapper. Check the water level in the tank. It should be ½ to 1 inch below the top of the overflow pipe. If it's too high, bend down the metal arm on the float ball, or adjust the screw at the top of the inlet assembly. To adjust a float cup that wraps around the inlet assembly, squeeze the clip that attaches the float cup to the adjustment rod, and move the cup down.

Also check the float ball. If it's old or leaking, it might be taking on water and holding the inlet valve open unnecessarily. Unscrew the float ball and replace it. If you can't unscrew it, don't force it, because you could damage the inlet assembly; unscrew the float arm from the inlet assembly, thus giving yourself more room to maneuver, then unscrew the float ball from the arm—or replace the arm and ball.

Full Flushes

If the toilet isn't flushing completely, the flush passage (up inside the rim of the toilet bowl) could be partially clogged. A good scrubbing can help, but if that doesn't work, take a wire and carefully poke it into the holes to clean them out (use a handheld mirror under the rim to see the holes more easily).

Check that the bowl-refill tube (which stretches from the intake assembly to the overflow tube) is positioned so that water flows into the overflow tube; reposition or bend the bowl-refill tube as necessary.

The water level in the toilet tank could also be the problem. As previously mentioned, it should be ½ to 1 inch below the top of the overflow tube. If it's too low, raise the float ball by bending the metal arm up, or adjusting the screw at the inlet assembly. To adjust a float cup that wraps around the inlet assembly, squeeze the clip that attaches it to the adjustment rod, and move the cup up.

Clearing Blocked Drains

Sooner or later, everyone has to tackle the dreaded blocked drain. It's tempting to chuck a chemical solution down there, but not only is that bad for the environment, it can degrade rubber gaskets in your plumbing and even some plastic piping. Try the easiest fix first: a plunger.

ALERT!

Always wear rubber or latex gloves when working with wastewater, and avoid splashing. A mask and safety goggles will protect your mouth, nose, and eyes from stray splashes. This is especially important if you've attempted to unclog the drain with any chemical solution.

Taking the Plunge

Plungers work best if they can seal around the drain properly. First, choose the right plunger. A toilet plunger has an inner lip that improves the seal. Lining the plunger with a little petroleum jelly will also help the seal.

Plug any overflow hole in the sink or tub with a clean rag, and if you're dealing with a double sink, seal the drain that you're not plunging with a plug or wet cloth. To create the seal, insert the plunger at an angle to reduce the air it traps inside it, and bring the water level up to at least 2 to 3 inches around the plunger.

Pump the plunger fifteen to twenty times without breaking the seal. If this loosens the clog, run water down the drain for several minutes to continue pushing the clog through your pipes. If it doesn't, bend a coat hanger into a long wire with a hook on the end and feed it through the drain to pull out the blockage.

Snakes and Augers

If you're still clogged, use a hand auger (sometimes called a drain-and-trap auger or plumber's snake) for most drains; use a closet auger for toilets. You operate the auger by feeding the flexible tube into the drain and cranking the handle to extend the tube. (For a tub, unscrew the overflow plate and insert the auger through the overflow hole, rather than the drain.)

Go gently, because these tools can scratch sinks, tubs, and toilets, and can damage pipes. When you feel a blockage, crank the coil back a little, then forward again, trying to break up the clog.

Keep a bucket or heavy-duty plastic bag handy, because the auger will be wet and mucky when it reappears. The worst of the water can be soaked up with a rag held around the auger tube as you crank it back out of the drain, but you'll need to wash and disinfect it before storing it.

Traps and Drain Clean-Outs

If the plunger or auger doesn't work, you may need to take the drain apart. A sink trap often has a clean-out plug at the bottom of its bend. Place a bucket under the trap, and unscrew the plug. Push a hooked wire up into the pipe in both directions of the bend to dislodge the clog. If this doesn't work, or if your trap doesn't have a clean-out plug, take apart the trap itself.

This is a straightforward job. Loosen the two nuts on either side of the trap (these connect the trap to the sink pipe and to the house's plumbing system). The trap should then come off, allowing you to clean it out and to insert an auger directly into the pipes if necessary.

Unfortunately, the trap's nuts can seize, and the trap itself can corrode, forcing you to cut the pipe with a hacksaw and replace the trap. This is still a relatively quick fix. Cut off the old drain trap, leaving as much straight pipe as possible running down from the sink and out from the wall or the floor. Measure the length and diameter of the pipe that's left, and take photos or make sketches if necessary.

Take the old drain trap and the photos/sketches to the home center, and have the staff help you find the right compression fittings and trap pieces to create a new drain trap bend and attach it to the old pipes. With most of these fittings, you'll simply slide a slip nut and then a slip washer onto the old pipe, and then push the new drain trap pipe over the old pipe so that it sits over the washer. Tighten the nut with groove-joint pliers approximately a quarter-turn past hand-tight against the washer to create a snug seal. Run water through the sink. If the drain trap leaks, tighten the nut a little more.

To clear a blocked toilet drain, you may have to take the entire toilet off the floor (see Chapter 18, under Reseating a Toilet). For other drains, look for the sewer line clean-out that's closest to the problem. Open it, and try again with the auger—but be aware that this is beyond a "quick and easy" fix. If in doubt, or this doesn't work, it's time to call the professionals.

Eliminating Odors from Drains

Most drains, including floor drains, incorporate some sort of bend, or trap, directly below where the water enters the pipe, in a U-, P-, or S-shape. These retain a small amount of water that forms a barrier against gases and odors from further down the pipe. If the drain isn't used much, the water in the trap can dry out, allowing sewer gases into the house. This is a common cause of basement sewer odors, especially in older homes. Solve this by pouring a bucket of water into the drain each month to keep the trap full.

Freeing Sticky Doors

Doors can refuse to close properly for a variety of reasons, including loose hinges, settling house walls, or even humid weather. Before you tackle any repairs, find out why it's sticking. If the problem is related to settling and is getting worse or affecting several doors or windows, you may have a more serious problem on your hands. If this is the case, call a house inspector.

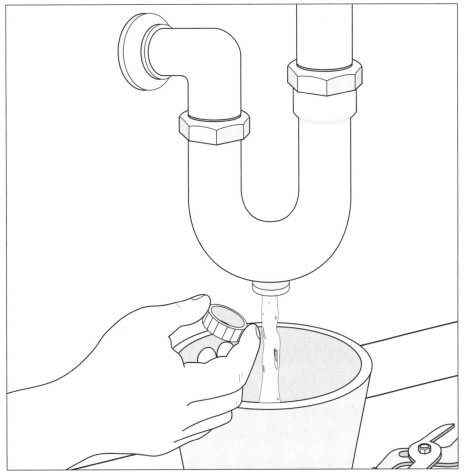

▲ If you've lost a small item—like a piece of jewelry—down the drain, you may be able to retrieve it by unscrewing the drain trap's plug or by taking the trap apart.

Too Much Moisture

If humidity is a long-term problem, consider adding a dehumidifier to your house or reducing the humidifier setting if you have one on a forced-air furnace. If the humidity is unusual, tolerate the door until the weather returns to normal. If the door also returns to normal, seal all its edges with paint or varnish to prevent moisture from making the wood swell during future humidity. If it's still binding, fix it (see the following), and then seal the edges and any areas that have been sanded or planed.

Medium-density fiberboard (MDF) is known for soaking up moisture from humidity and swelling up. To prevent this, ensure that all door edges and surfaces are well sealed with paint or varnish—including the often-forgotten top and bottom of the door.

Loose Hinges

When faced with a sticky door, first check the hinges. Are any screws loose on either the door or the door frame? If so, the fast fix is to tighten the offending screw. It's likely, however, that the motion of the door has ripped the wood around the screw's threads, so that the screw hole is "stripped."

Since finding a new hole isn't possible, repair the old one. Remove the screw and clean out the hole as much as possible. Fill the hole with wood glue and small pieces of wood such as matchsticks or a golf tee, let it dry, and then trim off any protruding wood. Redrill the hole and insert the screw. To support the door and ease any strain on the hinges while you're working on hinge screws, insert a doorstop under the door.

Sanding and Planing

If the hinge screws are okay, stand just beyond the door frame so that you can pull the door toward the frame. At the moment that it starts to stick, use a pencil to draw a line on the door, using the door frame as your guide. The line will show you how much of the door is causing a problem (these areas also show up as worn or shiny paint on the door edge) and will provide a depth guide for sanding or planing.

To remove a small amount of material from the door edge, sand it down until the door closes smoothly (depending on where you're sanding, you may need to take the door off the hinges). A more substantial area of binding may require planing. Sand or plane just a little at a time to avoid removing too much material, especially on hollow-core doors. Work from the end of the door edge toward the center, to avoid splintering the edge. Prime and/or touch up the paint where you've sanded or planed.

Another option—rather less quick and easy—is to reseat or shim one or more of the hinges (see Chapter 16).

FACT

When removing a door, undo the hinges from the bottom up. (Otherwise, the door can twist, ripping the wood around the bottom hinge screws.) To remove the pivot pin that joins the two hinge halves, rest a nail against the bottom of the pin or insert a flat-bladed screwdriver between the hinge and the pin's head, and tap gently with a hammer.

Sometimes, the longest part of a fix-it job is trying to avoid doing it. These quick and easy fixes, including toilet troubles and blocked drains, prove that repairs don't have to take hours out of your leisure time. A more detailed look at your house begins in the next chapter, which examines how healthy—or unhealthy—your home is. It's a bigger investment of your time, but it's worth making.

Chapter 4

Healthy Houses

Homes are the places that people turn to for comfort, safety, and well-being—so hearing that houses can harbor potentially unhealthy or even harmful substances can be unsettling, to say the least. But there's no reason to panic. Most of the time, all it takes is a few precautions and a little knowledge to turn health risks into health dividends for every family member. Read on, and breathe easier.

Water Testing

Do you know what's in your water? It's not just H_2O: minerals, chemicals, bacteria, and viruses all can be present, too, in quantities that range from harmless to health compromising. The difficulty is that some easily recognized water quality issues—such as color, taste, and hardness—may be no more than a cosmetic problem. And some very serious risks, such as lead or bacterial content, won't reveal themselves in color, taste, or odor.

The only way to properly determine the health of your water is to test it. This is particularly important if you receive your water from a well. Chemicals and microorganisms can leak into wells from above, or enter them via the ground water that the well taps into.

Even if you're not using well water, testing can be worthwhile. Although water utilities are now required to produce annual Consumer Confidence Reports, letting you know what's in the water that they're supplying to you, water can become contaminated after it leaves the utility supply and enters your home (especially if you have lead or copper supply piping). And utilities aren't perfect, either. Heavy rainfall or water runoff can overwhelm their systems, degrading the quality of their treatment processes.

How to Test Your Water

Depending on your local health department, and the specific elements that you need to test for, water testing ranges from free to hundreds of dollars. The basic tests, however, cost about $20 to $30. You can buy do-it-yourself test kits for some contaminants (usually mineral content) at home centers, but state-certified laboratories provide a fuller range of tests and more accurate or sophisticated results.

The laboratories provide containers and instructions for gathering water samples, and they will send you written reports identifying specific contaminants, their levels, and whether those levels comply with safe drinking water standards. Ask whether the test would be most effective after a period of rainy weather (when it's more likely that contaminants could have been washed into your well or ground water).

One of the best information sources for testing requirements and potential contaminants is your local or state health department (check the government pages in your phone directory).

When to Test Your Water

If you rely on well water, test it annually for fecal coliform bacteria (which come from human or animal waste and can cause severe gastrointestinal illnesses) and nitrates (which come from human and animal waste, and fertilizer, and can interfere with the body's ability to carry oxygen, especially in babies). Other tests may be indicated, depending on local risk factors. Talk to health departments and local labs to help you identify which tests you need and how often you need them. Testing is also called for if you've repaired your well or water pump system, or installed a new well.

Whether you're on well water or a utility supply, test your water under the following circumstances:

- Members of your household are having repeated bouts of gastrointestinal illnesses (such as diarrhea).
- Your water comes into the house through lead or copper supply pipes.
- You live near an area where pesticides or fertilizers are often used.
- There's a landfill, refinery, mine, or gas station nearby.
- Radon gas might be a problem in your area.
- You have concerns about the appearance, odor, or taste of your water.
- Before and after installing a water treatment unit, test the water to check on the unit's effectiveness.

How to Improve Your Water Quality

If a test indicates high levels of any contaminant, immediately switch to a reputable brand of bottled water for drinking and cooking, retest your water supply, and take steps to fix the problem. If you need assistance, call your local health department.

For high bacteria levels in well water, you may need to disinfect your well. Other contaminants may be controlled using water treatment systems or filters, but in some cases, drilling a new well might be required. If you're not on well water, report the problem right away to your water utility and local health department so that they can help investigate and solve the problem.

A variety of water treatment systems is available, in two basic types: point-of-entry systems that treat all the water entering the house; and point-of-use systems that treat only the water going to a specific faucet (such as the kitchen sink). The systems use various technologies, including carbon filters, ion exchangers, reverse osmosis, and distillation. Use your test results to determine which contaminants are a problem, and then choose a system designed to screen them out.

Wherever you obtain your water from, try to reduce your use of potential contaminants such as pesticides. Never store such contaminants near a well, and use them carefully to prevent runoff into ground water. Always take hazardous wastes such as pesticides, paints, solvents, oil, and batteries to approved collection sites. If they're dumped into drains or septic systems, or left in landfills, their chemicals can contaminate water supplies. You should also pick up pet feces.

QUESTION?

Where can I find more information about choosing the right water treatment unit?
The Water Quality Association (✐ www.wqa.org) and the U.S. Environmental Protection Agency (EPA) Safe Drinking Water Hotline (✐ www.epa.gov or ✆ 1-800-426-4791) have background information on water contaminants and treatment strategies.

Well Maintenance

Inspect and maintain your well regularly. First, look at its location. Is it on high ground, and does the ground slope away from it, without any low spots nearby where rainwater could collect? Wells should be located where rainwater and melting snow can't run toward or into them, and where there's no risk of contamination from a nearby septic system.

The well should be protected from tampering, with a cap or seal. Casings, caps, and seals should be in good condition, and the well casing should be above the ground, in accordance with local regulations. You should disinfect the well at least annually, and remove any sediment as necessary. Any wells on your property that are no longer used should be properly filled and capped.

Reducing Allergy and Asthma Triggers

Allergies and asthma are on the rise, and our homes may be contributing to the problem. The following strategies will help reduce troublesome substances such as dust, cleaning products, and pollens. The trick is to identify what triggers are causing problems for people living in the house (usually in consultation with your doctor), and target those first.

To start with, choose cleaning products carefully, reducing the hazardous chemicals or fumes associated with them. Use pump sprays, for example, instead of aerosol spray cans. For drain maintenance, choose enzyme treatments and augers, rather than chemical drain cleaners. Using cleaning products in a well-ventilated area will help, too.

Also limit your use of substances such as pesticides and fertilizers, especially those containing synthetic organics, and keep your doors and windows closed if your neighbor is applying them. In general, avoid or limit the use of any product with label warnings that include the words corrosive, explosive, or poisonous.

One key action to improve your home's health is to stop smoking. Period. If you can't quit, at least smoke outside the house, especially if you have children at home.

Dust and Dust Mites

Dust can contain all sorts of unpleasant things, from dirt and food particles to pet dander and dust mites (microscopic insects that feed on the substances in dust, including invisible flakes of skin). Reactions to these range from irritating (sneezing and watery eyes) to dangerous (asthma attacks).

The key to reducing dust is twofold: Choose furniture and décor elements that are easy to clean, and clean them regularly. Wood, vinyl, and tile, for example, clean more easily than carpets, which can trap up to 70 percent of dust particles even after vacuuming. Window blinds are easier to clean than curtains, as is furniture with a smooth finish and few intricate details.

Dust surfaces including windowsills and furniture weekly, with a water-dampened or specialty dusting cloth (aerosol cleaning products can emit harmful substances themselves, while dry cloths just spread the dust around). Vacuum after dusting, using either a central vacuum system vented outdoors, or a stand-alone vacuum with a high-efficiency filter (these reduce the dust from the vacuum's exhaust). Replace vacuum bags or clean dirt receptacles frequently.

If you're removing old carpets, vacuum them first to reduce the dust that they'll raise. If they're dirty, dusty, or moldy, protect yourself with gloves, safety glasses, and a nose/mouth mask.

Bedding such as sheets and pillowcases should be washed weekly in hot water and dried in the dryer (hanging sheets and clothes to dry outside is great for reducing utility bills, but the items can end up covered with pollens and dust). Mattresses and pillows can be sealed in dust mite–proof (sometimes known as hypoallergenic) covers. Curtains, area rugs, bathmats, cushions, and pillows should be washed regularly.

Cleaning tasks should also include washing or replacing filters monthly on such systems as forced-air furnaces or air conditioners. To reduce outdoor allergens in the house, caulk or weather-strip your doors and windows. To help eliminate indoor pollutants, maintain good ventilation; range, bathroom, and clothes dryer vents should be installed and vented outside the house.

Pets

As wonderful as pets can be, they can contribute to allergies and asthma difficulties. If you want to keep your pets but are concerned about the dust and dander that they generate, consider a few precautions. Keep pets out of sleeping areas and away from upholstered furniture and stuffed toys. Brush their coats regularly, outdoors if possible. Train dogs to wait for their feet to be washed or brushed off when they come inside. If you can, choose pet breeds that tend to have lower allergy triggers.

In severe cases, you may be forced to find a new home for your pet. If you can't find good adoptive homes yourself, take your pet to the local humane society or animal shelter. Never abandon a pet.

Volatile Organic Compounds

That "new smell" that comes with recent furniture purchases or construction may be a warning sign. Many items—including carpets, furniture made from particleboard or plywood, plastics, paints, and cleaning products—give off high levels of volatile organic compounds (VOCs) when they're new. Some VOCs include formaldehyde, benzene, and toluene, which aren't exactly substances that you want in your home.

The best defense against VOCs is prevention. Choose furniture and construction materials that don't release (or off-gas) these particles: solid wood, products labeled as low-emitting or containing phenol formaldehyde (softwood plywood) rather than urea formaldehyde (hardwood or finished-grade plywood), and fibers such as wool, cotton, or nylon. Avoid urea formaldehyde foam insulation (a type of expanding-foam insulation).

Cost can force you to choose higher-VOC substances such as plywood, but sealing exposed edges and surfaces by painting or laminating them will help.

If you can, leave new items such as furniture or carpets (unrolled) outside or in a garage for a few days. Inside, protect them from direct sunlight or heat. VOC release is highest during a product's first few weeks or months and tends to increase with higher temperatures and humidity levels. If you need to have the item indoors right away, open the windows to increase ventilation.

Backdrafting

If your home is not ventilated properly, it can create a phenomenon known as backdrafting, in which exhaust gases from furnaces, stoves, and fireplaces are drawn back into the house. These contain combustion gases, which can irritate breathing passages, aggravate existing breathing problems, and even cause death, in the case of carbon monoxide (there's a good reason why these gases are exhausted outside the house).

To maintain a good ventilation system, ensure that any appliance that burns fuel (e.g., furnaces and stoves) is adequately supplied with fresh air. In addition, these appliances and their intake and exhaust systems should be inspected and serviced annually by a qualified technician. You can help by changing or cleaning any filters regularly and by updating the technology whenever you can to replace older, less efficient models. Also ensure that range hood, clothes dryer, and bathroom exhaust fans are vented outside the house.

FACT

An air-cleaning or air-purifier system can reduce the allergens and hazardous substances in your home's air—but they need careful installation and maintenance, because they can produce ozone, which itself irritates breathing passages. Clean system filters regularly, and consider the benefits of the systems versus the risks.

Managing Mold and Mildew

Warm, damp conditions are perfect breeding grounds for mold and mildew—which is why bathrooms and basements or crawlspaces are the perfect hiding places for them. You can also find the culprits in enclosed spaces such as under sinks, in closets, behind furniture or under carpet that's next to an exterior wall or floor, within walls, and anywhere you have condensation or leaks. They're certainly easy to spot, showing up as black, white, or green stains, or an earthy or musty smell. While most molds are merely irritants, some strains can cause more serious health problems, ranging from allergies to fatigue or flulike symptoms.

Mold Cleanup

Even cleaning mold and mildew can cause problems, because you generally need a bleach solution—and the chlorine in bleach can harm your lungs. Plus, you don't want to release particles from the mold into the air, where you might breathe them in. A small, contained area may respond to scrubbing with hot water and detergent. On larger areas, try a solution of 1 part bleach to 4 parts water. Some commercial cleaners may also help, but likely contain strong, possibly corrosive chemicals, so use caution.

When cleaning mold, protect yourself with strong gloves, safety goggles, and a nose/mouth mask (with a respirator if it's a large area). Seal any used cleaning rags or paper towels in a garbage bag and take it outside immediately. Moldy carpets, ceiling tiles, and other porous surfaces are extremely difficult to clean; consider removing them.

If your furnace humidifier or your air-conditioning system contains mold, stop using it and have the system, including ductwork if necessary, cleaned and serviced professionally.

ALERT!

Never mix chlorine bleach with other cleaning products. If they contain ammonia, the combination can produce highly toxic fumes. Always keep cleaning products in their original containers, and don't reuse empty containers (recycle them).

Mold Prevention

Preventing molds and mildew from gaining a foothold in your home is much easier than cleaning them up. First, reduce moisture levels. Relative humidity should be between 30 and 50 percent (a widely available tool called a hygrometer measures humidity). Excess condensation on windows and other surfaces indicates that your humidity is too high, so reduce the humidity level on the furnace if you have one, consider installing a dehumidifier or air conditioner (depending on local weather conditions), and ensure that your house is properly ventilated. Install and use exhaust fans in bathrooms and kitchens.

Mold can start growing within twenty-four to forty-eight hours of a flood or water accumulation, so working fast reduces the problem. Immediately fix leaks in plumbing, roofs, windows, or walls. Reduce condensation on toilet tanks and cold-water pipes by insulating them with products available at home centers. Keep drip pans in appliances or systems such as fridges and air conditioners clean and dry.

Avoid storing newspapers, clothes, and other materials that can absorb moisture in areas with poor ventilation (including basements). Storage systems and shelves should allow air to move freely. Carpets should not be used in potentially damp areas, such as bathrooms or utility rooms. If mold is a problem, consider replacing carpet with a nonporous option such as ceramic tile or parquet flooring—after you've solved the underlying moisture problem. (Area rugs can always be used to add a sense of warmth to the area.)

Houseplants can help clean the air in your home, but trim any stems and leaves that rest on the soil, to prevent soil molds. And don't bring damp firewood into the house—let it dry outside, under shelter if necessary.

Getting the Lead Out—Or Not

If your house was built before 1978, chances are good that one of the layers of paint or possibly your plumbing contains lead. In fetuses and young children, lead affects brain and nervous system development. In adults, it can cause insomnia, headaches, anemia, and kidney and brain damage.

The risk to you and your family depends on where the lead is and what condition it's in. If it's in a paint layer that has been painted over or sealed in some way and isn't flaking, peeling, or chipping off, it's likely safer to leave it where it is. Removing lead paint can release lead into your home if it's not done properly—and it's expensive.

If, however, the paint layer is damaged (in a window frame, for example, where layers of the paint have worn away to reveal the lead-based paint), it creates lead-containing dust that's possible to breathe or swallow. You'll need expert assistance to deal with it.

Testing for Lead

According to the National Safety Council, about two-thirds of homes built before 1940 contain lead-based paint. That figure drops to one-half for houses built between 1940 and 1960, and it drops even further from 1960 to 1978, when lead was banned.

If your house may contain lead paint, test it. Do-it-yourself kits are available, but their reliability has been questioned. Have a qualified lead specialist investigate your house, or use a certified laboratory to test paint chips that you take yourself, carefully following their instructions.

Test for lead prior to doing any work that might disturb paint, including renovations or redecorating, or if you're concerned about the age of your house and the condition of its paint or plumbing. Also test water for lead levels. Lead pipes, or copper pipes that were sealed with lead-containing solder, may leach lead into water. If lead content shows up anywhere, or if you have reason to believe that it could, all house occupants should have a blood test to show whether their lead levels are elevated.

Dealing with Lead

Your first step is to consult a qualified lead specialist who can tell you if the lead can be sealed safely, or if it must be removed. To control areas of lead paint, you can seal walls with wallboard or stucco. Walls in good condition can be painted over or sealed with shellac. Doors and trim can be replaced, sealed with new paint or varnish, or removed from the house for stripping and repainting. (Use a contractor certified and experienced in lead paint removal.)

FACT

For more information on lead in your home, contact the National Lead Information Center at ✍ *www.epa.gov/lead/nlic.htm* or ✆ 1-800-424-LEAD.

Consider replacing lead pipes or lead-soldered joints where possible and practical. Where it's not, install a filter for all sources of drinking or cooking water, and let the water run for a few minutes before using it any time water hasn't been used for a while, such as overnight (water that has been sitting in pipes is more likely to contain lead than water that has run briefly through them). Also, use only cold water to fill kettles and saucepans, because hot water is more corrosive and could therefore contain more lead.

Other precautions include not allowing children to chew on windowsills or wall corners, pick up paint chips, or play in soil that could contain lead. Hands should be washed frequently, as should toys, stuffed animals, and bedding. Surfaces in the home, including windowsills, should be cleaned regularly. And if you're renovating or having the lead-based paint removed, children and pregnant moms should move out of the house, to reduce exposure.

Radon Gas

Radon is a radioactive, invisible, odorless gas produced when uranium (which can be present naturally in the soil) decays. The gas can seep into your home through cracks or openings in basements, walls, crawlspaces, and exposed earth surfaces (often found in older basements), and into well water. As it breaks down, it becomes part of the dust that you breathe, and inhalation can lead to an increased risk of lung and other cancers.

Radon gas levels can vary greatly over small distances—even in houses on the same street. It's important to have your own house and water tested, rather than relying on neighborhood results.

If radon is found, a number of solutions can be considered, including pressurizing the basement (to keep the gas out), ventilating subflooring (to carry the gas away from the house), and covering any exposed earth or rock with a polyethylene material to act as a barrier. You should also seal cracks or openings (including where wiring or pipes enter the house), and protect floor drains with a backup valve or gas trap. Charcoal filters or aeration units can remove radon from well water.

A retest for radon should follow any of these measures to ensure that they've been effective. You can also use these strategies if you live near a landfill or fuel refinery site, which can also release various gases through the soil if they leak. (If you're concerned, have your soil and air quality tested.)

Asbestos

Asbestos occurs naturally and was mined for years before people realized that its long, flexible fibers can cause breathing problems and even cancer after prolonged exposure. It is, however, an effective insulator and fireproofing material, and it was used in a variety of home products, from ironing board covers to roof shingles and exterior siding.

Even if you have asbestos-containing products, they're not likely to cause problems as long as they're in good shape, because the fibers are sealed. Once asbestos is cut, damaged, or worn, however, the fibers can become friable, or loose in the air—which is a problem.

If you know you have asbestos-containing materials, check their condition. If they're in good shape, you may not need to do anything except be aware of them, or seal surfaces with paint or a new layer of wallboard or stucco. If their condition is worn or deteriorating, or if you have any concerns, seek expert advice; you need to bring in a qualified contractor to seal or remove asbestos safely.

As you've seen in this chapter, making your house as healthy as possible is often just a matter of knowing which problems to look for. Although you may need expert help to find solutions, your awareness and understanding is the first, and essential, step. Making your home environment healthier and more comfortable is also the focus for Chapter 5, which looks at how to keep the weather outside the house from affecting you inside. Ⓔ

Chapter 5
Weather Wise

Your house shelters you from the worst of weather conditions: wind, rain, snow, and heat. Over the years, exposure to these elements takes a toll on the house. To keep it from taking a toll on you (and your wallet), aim for regular maintenance and preventive measures. If the weather turns nasty, preparation can seriously limit the damage that Mother Nature dishes out.

Fall Maintenance

Most fall weather-related maintenance involves preparing the house for cooler temperatures and rain or snow. Start with the roof. Has tree growth caused any branches to overhang? These can create shady, damp areas on the roof that contribute to moss or mildew growth, and can damage roof surfaces in windy weather. Prune the branches as necessary. (If the tree variety shouldn't be pruned in the fall and the situation isn't urgent, mark the task down so that you remember next spring.)

Check roof vents and the vents in the soffit, the flat area under the eaves where the roof overhangs the house, to ensure that they're free of debris, and check that flashings and chimneys are in good shape. Also watch gutters and downspouts on a rainy day to make sure they're ready for heavy rains or snowmelt. Splash blocks or downspout extensions should be positioned so that water runs away from the house without wearing away the soil under the downspout.

This is the time to remove window air conditioners and to install storm windows. Weatherproof doors, windows, vents, and any other potential air-leak sites on the house exterior.

Have heating systems, including ductwork, chimneys, and appliances, serviced and/or cleaned professionally. Winterize exterior faucets if they're not frost-proof, and insulate interior pipes if any are vulnerable to freezing. Test exterior GFCI outlets to ensure that they're ready for vehicle block-heater use if necessary in your area, or for holiday lights. Clean, oil, and store gardening tools for the winter, and service or prepare any snow removal tools.

Check any culverts or drains on your property to make sure they're not blocked, and protect tender shrubs and trees for winter. If you have a wood-burning stove or fireplace, make sure you're well stocked with firewood.

Spring Maintenance

Spring weather-related maintenance generally involves assessing any damage or wear and tear done over the winter and getting ready for a season of garden growth and hot temperatures.

Again, start with the roof. Did the winter damage any shingles or other roof coverings or flashings? If so, replace damaged areas or assess the situation to see if replacing all of the roof covering is necessary. Although binoculars can help you see the roof, another sign of shingle deterioration is a heavy accumulation of shingle covering, such as gravel, coming down through gutters and downspouts.

Have cooling systems, including appliances and any related ducting or venting, serviced professionally. Keep outdoor air conditioners free of leaves and other debris. If you have heating oil tanks, fill them up for the nonheating season—this helps to prevent condensation that can contribute to rust or bacterial sludge problems.

Remove any broken or damaged tree branches, and clean and repair gutters as necessary. If the ground surface is sloping toward the house, spring is a good time to correct it.

If your storm windows are removable, now's the time to take them off. Repair damage now so that they're ready for next season. Also install or repair window screens as necessary. Install window air conditioners, and check the seals around them to ensure that they're tight. Examine windows for signs of leaks or rot, and repaint or reseal them as necessary.

Check the condition of your exterior walls, foundations, trims, porches, decks, sidewalks, driveways, and fences. If repairs need to be made, schedule them for warm (but not hot) weather. Pressure-wash your roof and walls, as well as the garage floor if road salt has accumulated. Ensure that all vents and openings in the house wall are either sealed or screened to prevent animals from entering.

Test exterior GFCI electrical outlets to ensure that they're ready for use. Inspect gardening tools for rust and smooth operation, and service lawnmowers. Inspect the house for signs of insects such as termites. Prune plants that are encroaching on house walls, and repair lawns. Also watch for signs of erosion in the yard.

Exterior Weatherproofing

Weatherproofing your house basically means preventing the outdoor environment—whether it's too cold or too hot for comfort—from interfering with the indoor environment. This has the added advantage of preventing heated or cooled air inside from leaking out, thus reducing utility bills. Adapt the following exterior weatherproofing strategies as applicable, and see Chapter 6 for interior weatherproofing strategies.

Caulking and Sealing

Where possible, remove the old caulking and any loose paint around joints in windows, doors, and vents, and clean the surface. This will provide better adhesion for the new caulking, which can be applied using a tube and gun, or (for small areas) a tube that's squeezable by hand. An exterior-grade, silicone acrylic latex caulk is a good all-purpose choice.

Cut the tip of the caulking tube at a 45-degree angle to produce an opening about ⅜-inch wide, and use a nail or awl to puncture any inner seal. Holding the gun or tube at a 30- to 45-degree angle, apply the caulking in a long bead all around the joint. Use steady pressure and even movement to get the best results. If the bead of caulking is bumpy or uneven, wet the back of a spoon and run it along the bead to smooth it out (you can also use your finger, but wear latex or similar gloves). Caulk-smoothing tools are also available, which produce a professional-looking finish.

ALERT!

Don't caulk over weep holes in masonry and window frames, or masonry joints left purposely mortar-free—these allow condensation and other moisture to escape, and if blocked will cause water damage.

Caulking works best on fairly thin seals, usually less than ½-inch wide. Fill a bigger gap with expanding-foam insulation first, or place a backer rod inside it, then caulk on top to finish the seal if necessary.

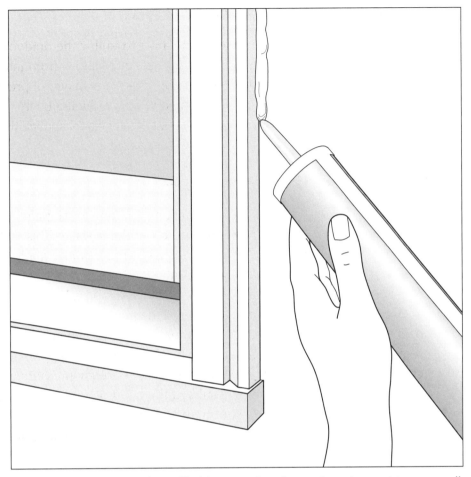

▲ Choose a caulk color that will either match or be unobtrusive next to your wall.

Weather-Stripping a Door

To check potential drafts through exterior doors, place a piece of paper between the door and the frame and close the door, or have someone shine a flashlight around the edges of the closed door. If you can easily slide the paper out, or see light from the flashlight, the door's seal needs help. A variety of kits is available for this, offering flexible tubing or other material that's often aided with a strip of thin metal. Basically, you cut the weather-stripping material in the kit to fit the sides and top of your door, and nail, screw, or stick it in place. Ensure that it touches the door but doesn't prevent it from closing properly.

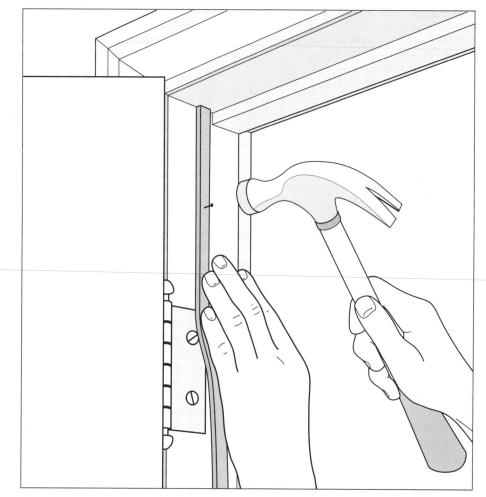

▲ Weather-stripping a door not only seals the door against cold or hot air, but also prevents pollens and dust from entering.

Door Sweeps

Door sweeps, or bottom seals, close any gaps between the bottom of the door and the threshold. Buy a door sweep kit that suits your door and décor. They generally combine a metal strip that screws onto the door with a flexible seal that hangs below the door. Depending on the sweep, your door, and your threshold, determine whether the sweep fits better on the interior or exterior of the door. Measure the bottom edge of the door, and trim the door sweep to fit. Hold the sweep against the door and mark the screw positions. Predrill the holes, and screw the sweep to the door.

▲ A door sweep can seal the bottom of a door very effectively and takes only minutes to install.

Window Well Covers

These plastic covers come in a variety of shapes and sizes designed to cover the metal "well" that usually surrounds a basement or ground-level window. Purchase covers that fit your window well. The covers generally have a long strip built into their top that allows you to insert it between two pieces of siding. Follow the cover's instructions for fastening it to the rest of the house, and caulk the seal if you need extra protection.

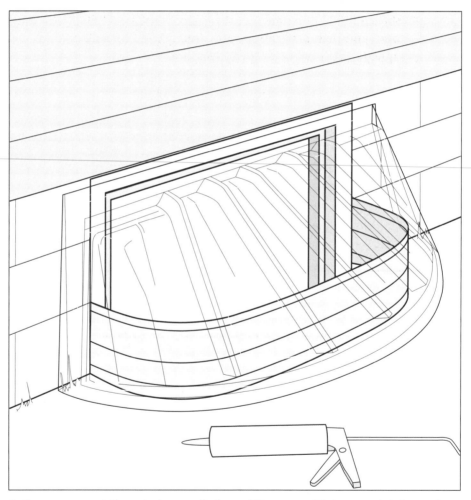

▲ Covers prevent the window wells from filling up with leaves, debris, and even water.

Windows and Walls

If your windows are older, the glass is likely sealed to the window frame using glaze or putty. If this cracks or crumbles, drafts result. To replace it with glazing compound, scrape out the old putty, and apply glazing compound as described in Chapter 17 for replacing the glass in a wood-frame window.

Check your exterior walls. There's often a gap behind the bottom piece of siding, between it and the wall. This can be sealed using thick backer rope or foam caulking. Simply buy the required length of caulking or rope, and insert it between the siding and the wall. You can seal the result with a caulking gun if necessary.

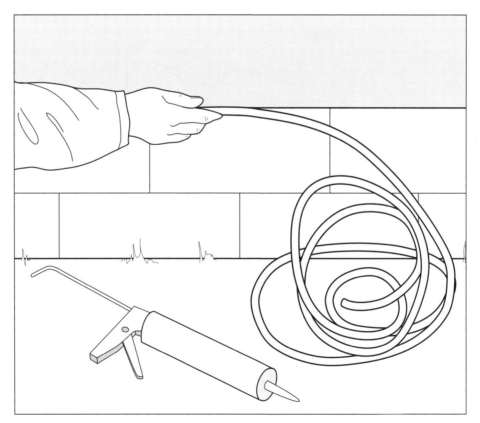

▲ When installing the rope or caulking, beware of sharp pieces of siding or protruding nails that could catch your fingers.

Dealing with Frozen Pipes

The easiest way to deal with frozen pipes is to prevent them. Before the cold season, inspect all of the plumbing pipes that lead into and through the house. Any that run through an unheated area, or against outside walls where they could be exposed to cold temperatures, should be insulated. A number of commercial products are available for this, including foam insulation tubes that snap around the pipes and can be cut to the right length.

If freezing pipes are a recurring problem, or the cold is so extreme that insulating alone won't help, consider having a qualified technician wrap the pipes with electrically heated wire or cable.

ALERT!

Don't use propane or other torches to thaw pipes. The flame can be unsafe, and it can heat the ice so quickly that it turns into steam, which expands rapidly and can burst the pipe.

To handle an isolated case of cold weather, open the faucets just enough to keep the water trickling through them so that the water doesn't have time to freeze—and never turn the heat down so far (below 45°F) that the pipes could freeze.

If the pipes have frozen, but not burst, open at least one of the faucets that the pipe leads to. As you're thawing the pipe, this will allow melting water to escape from the pipe, rather than bursting it. Try these tricks to find the frozen area (if they don't work, start thawing the pipe at the faucet, and work back along the pipe until the water is running again):

- Run your hand along the pipe, feeling for a cold spot.
- Look for condensation or frost on the pipe.
- Run a thermometer along the pipe to find the coldest part.
- Run a damp cloth along the pipe until you see frost forming.

Using a handheld hair dryer on a "hot" setting or a heat gun, start warming the pipe at the side of the frozen area that's closest to the faucet (again, so that melting water has an escape route). Other thawing methods include wrapping a towel soaked with hot water around the pipe or using electrical heating tape around the pipe.

If the pipes have burst, shut off the water supply. A small burst might be solved by the leaky pipe fixes in Chapter 3. If it's more serious, use compression fittings to replace the damaged pipe section (see Chapter 18), or call a plumber.

Putting the Chill on Outdoor Faucets

In cold climate areas, fall frosts signal that it's time to winterize outdoor faucets. Garden hoses need to be removed from faucets, drained (hanging them over a clothesline works well), coiled, and stored for the winter. Faucets that sit on the house exterior (known as sillcocks or hose bibs) generally have a shutoff valve on the pipe leading to the faucet, inside the house. (If they don't, you should install one.) To avoid having the faucet freeze and burst during cold weather, turn off the shutoff valve, and then open the faucet to drain any water that remains in the pipe. In the spring, reopen the valve.

Of course, shutting off the water means that you no longer have running water outside the house. For mild areas, you may be able to avoid shutting off the water by buying an insulated cover for the faucet. In colder areas, however, you'll need a frost-proof sillcock. These extend a long tube into the house, inside which is the valve that opens and closes the water supply—handily located beyond the freezing temperatures.

To replace a regular faucet with a frost-proof sillcock, first check the existing pipes to ensure that you have room to install the sillcock's longer tube. Talk to your plumbing store staff, perhaps bringing with you a Polaroid or digital photo of your current setup so that they can properly advise you on the right sillcock to buy.

Close the existing faucet's shutoff valve or the house water supply, and use a pipe cutter or hacksaw to cut the water supply pipe at the point where it needs to meet the end of the new sillcock's tube. Replace the old sillcock with the new one, fastening its collar loosely in place on the exterior house wall. Double-check that the sillcock tube meets the water pipe and that the sillcock is installed at a slight downward angle to let the water automatically drain out of it.

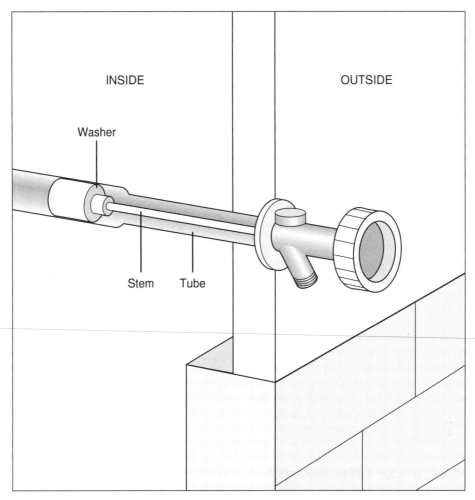

INSIDE

OUTSIDE

Washer

Stem   Tube

▲ Frost-proof sillcocks, or faucets, mean that you have access to water outside all winter long—even when the temperature dips below freezing.

Most instructions now tell you to solder the two copper pipes and their fittings together, but if you're not comfortable with this, talk to your plumbing store about fittings that will connect the two ends without the need for flame. Tighten up the screws that fasten the sillcock to the outside wall, and caulk any gaps. Turn the water back on, and check for leaks.

Eliminating Ice Dams

Ice dams form on roofs when warm attic air melts the bottom layer of snow that's sitting on the roof. The snowmelt runs down the roof and builds up along the colder edge of the roof, freezing into an icy mass as it does so. This can seriously damage the roof, because it forces water up underneath the shingles and into the roof structure, causing it to leak or rot.

If you notice ice dams building along your roof, try running a garden hose attached to your hot-water tap over one spot in the dam, to create an escape route for the water and stop the dam from expanding. Chipping the ice away from the roof yourself is *not* recommended. It's easy to damage the shingles or roof covering—and balancing on a ladder in icy weather is a good way to fall off it. Call in a professional to thaw the ice dam if it's serious; they use steam equipment that's less likely to damage your roof.

FACT

Insulating and ventilating the attic is the best way to prevent ice dams from forming. Take photos of the ice dam so that you'll know later where in the roof or attic you need to improve the insulation or ventilation.

Natural Disasters

Basic emergency preparedness measures are easy and inexpensive, and they can help prevent both injuries and property damage. First, know the emergencies most likely to occur in your area. Check your home insurance policy to ensure that you're covered for these possibilities, and consider purchasing additional insurance as necessary.

Depending on your situation, and how vulnerable you are to the effects of a power outage, consider alternative sources of electricity and heat. These range from generators to solar power, and from wood stoves to battery backups. Whichever you choose, ensure that it is installed and maintained properly so that it's always there when you need it.

You can also prevent damage to your house, garage, or yard by having a professional arborist inspect trees for signs of rot or disease once every five years, and by dealing with damaged or weak tree branches as you see them. It's better to cut them down under control than to have them crash down during a storm.

A National Oceanic & Atmospheric Administration (NOAA) Weather Radio can alert you to weather watches or warnings in your area. Your household should also have a disaster plan, similar to a fire escape plan, that lets each family member know what to do, how to contact each other, and where to meet if you're separated during a disaster. Ensure that pets are included in planning, as most emergency shelters can't take them.

If you need to evacuate your house, and you have sufficient time, unplug appliances, shut off utility supplies as necessary, lock your doors and windows, and prepare your house for cold temperatures if necessary.

For detailed information on disaster preparedness, contact the Federal Emergency Management Agency (FEMA) at ☎ 1-800-480-2520 or 🖱 *www.fema.gov*. Ask for their publication *Are You Ready? A Guide to Citizen Preparedness.* They also have a range of publications about preparing for and dealing with specific disasters.

Electrical Storms

Because lightning can cause power surges through your home's electrical circuits, it's best to unplug sensitive electronic appliances before a storm—TVs, microwaves, computers, and stereos, for example. If the storm has already begun, however, don't unplug them; you don't want to be holding the plug if there is a power surge. Another option is to have all such appliances plugged into a surge-protected power bar, as are commonly used for computers. Stay off land-based corded phones during a storm (cordless or cell phones are okay), and don't shower or have a bath (plumbing can conduct electricity).

When lightning strikes a house, it can spark electrical fires within the walls. Whether or not you can see or smell smoke, evacuate the house, and call the fire department so that they can check it out.

FACT

Major electrical storms, freezing rain, and other weather phenomena can all cause power outages. If a major storm is in the forecast, turn up your freezer and fridge to the highest settings. If the power goes out, the deeply chilled food will last longer before beginning to thaw.

Freezes

If the house is going to sit at below-freezing temperatures because of a power cut for an extended period, unplug your appliances. When the power is restored, let the appliance warm up a little before plugging it back in, as most are not designed to operate in freezing temperatures.

To prevent your water supply from freezing, turn off the main water shutoff. Open all faucets and flush the toilets. If you know the house will freeze, put nontoxic antifreeze in all traps, such as toilets, sinks, washing machines, and floor drains.

Floods

Limited flooding can be kept from your house by sandbags or other temporary barrier systems, especially when combined with a sump pump, but a serious flood may overwhelm these. If you have advance notice of floodwaters, move all furniture and belongings to the highest floor in the house, shut off all utilities and appliances such as heating and air-conditioning systems, and take important papers or items with you when you evacuate.

To limit the damage from contained flooding, such as that coming into the house from a damaged roof, line the floor with a plastic tarpaulin or other heavy-duty plastic sheet, taping it partway up the walls. This should keep the worst of the water from running through the house and will give you a contained area to either bail or mop. Plastic sheets can also be stapled to the roof itself, but don't venture onto the roof while it's wet, during a storm, or if it's so badly damaged that it might no longer be sound. Think safety first.

Floodwaters can be contaminated with wastewater, sewage, and pesticides or manure from nearby fields; protect yourself with boots and gloves, and use the disinfecting solution advised by your local emergency measures organization. Inspect your house foundation for cracks, and watch for signs of settling inside the house, in case the flood affected the foundation.

ALERT!

Remember that water can become electrically charged if it's in contact with a live electrical circuit. If your house is flooded and the electrical panel is still switched on, wait for emergency services personnel to assist you in shutting it off, even if the area's electricity is down (you don't know when it might be restored, and you don't want to be standing in the water when that happens).

Wind

Hurricanes and tornadoes can do significant damage, but they differ in how much warning time you'll receive. Hurricanes are usually predicted several days in advance; tornadoes may occur without warning, although they're often associated with hot humid weather and thunderstorms.

To prevent wind damage, keep trees around the house in good shape, maintain gutters and downspouts, and ensure that structural elements such as roofs comply with local building codes. These usually require some kind of extra strapping or clipping to secure the roof structure in areas vulnerable to wind storms. In these areas, you should also consider permanent storm shutters for your windows. If you don't have them, board up windows with $5/8$-inch marine-grade plywood.

If you have time, store or tie down any objects that could fly around in a windstorm. Also consider building a wind-safe room within your house, if the risk of tornadoes is very high in your area.

Wildfires

Help protect your home from wildfires by creating a space between your house and any vegetation or material that is likely to bring a fire your way. This space should extend at least 30 feet out from the house and shouldn't contain thick brush or trees, firewood, or flammable materials. In fire-risk areas, investigate fire-resistant plants, and consider replacing wood-based exterior materials with those that are more resistant to fire, like brick, stone, or metal.

Earthquakes

To lessen the damage an earthquake can cause, inspect your home for any appliance, furniture, or fixture that could tip or fall. Free-standing bookshelves, for example, can be fastened to walls, and heating and air-conditioning units can be bolted down. Also investigate whether your house fully complies with earthquake safety requirements. Are gas and water lines protected with flexible joints and do you have an automatic gas shutoff?

Heat Waves

While an air-conditioning system can prove a lifesaver—quite literally—during extreme heat, it needs help. Weather-strip or caulk around windows, vents, and openings in the house, to help keep the cool air inside. Try to limit the heat building up inside your home. Line windows with aluminum foil to reflect heat, or shield windows with curtains, blinds, shutters, or awnings. If the heat eases at night, consider turning off air conditioners and opening windows.

Emergency Supplies

Depending on where you live and what emergency you're likely to face, consider storing the following items in easily accessible, portable waterproof containers. (Batteries, food, water, and other perishable supplies should be replaced every six months or as necessary.)

- Flashlight and radio with spare batteries
- First-aid kit
- Candles and matches/lighter
- Extra car keys and cash
- Basic tools, such as a shovel and adjustable wrench
- Important papers such as ID and personal documents
- One sleeping bag and change of clothing and footwear per person
- Toilet paper and personal supplies
- Medication
- Whistle
- At least a three-day supply of water (allow 1 gallon per person per day)
- Ready-to-eat foods for at least three days
- Manual can/bottle opener
- Games and supplies appropriate to children's ages
- Pet food and supplies

Being weather wise around the house will not only help protect you from natural disasters, but also allows you to identify wear and tear on the house exterior before it becomes a major problem. This, of course, creates a much more comfortable interior environment—as do the tips from Chapter 6, which focus on saving energy but have the added advantage of making your house a more comfortable place to be. (E)

Chapter 6

Energy Savers

According to the EPA, the average American family spends $1,300 a year on energy bills. What would you say to cutting that by 20 to 30 percent—a savings of $260 to $390? It's not difficult to achieve these savings, if you focus on two strategies: fixing or replacing house components, and fixing your household's habits. Take a look around your house—you can make a difference in just a few hours.

Identifying Energy Wasters

For a comprehensive report on where and how to improve your home's energy efficiency, have your local power company or energy contractor conduct an energy audit (some power companies offer these audits free or at a significant discount). These use inspections and tools such as infrared photography or blower tests to identify where the house is losing energy.

An audit provides detailed, quantifiable results, but you can also conduct basic visual tests yourself. If your house has drafts, unevenly heated or cooled rooms, high utility bills, and frosty windows or walls, you already know there's a problem. To find the source(s), light an incense stick and slowly pass it near areas where two materials or house components meet: window and door frames, light fixtures, electrical outlets, vents, chimneys, plumbing, and holes where services come through an exterior wall. When the smoke blows about, you've found energy being wasted, and a good place to start weather-stripping or sealing.

Reducing Utility Bills

Although energy efficiency has huge environmental benefits, the most obvious advantage to you is lower utility bills. A home renovation is the ideal time to incorporate major energy conservation measures (such as windows with low-emissivity coatings), but you can accomplish a lot with everyday options.

FACT

When shopping for new appliances—from ceiling fans to dishwashers to furnaces—look for the Energy Star label. It means the product has met strict energy efficiency guidelines from the EPA and the U.S. Department of Energy, and will help you save money. Similarly, choose compact fluorescent or halogen light bulbs, which last longer and use less electricity than incandescent bulbs.

Creating an Energy-Efficient House

Begin with the heating or cooling system. Clean or replace your furnace or air-conditioning filter monthly, or as recommended by your model. (Dirty filters make heating and cooling systems work harder.) If your system is more than ten or fifteen years old and needs frequent repairs, it may be more cost-effective to replace it with a new, energy-efficient model. Invest in a programmable thermostat, which you set to automatically lower the house temperature at certain times, such as when you're at work or sleeping. Also check that your humidity level is between 30 and 50 percent (if it's too low, it could be making the air feel cold).

With forced-air systems, examine your ductwork. Air leaks at joints should be sealed with duct tape. If specific rooms are too hot or cold, adjust the dampers (baffles that block or redirect airflow), identified by a metal handle on a duct. Close it to see what area it affects, and label the handle with this area and its seasonal settings (in the winter, you may want to partially close a damper leading to upstairs rooms, because warm air rising from downstairs may be heating them—which is known as the "stack" effect).

Dampers can also be located on individual floor or wall registers. Position these dampers to direct heated air across the floor, or at least away from exterior walls and windows. Plastic shields (deflectors) placed over the registers will move the air away from obstacles such as curtains and furniture. You should also position furniture, rugs, and appliances so that they don't block the registers.

Partially close dampers in small or unused rooms (don't reduce the heat so much that you risk freezing pipes or room contents), and fully open them in large rooms. In addition, close fireplace dampers when the fire's not lit. For hot-water heating systems, the heat in specific rooms can be adjusted using the valves on branch pipes or radiators.

Once you've made your heating or cooling system as efficient as possible, it's time to focus on keeping the warm or cool air inside. This means insulating, caulking, and weather-stripping any place where unheated or uncooled areas (such as crawlspaces and attics) can affect the house's living areas.

Operate ceiling fans counterclockwise during hot weather, for a cooling effect. Operate them clockwise during cold weather to help distribute warm air throughout the room.

Creating an Energy-Efficient Household

Energy efficiency isn't just about your house—it's also about how your household uses the house and its systems. Consider turning down your hot-water tank's temperature to 120°F (which also reduces the risk of scalding), and positioning the fridge away from heat sources like stoves, dishwashers, and even sunlight (which make it work harder to cool food). It also helps to maintain your appliances. Clean fridge and freezer condenser coils and defrost freezers regularly, and clean dryer lint filters with every load.

Take advantage of "passive" (and free!) solar heating in cold climates: Open curtains and blinds when it's sunny, and close them when it's dark. In hot climates, shield windows that face east, west, and south with shade panels, awnings, shutters, blinds, or curtains. For a more permanent solution, apply a reflective film to the window glass that lets light, but not heat, into the house (see Chapter 17). Deciduous trees (whose leaves drop in the fall) can reduce the heating effect of summer sun while still allowing winter sun to warm up the house.

Operate appliances such as dishwashers, washing machines, and clothes dryers only on full loads and on the shortest and coolest cycle that will do the job. Use dishwashers and fridges on energy-saving settings. When possible, air-dry dishes and clothes. (If you're drying laundry on the line, turn clothes inside out to reduce fading, and shake the clothes to get rid of pollen, dust, and insects.)

To further reduce electricity use:

- Turn off lights and appliances such as stereos when you leave a room.
- Choose toaster ovens, microwaves, and electric skillets instead of the oven.

- Turn off your computer monitor (even if you leave your computer on).
- Use a timer to switch on your car's block heater just one to three hours before it's needed.

The Benefits of Insulation

When you're talking about insulation, you'll hear the term "R-value" a lot. R-value means "resistance" value—it measures the insulation's ability to resist conducting heat. The higher the R-value, the more the material insulates. Insulation comes in several different varieties, with varying R-values. Fix-it jobs generally involve fiberglass batts, which have an R-value of about 3 per inch of material. Loose-fill cellulose, which is also common, has about 3.3 per inch.

Your local building code will tell you what insulation level you need in the house. Attics provide the greatest energy-efficiency return on insulation investments, and it's relatively easy to have additional insulation laid or blown in to bring attics up to standard (see Chapter 15).

You may also be able to insulate areas such as unfinished basement walls and crawlspace ceilings yourself (see Chapter 11), but insulating inside wall cavities is not a fix-it job. If you've ever seen frost on the inside of an exterior wall, you've seen a need for improving the wall's insulation. The most effective methods involve pumping in loose or expanding-foam insulation through holes drilled in the walls—it's a major undertaking, and requires qualified contractors.

FACT

According to the American Society of Home Inspectors (ASHI), many older homes have just 4 to 6 inches of insulating material in their attics—when the standard in many colder areas of the country is 12 inches, for an insulating value of about R38. (If you measure the insulation depth on the attic floor, you can figure out its R-value. Multiply the number of inches by 3.3 for loose insulation, or by 3 for fiberglass.)

When you're examining your house's insulation, be aware that some things shouldn't be insulated, including attic vents (essential for house ventilation), and anywhere that the insulation could catch fire (recessed lighting, chimneys, flues, and electrical fixtures, where specific fireproof insulation is needed).

Easy Insulation Fixes

There's nothing like a warm blanket to hold in the heat—which is exactly the principle behind wrapping an insulating cover around ductwork, hot-water pipes, and hot-water heaters.

Ductwork

First, check the joints in your ductwork. You can seal any that leak air by wrapping them with an overlapping layer of metal-backed or duct tape (duct tape can't handle very high temperatures, so it shouldn't be used around chimneys or flues).

If ductwork from a forced-air heating or cooling system travels through an unheated (or uncooled) space, insulate the ducts. Wrap the ducts with batts of foil-backed fiberglass insulation or foil "sleeves" available at home centers. Tape the ends of the batts together with duct tape (if you scrape a little insulation off the foil backing, this provides a "lip" that can be wrapped over the neighboring batt to make taping easier).

Fiberglass insulation can irritate eyes, lungs, and skin, so take precautions when handling it. Wear gloves, a hood, long sleeves, and long trousers (coveralls work well), and use a respirator mask and safety goggles.

Hot-Water Pipes

You should insulate any hot-water pipes that run through unheated areas of the house and are vulnerable to freezing. You can also insulate the hot-water pipe as far as possible after it leaves the hot-water tank, even in heated areas. This helps the hot water inside the pipe to retain its heat for longer, and thus reduces the time it takes for hot water to reach your faucets. The easiest insulation to use is the sleeve- or tube-style that has a slit running down its length.

Wait for the hot-water pipes to cool down sufficiently to be safe to work around. Cut the insulation tube to fit the pipe length as required, and slip it over the pipe (measure your pipe diameter before buying the insulation to make sure you choose the right size). If the slit has self-adhesive backing, remove the tape and seal it. Seams can be duct-taped together.

Hot-Water Heaters

You can buy insulating kits to fit your hot-water tank. Just wrap the insulation around the heater as directed in the instructions. Be careful, however, as there are some areas that insulation shouldn't cover, including the top of the tank, temperature controls, and drain and pressure-relief valves. For gas heaters, keep the burner inlet, pilot access plate, and draft hood clear. For oil heaters, keep the peep sight, flue pipe, and oil burner mechanism clear. And for electric heaters, keep the power connection and element access panels clear.

Roofs

If your roof has a dark covering, heat can build up in the attic, straining the air-conditioning system. Try a heat barrier, which consists of foam sheets with an aluminum layer that blocks the heat—staple the sheets to the underside of the roof (aluminum side against the roof).

Interior Weatherproofing

Exterior weather-stripping and caulking (covered in Chapter 5) is important to keep weather from penetrating the house, but it needs to be matched by interior weatherproofing for the best possible energy savings. The most useful materials are caulking (for sealing gaps of less than ½ inch), expandable (spray) foam and caulking backer rope for larger gaps, and weather stripping (ideal for sealing parts that move, such as windows and doors in their frames).

Weather-Stripping Windows

Since most modern vinyl or metal windows come with weather stripping or sealing materials built into the window design, the most likely window types that you'll need to weather-strip are casement or sash windows. Various types of weather stripping are available, including vinyl self-adhesive V-stripping, and combinations of metal strips with vinyl, rubber, or felt lining, or a spring action. Removable caulking is also useful for sealing the gaps between windows and frames, as long as you don't want to open the window during the heating (or cooling) season. The type that you choose will depend on how long you need it to last (metal strips that are nailed to the window or frame last longer than self-adhesive strips), ease of installation (V-strips are supereasy), and looks (a matter of choice).

Regardless of the type of weather stripping, your first job is to remove any old weather stripping and to clean the window frame; then, for casement windows, you can stick self-adhesive foam strips to the frame where the window closes against it. For sash windows, V-strips can be inserted into the channels in which the sashes move up and down, on the bottom of the window sash where it meets the window frame, and on the lock rail of the top window sash where it meets the bottom window sash.

Measure the V-strip to fit the lock rail, sash, or channels (for the latter, the strips should be 2 inches longer than the window), and cut. Crease the V-strip, and position it in place. For window channels, the open part of the V should face outdoors. For the bottom sash and lock rail, the V should face down.

Metal weather stripping can be inserted in the same places as the V-stripping, and nailed in place. You may need to bend the metal out slightly using a screwdriver or putty knife blade to adjust the fit to the window.

Shrink-to-Fit Window Film

Shrink-to-fit window film that seals over the interior window frame can reduce heat lost through the window by 25 to 50 percent. It's also

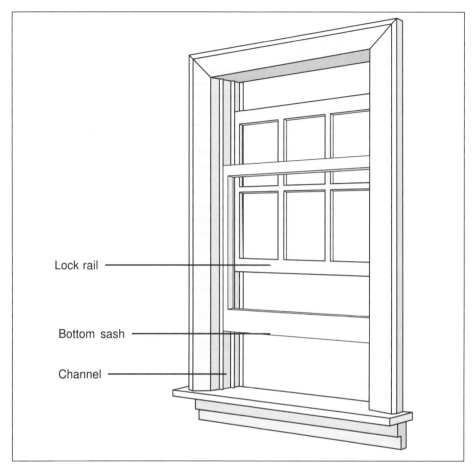

Lock rail

Bottom sash

Channel

▲ V-strip weather stripping seals all four edges of sash windows.

inexpensive, supereasy, and removable at the end of the heating or cooling season.

To install it, remove or hook back any curtain coverings and clean the window frame. Apply the kit's two-sided tape to the edge of the window frame. (Avoid taping to wallboard, because although the tape pulls off most surfaces without removing paint, it may damage wallboard.) Peel off the tape's backing.

Cut the plastic film to fit the window plus about 4 inches all around. Apply the plastic film to the tape, starting at the top or one corner, working down and around the window. At this point, you should be able to remove the plastic from the tape fairly easily if you need to reposition it. Aim for a snug, but not tight, fit.

To shrink the plastic, apply heat using a hair dryer. Hold the dryer a few inches from the plastic, starting at one corner and sweeping across the window. The plastic will shrink rapidly and wrinkles will disappear. Check the tape to ensure a tight seal at the edges of the window, and trim off any excess plastic. When you need to remove the window film, pull off the plastic and tape. If it resists, warm the tape with a hair dryer.

Although it's unlikely that weather stripping will seal an older house well enough to make it too airtight, watch for increased condensation, musty or lingering kitchen odors, or molds—these indicate a need for ventilation. Use bathroom or kitchen fans (exhausted outside), remove some weatherproofing, or improve your ventilation system.

Baseboards and Cover Plates

Baseboards often have a gap behind them, between the wall and the floor, that causes drafts. A small gap between the baseboard and the floor can be sealed with caulking. If the gap is large, carefully remove the baseboards with a small pry bar (baseboards are generally nailed to walls). Fill the gap with caulking or expandable-foam insulation (which may need to be trimmed with a sharp knife to allow the baseboards to lie flat against the wall again). Replace the baseboards.

Alternatively, consider leaving the baseboard in place, using foam to seal the gap, and installing a thin piece of shoe molding against the baseboard to cover the gap attractively.

Drafts around light switch and electrical outlet cover plates on exterior walls can be reduced with store-bought draft sealers that fit under the cover plates.

Attic Hatches and Garages

Foam or vinyl tubing works well to seal attic access panels or hatches. Open the hatch or access, and stick or nail the weather stripping (depending on the type) to the attic opening. This creates a good seal when the panel is dropped back down or the hatch is lifted back into place.

Whether or not your garage is heated/cooled, if it's attached to your house, check out garage door weather stripping and insulating kits. The weather stripping is generally nailed or screwed to the bottom of the door, while insulating panels can be glued to the door interior.

Installing a Programmable Thermostat

The U.S. Department of Energy reports that decreasing the temperature by 10 to 15°F for 8 hours (while you're at work or sleeping) can reduce heating bills by 5 to 10 percent. Programmable (or set-back) thermostats allow you to program different temperatures for mornings, daytime, evenings, and nights, on a different schedule for weekdays and weekends. Because you don't need to remember to change the temperature setting yourself, these thermostats (which start at about $40) can save up to $100 annually.

FACT

Some people are concerned that it takes extra energy to heat the house back up after the temperature has been reduced—but studies have shown that the energy required to heat the house back up equals the energy saved as it cooled down. You still save the energy that's conserved while the temperature is stable at the lower level.

Your thermostat should be placed in an area that's not prone to big temperature swings (such as beside an exterior door), but if you're replacing your existing thermostat, you may be limited to putting it where the old one was. This is a simple job that will take about an hour, but if you're uncomfortable with the idea of working on electrical components (even though most programmable thermostats are low voltage), or your local building codes require an electrician, call an expert.

Otherwise, turn off the power to the thermostat's circuit at the house's main electrical panel. Remove the old thermostat's cover, and examine how it's wired. One by one, loosen the screws that hold the wires in place, unhook the wires, and use masking tape to label them with the terminal screw color (not necessarily the wire color) so that you'll know which terminals they need to be reattached to. (Some thermostat kits come with special labels, or you can use masking tape.) Either spread the wires apart or wrap them around a pencil to stop them from falling back into the wall.

Remove the screws that hold the thermostat to the wall and take off the thermostat, carefully moving it past the wires to avoid tearing off the labels. Place the new thermostat on the wall, level it, and mark the new screw locations. If necessary, remove the thermostat so that you can drill holes for wall anchors.

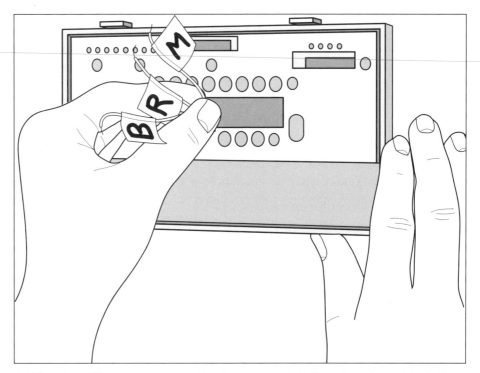

▲ When installing a programmable thermostat, labeling the wires with their terminal screw color ensures that you refasten them on the correct screw.

Screw the thermostat to the wall and reconnect the wires, carefully matching them to the right terminal screw. Insert the batteries (if required) and snap the thermostat cover in place. Then program the thermostat to the lowest comfortable temperatures.

Not all thermostats operate all systems. Take your furnace details with you to the store, and ask staff to help you choose the right model for your furnace and your household needs. Look for a model with batteries, as it may be more reliable than one that relies solely on the electrical circuit.

Reducing Water Consumption

Conserving water can also reduce utility bills. The EPA reports that the average household uses almost 100 gallons of water per person daily. The bathroom sees the house's largest water use with a whopping 41 percent literally going down the toilet. Again, there are two strategies for water conservation: dealing with water-using fixtures, and dealing with water-using people.

First, repair running toilets or dripping faucets (see Chapter 18)—a leak of a water drop per second adds up to some 2,700 gallons wasted annually. For inexpensive and easy fixes, replace showerheads with low-flow options, install faucet aerators, and reduce toilet flush capacity (see the following).

When choosing new appliances, the Energy Star label can help. A qualified clothes washer uses about half the 40 gallons per load of a standard machine, and it removes more water during the spin cycle, reducing drying times. (If you're looking at low-flow toilets, be aware that their design has improved over the past several years.)

Once you've dealt with fixtures and appliances, it's time to deal with people—which is all about minimizing water use. Choosing showers instead of baths will help conserve water, as will turning off the faucet while brushing your teeth or doing dishes. Water that would be wasted while you're waiting for it to warm up can be collected for watering plants. Sink-based garbage disposals are water hungry—putting vegetable and fruit waste into a compost bin instead will also keep your garden happy. Finally, run dishwashers and clothes washers only when they're full, and on the shortest possible cycle. (If it's a small load in a clothes washer, reduce the fill level.)

Going Low Flow

With low-flow toilets using 1.6 gallons of water per flush and conventional toilets using 3.5 to 5 gallons, the potential savings are clear. If you don't need to replace your toilet, you can at least make it behave like a low-flush model. To save a gallon per flush, fill a plastic container (like a milk jug) with pebbles and water, and place it in the tank where it won't interfere with the flush mechanism. Or, purchase toilet dams that save 1 to 2 gallons per flush. (Reduce the size of the container if it's causing incomplete flushes.)

Standard showerheads use about 4.5 gallons of water per minute; this drops to 2.5 gallons with a low-flow showerhead (most of which are designed to maintain the shower quality). See Chapter 3 for replacing showerheads.

If your faucets don't have aerators, head to the store. Aerators attach to the end of the faucet and—by mixing air with the water—save as much as 60 percent of the water flow. Most just screw on, but you'll need to bring details of your faucets into the store to choose the right model (digital or Polaroid photographs will help).

Landscaping

This is all about the right plant in the right place. Native plants tend to be much more drought resistant than non-native plants. If they need help, water in the morning or evening, when temperatures are lower and less water will be lost to evaporation.

Lawns need about 1 inch of water per week. Place the sprinkler so that the water's hitting the lawn, not running off over sidewalks and driveways (which should be swept, not hosed off), and don't overwater. Adding rain barrels to your downspouts will catch water coming off the roof for later use.

To take water conservation to a fun extreme, try xeriscaping. This uses garden design, soil analysis, mulching, maintenance, and plant choice to create a garden that's high on conserving water and low on producing pollution.

As you've been working on weatherproofing and saving energy in every part of your house—from its heating and cooling systems to the walls around you—you may have discovered components such as shingles or siding that need repair. That means that it's time to tackle those bigger fix-it jobs. To start, check out Chapter 7's focus on your home's exterior envelope.

Chapter 7

The Exterior Envelope

From the foundation to the roof, the exterior envelope that encloses your house takes the brunt of time and weather. Fixing problems as soon as they occur will protect the house's exterior and keep your home looking its best. Before attempting any repairs, check the material's guarantee or talk to the installation company or manufacturer—you may be able to have the repair handled professionally (and for free) under the warranty.

Foundations and Masonry

Besides supporting a house's four walls, the foundation is one of your home's most important defenses against cold (or heat), water, and unwanted houseguests such as insects and mice. Concrete and brick (masonry) are the most common foundation materials, although you may also find fieldstone and wood.

While weatherproofing strategies covered in Chapters 5 and 6 help to seal the foundation against water and weather, other problems may turn up. Small cracks in concrete foundations are common and aren't usually causes for concern. If the cracks are wider than $\frac{1}{8}$ inch, the edges of the crack don't match each other, or the foundation is bulging or bowing, call a professional to assess whether the crack is a symptom of a more serious settling problem.

In addition to keeping water away from the foundation (by sloping the ground away from the house and keeping gutters in good shape), you can tackle narrow cracks or small areas of foundation wall damage as a fix-it job. Be sure to first fix whatever caused the damage; if you repair a crack that was caused by water leaking down the wall without also fixing the leak, the repair won't last.

FACT

If you have vines growing over your house, be sure that they're a noninvasive species. Many vines invade mortar joints, causing the mortar to crumble, and seriously damaging the wall. Even noninvasive vines should be monitored to ensure that they're not allowing mold or mildew to grow.

Concrete Cracks

You can use similar techniques to seal cracks in concrete whether the surface is a vertical wall or a horizontal sidewalk or basement floor. Home centers offer good-quality concrete patching compounds, but their use can differ depending on where the patch is needed, how large it is, and your comfort level with various materials. Talk to the staff about which compound best suits your problem and how much of it you'll need. Before you start the repair, check the product label for detailed mixing, bonding, and curing instructions.

First, clean any oil, grease, or paint from the concrete surface (use TSP or a concrete cleaner). If it's just a hairline crack, you may be able to brush it out with a stiff brush and pour in crack filler, apply a concrete caulk with a caulking gun, or a patching compound with a putty knife. (Check your product to see if you first need to paint on a bonding agent.) Scrape off any excess compound, and let it cure according to the product's instructions, keeping it moist if necessary.

If it's a larger crack, you'll need to chisel it out. Use a cold chisel and a ball-peen hammer to shape the crack into a wedge (undercutting the top edge of the crack so that the bottom of the crack is wider than its surface) to prevent the patch from popping out. If you uncover any rebar (iron reinforcing bars), chisel about 1 inch of concrete out from behind it to create a good bonding area for the patch. Clean any dust and loose concrete out of the crack with a brush, air compressor, or hand bellows. The crack's interior surface should be rough and uneven.

If your patching compound requires the crack and its surrounding area to be damp, spray it with water and sponge up any excess so that the area remains damp but not puddled. (The existing concrete may pull the moisture out of the patching compound and interfere with the curing process if it's not dampened.) Also check to see whether your compound requires a bonding agent.

Mix your patching compound as necessary, and apply it to the crack with a pointing trowel. Packing it first against the sides of the crack ensures a strong bond with the existing concrete. For wall cracks, work from the bottom up. Once the crack is a little more than full, smooth the compound so that it's level with the existing surface, overlapping it slightly to blend it in.

If the compound requires moisture for the curing process, cover the repair with water-saturated burlap, and keep the burlap moist. Or, mist the patch with water and cover it with plastic. Check your compound's instructions for specific curing times and details.

 **ALERT!**

Always protect yourself when using a chisel. Wear safety goggles to shield your eyes from stray chips, and wear work gloves to protect your hands from the patching compounds. Using a chisel holder also keeps your fingers out of harm's way.

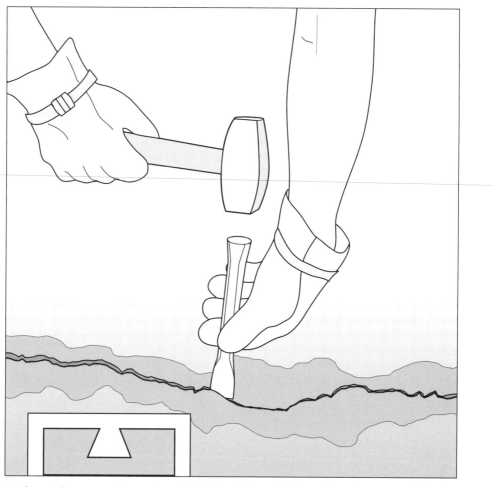

▲ Shape the concrete crack so that it's wider at its base than its top to help the patch stay in place.

Stucco

Stucco is a veneer of masonry that covers another surface, such as concrete or wood. It's often finished decoratively, but also helps to seal the interior surface. If it's damaged in a small area, you can try patching, but it's difficult to match a repair to the surrounding stucco's appearance. Larger repairs should be handled by professionals.

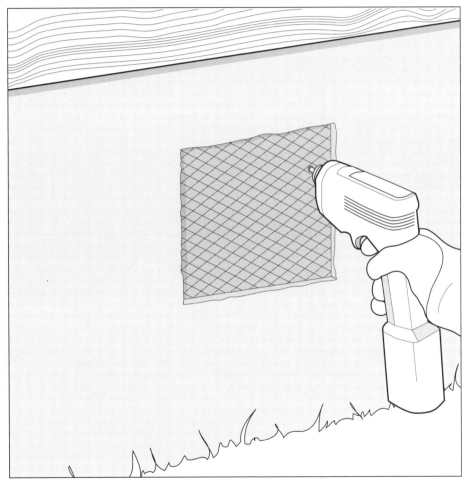

▲ Depending on the material under the stucco, you can nail, staple, or screw a new piece of wire mesh to the wall to provide a backing for the stucco repair.

For hairline cracks, use a flexible, all-purpose caulk. Larger cracks should be chiseled out as for concrete cracks. Brush out and moisten the crack, and apply a stucco-patching compound (in successive layers if the crack is deep). Try to match the finished texture to the existing stucco (broom heads can be used to stipple or sweep the surface). Check the compound's curing instructions; it probably needs to be kept damp for several days.

Stucco might also crumble away from its wire backing, creating holes. If the area is less than 6 inches wide, it's still a fix-it job. Break away any loose pieces, clean the area, and check to make sure that the wire backing is intact. If it's not, patch it by attaching a piece of wire mesh over the damaged area (you may need to cut the damaged part away with tin snips), with a couple of extra inches overlapping the old metal on each side. Moisten the area, apply the stucco-patching compound, and cure as required.

Brick

There are two repairs you can tackle for brick surfaces: repointing them (replacing the mortar in the joints between the bricks), and replacing individual bricks. To repoint an area of crumbling or missing mortar, first use a chisel to remove as much of the old mortar as possible, to a depth of at least ¾ inch. Brush out and moisten the joints, and then fill the joints with the mortar using a pointing trowel. A premixed mortar is much easier to use than one you have to mix, but it's more expensive. Ask home center staff to help you choose the right mortar, especially if you're dealing with older bricks.

Let the mortar dry just to the point where it doesn't come off on your glove when you press a finger down on it. Now, it's ready to be "struck," or smoothed. Run a smoothing tool or the point of the pointing trowel along the joints (vertical first, then horizontal) to compress the mortar. Scrape off any excess mortar, and strike the joints again. Follow the curing instructions for your mortar.

To replace one, or several, bricks that are broken or crumbling, use a chisel and hammer to remove the mortar in the joints around them and to break the bricks apart so that you can remove them. Clean the space, flush it with water, and soak the new bricks in water for about five minutes. Apply the mortar with a pointing trowel to the bottom and sides of the space, about 1 inch thick, and to the tops and ends of the bricks. Place the bricks in the cavity, tapping them gently into place with the trowel handle. Add more mortar if necessary to fill the joints, and then let dry, smooth, and cure as previously described.

If a replacement brick goes in so crooked that you can't tap it into place, it's best to remove it, take off all the mortar on it and the cavity, and start again with a new layer of mortar.

Caring for Siding

Many houses are covered with some kind of siding: aluminum, vinyl, or wood, installed either horizontally (e.g., clapboards) or vertically (e.g., board-and-batten). Although aluminum and vinyl siding are largely maintenance free, their surfaces can still fall victim to scratches, cracks or dents, and individual pieces can come loose. While the damage can be repaired, it's usually noticeable, so it is best used in a less noticeable area, or artfully hidden behind vegetation.

Siding also needs a good annual cleaning. Use a power washer (which you can rent) to spray the siding, washing from the bottom up to the top of the house, and rinsing from the top down. Work in the shade or on a cloudy day, and avoid driving the water up behind the siding. If needed, a nonabrasive cleanser can be added to the power washer; follow the washer's instructions to pick the right cleanser.

Repairing Aluminum Siding

For small scratches or rusty areas on aluminum siding, use a wire brush or sander to remove loose paint or rust. Take the surface down to the bare metal. Prime and then paint the area with metal paint to match the rest of the siding.

Dents in aluminum siding can be fixed by drilling a hole through the dent. Place several washers over a self-tapping screw, and insert the screw into the hole. Use pliers to pull on the screw head—as you pull on the screw, the dent will come up as well. Remove the screw and fill the hole with aluminum or steel filler. When it's dry, sand it smooth, and prime/paint it to match the surrounding surface.

Larger cracks or damaged areas may mean that you have to patch the damage. First, cut away the damaged area using tin snips. Make a vertical cut on either side of the damage, extending just above the damaged area but not up through the nailing strip on the top edge of the siding. Cut horizontally between the vertical cuts to remove the damaged area.

▲ Wear gloves while handling the aluminum siding patch, because its cut edges will be sharp.

Cut a patch sized at least 3 inches longer and wider than the damaged area, removing the nailing strip. Apply roofing cement around the area on the siding where you cut out the damaged area, and to the back of the patch. Place the patch over the gap, and press firmly to seal it.

Repairing Vinyl Siding

You can tackle small cracks in vinyl siding with a siding repair kit from your home center or siding supplier. Gently lift up one edge of the crack, apply the repair glue inside it, and press the edges down firmly. Work on a warm day, when the vinyl will be pliable (it can crack or break when it's cold).

For larger cracks, replace the damaged area. The bottom edge of each piece of siding is shaped like a J so that it bends back and under the upper edge of the siding underneath it. You'll need a zip tool to unlock the two pieces of siding where the damaged areas need to be replaced. Slide the zip tool up, under, and along the J-channel, pulling down slightly (persevere, because this can be a hassle). Wedge the overlapping siding up to give yourself room to work on the damaged piece.

ALERT!

It's easy to tear or damage the paper that's wrapped around the building under the siding when you're tackling these repairs. Repair the damaged paper by applying a layer of roofing cement over it before you patch the siding.

Cut through the damaged piece from its bottom edge right up through the nailing strip (try to remove enough length that you have at least two studs to nail the replacement into). Remove the nails and the damaged piece. Cut a replacement piece that's about 4 inches longer than the damaged piece. On the replacement, cut away the nailing strip 2 inches from either end so that the nailing strip will fit into the original area but the siding itself will overlap the existing siding by about 2 inches on either side. (If you don't have a replacement piece of siding, glue a patch onto the back of the damaged siding and use it as the replacement.)

Insert the replacement siding. It's tricky to drive the nails into the nailing strip, because the strip is tucked up under the overlapping siding. With the overlapping siding still wedged up a little, place your ring-shank siding nail or roofing nail in the nailing strip. Place the end of a pry bar over the nail, and strike the pry bar with your hammer; this should drive in the nail. Then, use the zip tool to relock the J-channel.

When you're nailing aluminum or vinyl siding, never drive the nails all the way in. The long slots in the nailing strips are designed to let the siding expand and contract. If the nails are too tight, the siding can buckle or warp. Leave the nail heads above the surface just a little.

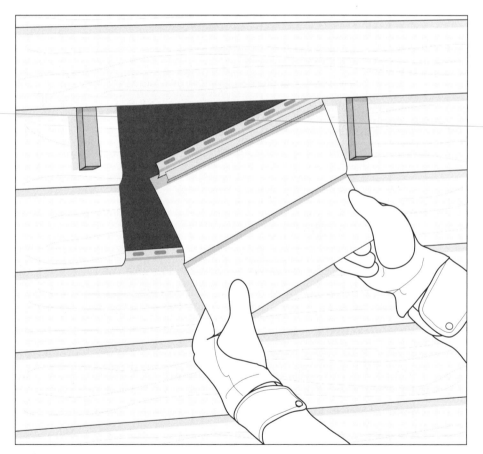

▲ If you're working with a small area, you can patch more than one piece of vinyl siding at a time—just lock the pieces together before you nail the top piece.

Repairing Wood Shingles or Siding

Small holes in wood shingles or siding can be filled with wood putty, sanded, and then painted to match the rest of the wood. Cracks can also be fixed in place. Gently widen the crack with a putty knife or chisel so that you can apply an exterior-grade wood glue to both its edges. Press the pieces back into place and insert screws (predrill the holes to avoid splitting the wood) on both sides of the crack to further strengthen the repair.

You can try to straighten warped wood siding by inserting screws into predrilled holes through the warped board into the wall studs. Otherwise, you'll need to replace the board.

FACT

Wood needs room to expand and contract with temperature changes. Whenever you replace wood shingles or siding, leave a ⅛-inch gap on either side of the replacement wood to give it room to move.

To replace damaged siding that doesn't have an overlapping style, cut around the damaged area, pry up its nails so that you can remove it, and nail a replacement into place.

Board-and-batten siding can be removed by prying up the thin battens that cover the joints between the boards. Remove the nails in the damaged area, take out the damaged wood, and replace it, leaving a ⅛-inch expansion gap on either side. Caulk the seams, and then replace the battens.

For overlapping styles, carefully pry up and wedge the board or shingle that overlaps the damaged area so that you have room to cut around the damaged piece (you may need to cut it into several pieces along its length). Slide a hacksaw blade up under the damaged wood or shingle(s) to cut off its nails flush with the wall surface. Remove the damaged area, and slide the replacement wood or shingle as far as possible into place. With a block of wood protecting the wood's bottom edge, tap it completely into place. Predrill holes, and nail or screw the shingle to secure it. Caulk the nail holes and the seams between the existing siding and the replacement, and finish to match the existing siding.

Soffits, Fascia, and Trim

One of the most common areas for trim damage is wooden windowsills that rot when water sits on them. If the rot extends several inches into the sill, you'll need to replace the sill (a job for a pro). If it's superficial, try a fix. First, chip away all the rotten areas of wood with a hammer and chisel, and let the wood dry out completely (this can take days to weeks, so be sure to cover the sill with plastic in case of wet weather).

Choose a wood filler and epoxy that suits your climate conditions. Apply the epoxy as directed to seal the wood, then apply the filler to re-form the sill. Once the filler is dry, you can sand and prime/paint the repair.

Many homeowners are choosing to replace wooden soffits (the flat area under the eaves where the roof overhangs the house) and fascia (the outward-facing boards that trim the roof) with aluminum or vinyl to reduce maintenance. If you're still dealing with wood, you can fix small areas of damaged soffit panels.

First, remove any decorative pieces of wood that hold the soffit in place. Mark straight lines on the soffit on either side of the damage, from the edge of the roof to the edge of the house. Use a jigsaw to cut out the damaged piece. Nail pieces of wood, such as 2" × 2" or 2" × 4", on two opposite edges of the opening, up inside the roof and extending into the patch area, to give yourself a surface to attach the soffit patch. Cut a soffit patch $\frac{1}{8}$-inch smaller all around than the damaged piece, and screw it into place. Caulk the seams, and then replace any decorative molding that you removed, and finish the wood to match the rest of the soffit.

Maintaining Gutters

Plan on reserving half a day in spring and fall for cleaning your gutters, and enlist a friend or family member to help. If you have particularly high roofs, however, use caution; a commercial gutter-cleaning service may be the safer option. Along with cleaning gutters, ensure that water is carried well away from the house, either using downspout extensions or splash blocks.

Cleaning Gutters

Head up the ladder (without leaning the ladder on the gutters themselves). If you have screens on top of your gutters, unclip them so that you can clean out anything that's slipped through. Remove large debris, such as leaf buildup, from the gutter with an inexpensive plastic gutter scoop.

Either toss the debris down (keeping it away from the house, because it can stain siding), or use a rope to haul a bucket up the ladder for the debris. Flush the gutters clean with a garden hose, aiming the water toward the downspout. Check for leaks, blockages, or areas where the water pools.

A common spot for blockages is the elbow joint at the connection between the gutter and the downspout. The best solution is to dismantle the joint and poke out any debris. If this isn't practical, use the garden hose or a plumber's snake/auger to shift the blockage, then install a leaf strainer at the top of the downspout.

If the blockage is in the downspout, run the hose into the downspout, increasing the water pressure by blocking the gap around the hose with rags. (It's safer to do this from the bottom of the downspout rather than while balancing on a ladder.) If the hose doesn't shift the blockage, try a snake/auger or a pressure washer. (Pressure washers can be rented by the hour, day, or week from many home improvement stores.)

Screening Gutters

Gutter screens don't eliminate the need for regular cleaning, but they do help prevent blockages in hard-to-reach areas. Most types snap or flex into place over the gutter. Buy enough to shield your entire gutter system, cutting the screens as necessary to fit between the gutter hanging straps.

Leaf strainers fit into the top of downspouts, to provide a further line of defense.

QUESTION?

My downspout blocks regularly. What can I do?
Along with installing leaf strainers and screens, check the length of the screws that hold the downspout pieces together. Long screws can catch debris and cause blockages, so replacing them with shorter screws can help.

Sagging Gutters

Gutters should run slightly downhill toward the downspout. If water pools anywhere, the gutter needs to be repositioned. This can be as easy as moving a gutter hanger to adjust the downhill angle, or adding another one to support a sag.

You may be able to reposition gutter hangers by bending the strap with a pair of pliers. If that's not enough, carefully lift up the shingle on the edge of the roof to give you access to where the strap is attached to the roof. Unscrew the strap, or remove its nails. Move the strap higher or lower on the roof, at least 1 inch away from the old hole (move the strap along the gutter if necessary), and reattach the strap to the roof. Seal the old nail hole with caulking or roof cement.

To move a sleeve-and-spike hanger, use a hacksaw to cut through the spike, move the sleeve along the gutter so that it's repositioned at least 1 inch away from the old hole, and nail a new spike through the gutter and sleeve. Seal the old nail hole.

You can also add hangers if necessary. You should see them every 2 feet on the gutters, and there should be one close to every gutter joint.

Leaking Gutters

Gutter joints can be weak links, particularly with aluminum systems. If the joint is leaking, take it apart, clean and dry it, and then apply new gutter caulking or sealant with a caulking gun.

If it's not practical to take the joint apart (such as at a corner), try repairing it. Dry the area, then use a wire brush or sandpaper to get rid of any rust or loose pieces. Apply a coat of roofing cement for holes smaller than about $1/2$-inch wide. For larger holes, apply the roofing cement, then place a vinyl or metal patch over it, and cover the area with another layer of roofing cement. Fiberglass auto-repair kits can also make good patches. On aluminum gutters, finish the repair with a coat of rustproofing paint.

Maintaining Roofs

Some roof repairs, such as sealing leaky flashing or replacing a small area of asphalt shingles, are quite straightforward, until you add the challenge of working on the roof. If you're not comfortable with heights, call an expert.

Similarly, you'll need expert help if your roofing material is more complicated, such as tile, slate, metal or asbestos, if you don't have the ladders necessary to reach the roof, or if the roof is steeply sloped (rising more than 6 inches over 12 horizontal inches).

Always observe ladder safety measures, and use a safety line attached to a strong anchor (such as a secure chimney) when you're on the roof. Don't work alone; have someone on the ground who can call for help if you run into trouble. Most roofs aren't designed for walking, so try to step only where the rafters are.

Never venture out onto a roof when it's wet, because roofs can be incredibly slippery. Similarly, power-wash the roof, if needed, from the ground or a firmly secured ladder to keep moss at bay, which makes the roof slippery and can damage shingles. Trim any overhanging tree branches.

ALERT!

When power-washing roofs, use low pressure and test the spray in a small area first. If it loosens the asphalt shingle's granules, stop; it's going to create more problems than it will solve.

First Aid for Roofs

If you have a roof leak and you're lucky, you'll be able to see water dripping from a hole in the attic roof, or light shining through the hole. In either case, insert a long wire up through the hole so that you or your roof contractor can easily find and fix the problem on the roof itself. For a temporary fix, you can apply a layer of roof patching compound on the underside of the attic.

Water can travel a long way before dripping into the attic, however. In this case, a nail driven through the roof where the drip is coming down will give you a clue once you're on the roof; look for the leak farther up the roof from where the nail comes through. (Always seal the nail hole with roofing cement once you've finished the repair.)

If you can't fix a leak right away, place a tarp over the damaged roof area, and nail it into place with strips of lath. Seal all the nail holes with roof cement once you've fixed the roof.

To fix a small damaged or blistered area on a flat roof, brush away the surface gravel and cut away the damaged section of the roof covering. Apply roofing cement or patch compound under the cut edges and to the patch area. Cover with a patch (check for patch kits at home centers) that's at least 2 inches larger on all sides than the damaged area. Apply another layer of cement, let it dry, and then brush the surface gravel back over.

Repairing Roof Flashing

Flashing is the name for the wide metal strips that you'll see sealing the joint wherever two materials meet on the roof—against the chimney or vents, or where two roof slopes connect. To reseal flashing, lift the shingles that overlap it, and cover about 6 inches of the flashing with roofing cement or patch compound. Replace the shingles, pressing them firmly into the cement.

For chimney flashing, caulk the seal between the chimney and the top of the flashing (remove any old caulking first), and the seal between the bottom of the chimney flashing and the edge of the roof flashing.

You can seal small holes in flashing with caulk or sealant, or with roofing cement and a flashing patch, or with an automotive fiberglass repair kit, but larger areas of damage mean that the flashing should be replaced.

Replacing Shingles

Loose asphalt shingles can be glued into place with roofing cement or nailed (use galvanized nails), with the nail heads sealed with roofing cement. A few curled edges of shingles can also be glued down with roofing cement, but be aware that curling edges are a warning sign that the shingles need to be replaced.

▲ If you can't lift up the overlapping shingle to insert the pry bar, slide a hacksaw blade up under the damaged shingle, and cut through the nails that are holding it to the roof.

You can temporarily fix a torn asphalt shingle by nailing the sides of the tear down and covering it with roofing cement, or by cementing a piece of sheet metal under the shingle—but it's not difficult to actually replace the shingle.

Lift up the bottom edge of the shingle that overlaps the damaged shingle, and use a pry bar to remove the nails holding the damaged shingle in place. Remove the damaged shingle. If the new shingle is self-adhesive, position it and peel away the backing. If it's not, apply a layer of roofing cement to the bottom of the new shingle, slide the top edge into place, and then nail it down. Cover the nail heads with roofing cement, and also seal the edges of the shingles that overlap the new shingle.

Replace wood shingles as you would wall shingles (described in the previous section), remembering to leave a $\frac{1}{8}$-inch expansion gap around the new shingle.

Many of the techniques described in this chapter, such as repairing concrete, can also be used to handle repairs in your yard. Detached garages and sheds also make good subjects for practicing your repair skills, because they're not on view the same way your house is, and the consequences of making a mistake are much less severe. Chapter 8 focuses on your yard—so stick around, outside the house. (E)

Chapter 8

The Great Outdoors

The area surrounding the house is an extension of an indoor living space. It's a place to play, garden, relax, and socialize—but it's also more than that. A well-maintained outdoor space adds curb appeal and financial value to your home. From improving the appearance of decks and fences to ensuring proper water drainage to keep your basement dry, maintaining your part of the great outdoors can make it one of your home's best assets.

Utility Lines

Before you tackle any outdoor project, look around. Where are the utility lines that bring electricity, phone, and cable service into the house? There may be overhead lines that stretch from a utility pole through your yard to the house, buried lines that you'll see as they come out of the ground at the house, or a combination of both.

Overhead lines should not rest on any surface (such as a garage roof), nor should they be within reach of tree branches or clotheslines. If you see any of these problems, call your utility company. All lines need a little "sag" in them so that they move with the wind instead of working loose at their connections, but utility crews may be able to tighten them up enough to bring them off a garage roof or away from a clothesline.

Some utility companies or municipalities have tree-trimming programs to handle vegetation that's encroaching on utility lines, but you may be responsible for hiring a contractor to prune trees on your property. (Pruning trees around utility lines is not a do-it-yourself fix. There's too much danger of accidentally touching the line or bringing a branch down onto it.) If the utility lines are still a problem, you may have to consider paying to either bury them on your property or relocate where they meet the house wall.

There's not much you can do to check the health of buried wires, but you should know where they are. Every state has a "Call Before You Dig" or utility notification telephone number. Before you put a shovel into the ground anywhere in your yard, you *must* call that number. Your utility companies will then come out and mark where the lines are (including any natural gas or sewer lines) so that you can avoid them.

FACT

When choosing trees for your yard, always consider their mature height to ensure that they won't reach as far as your utility lines or become a danger to your house. And phone your local "Call Before You Dig" number to make sure that the hole for the tree won't interfere with utility, gas, or sewer lines.

Clotheslines

Drying your clothes on the line is a great way to save money on your utility bills—but check municipality or county regulations before you install a clothesline. Some areas have bylaws controlling them (to keep the neighborhood looking "tidy"). Also determine whether a clothesline strung between two points or an umbrella-type collapsible clothesline would best fit your yard.

The umbrella-type is easiest to install. Most of these come with a metal sleeve that you insert into the ground—concreting it in is the most permanent way to secure it. Dig out the hole to the depth and width recommended by the clothesline instructions, and insert a cardboard concrete form into the hole. Mix the concrete (home center staff can help you choose the right mix), and pour it into the form, holding the clothesline pole support in the sleeve as you do so (check that it's level). Trowel off the concrete to a smooth surface, and cure as required.

Sagging or cracked clothesline can be tightened or replaced. For an umbrella-style clothesline, pull or insert the line between the umbrella's opened arms so that the line is taut, and tie it off. For line-style clotheslines, check the pulleys and hooks. If they're rusted, loose, or in poor condition, buy a new clothesline kit. If not, simply tighten the line using the cord tightener that should be on the line (if it's not, undo the line and thread one on). You can also replace a cracked line by threading a new line through the pulleys and tightener system (you may need to use wire cutters to cut the old line down).

If you're installing a new line-style system, choose its location carefully, where it won't interfere with traffic paths and is high enough for even large articles such as sheets to hang well clear of the ground. Screw the hooks into two anchor points—on the house or garage wall, or a post (it's best to line the posthole with concrete, as for an umbrella-style clothesline pole). Seal around the hook with silicon caulking if it's on the house or garage wall. Hang the pulleys on the hooks, and run the line through each pulley. If you don't have someone to help you, tie one end of the line to an anchor so that it doesn't pull out of one pulley as you're stringing the other). Cut the clothesline to fit, ensuring that you have approximately 12 inches of extra line. Run the two ends of the line through the tightener, and tighten as needed.

ALERT!

Never attach a clothesline anchor hook to a utility pole. If you need to install a post for the clothesline, phone your local "Call Before You Dig" notification number before you decide where to place the post.

Optimizing Water Drainage

Rainwater and melting snow need to be carried away from the house, so check the way the ground slopes. If it's level or sloping toward the house, it may be contributing to leaky basements or wet walls. You'll need to regrade the slope so that the ground drops about ¾ inch for every foot.

This can be a big job, but it's not difficult. Just work on a manageable section at a time. You can order topsoil from a contractor or home center. If the soil is going to sit on an area of grass for several days, put a layer of tarpaulins down first, to make cleanup easier and to protect the grass.

Tie or staple a string between two stakes, one placed next to the house and the other about 8 feet out into the yard. Keeping in mind that the top of the soil should ideally rest against a concrete foundation, keeping at least 6 inches away from wall materials such as wood, slope the string so that it follows the angle you need to achieve on the ground (if the ground has high points, dig them out). Add soil to any low areas, beginning at the house, to bring them up to the height of the string. Rake the soil evenly, following the string, and tamp it down lightly. Lay sod or seed the area for grass, or landscape it, remembering that shrubs should be kept at least 6 to 8 inches from the side of the house (or more if you have an insect problem or fire risk in your area).

▲ Grading the soil so that it slopes away from the house will help prevent water from accumulating around the foundation, where it can leak into basements, encourage mold, and attract insects.

If this process is going to be difficult around your house—because your whole yard slopes toward your house, for example—you may need a more complicated solution that involves digging drainage ditches and lining them with perforated pipe that takes the water to a better drainage area. You'll need expert advice to make this work properly and to ensure that you don't inadvertently direct the water toward your house, or a neighbor's.

Driveways, Patios, and Sidewalks

Whatever material your driveways, patios, and walkways consist of, you can maintain them by following a few guidelines. Water is their worst enemy, especially in cold climates where freeze/thaw cycles can break them up, so check that water drains off and away from their surfaces. If it doesn't, try to reslope the ground. If that's not possible, redirect water (using downspout extenders, for example), or consider having a drain system installed.

Any weeds, grass, or other vegetation should be trimmed from the edges of the drive or sidewalk and removed from cracks or mortar areas. Remove surface stains such as oil from concrete or asphalt surfaces as soon as possible.

To prevent accidents, also check that a driver entering or leaving your driveway has a clear field of vision and can easily be seen from the street.

Concrete

To clean stains, look for concrete stain removers at your home center, or try a solution of 5 percent muriatic acid, followed by TSP. Wear protective clothing, gloves, and safety glasses, and scrub the solution into the stain with a stiff brush.

Concrete should be sealed to help prevent water from entering it. Before sealing, check for cracks or holes that need to be patched. Cracks can be fixed as described in Chapter 7. The same general procedures apply to patching holes or damaged areas. Chip out any loose pieces, brush or vacuum away any dust, and clean the area. Paint on a bonding liquid if necessary to help the patch adhere to the concrete. Trowel the patching compound into the hole or over the area, and smooth it level with the surrounding concrete surface. Keep it moist as it cures, as required in the patching compound's instructions.

To seal concrete, first brush it clean and remove any stains. Once it's dry, the sealer can be applied with a roller, brush, or even a sprayer attachment for your garden hose.

Concrete Steps

For step edges or corners that are chipped or damaged, follow the general procedures for patching holes, but use either hydraulic cement (which sets up quickly and holds its shape), or place a wood form around the repair to prevent it from slumping away from the step while it dries (hold the wood in place with wedges or concrete blocks).

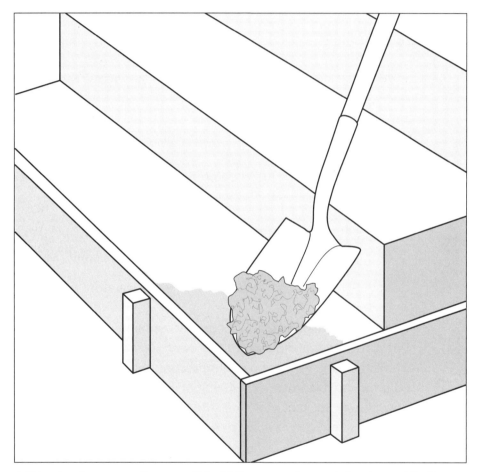

▲ Wooden frames, or forms, will hold the concrete repair in place while it cures.

Concrete blocks or paving slabs can heave or sink as the ground expands and settles. To fix this, pry up the high or low end with a crowbar, and prop it up with stones or a jack. Depending on the problem, either remove some of the underlying material, or add some (try sand and small stones). Lower the block down and tamp it firmly into place.

Iron railings are often secured to concrete steps with bolts—an attachment that can come loose over time. To repair it, chip concrete away from the railing post to make a hole about 2 inches wide and 2 inches deep. Patch it as described previously with a compound designed for bolt holes.

Asphalt

Periodic sealing of your asphalt driveway protects it from cracks and stains, and can also restore the appearance of the blacktop after you've repaired it. Try using an acrylic sealer; it's water-based, kinder to the environment, and easier to apply than tar-based products. You should expect to recoat every two years.

Patch any cracks or holes before sealing asphalt. Cracks less than $\frac{1}{2}$-inch wide can be sealed with asphalt crack filler. Clean any loose pieces out of the crack, and apply an asphalt primer. Squeeze the crack filler into the crack until the filler is just above the surface, and then smooth it out using a trowel or putty knife. Sprinkle sand over the patch before the filler dries to prevent it from sticking to car tires.

FACT

Watch the weather. Don't fix or seal asphalt if rain is forecast in the next twenty-four hours. Work in warm weather (usually above 60°F for sealer and 70°F for patching compound, but check product instructions) to ensure the best bond and easiest application, but avoid very hot sun, as it dries the sealer too quickly.

Larger cracks and holes need asphalt-patching compound. Clean out any damaged material, taking it down to an undamaged layer and undercutting the edges to help the patch stay in place. Apply the patching compound and compact it (in layers if the hole is deep) with the end of a 2" × 4", until the compound sits just above the surface. Place a piece of plywood over the patch and weight it down with concrete blocks or drive over it. Add more patching compound if necessary. Check the product directions to see how long the patch needs to cure before sealing.

To seal asphalt, first sweep the driveway or sidewalk to get rid of loose dirt and debris. Clean off oil and grease spots with TSP or a commercial cleaner/degreaser. Scrub it on, and then rinse with a garden hose. If stubborn stains persist, apply an asphalt primer to ensure the sealer adheres to the stain.

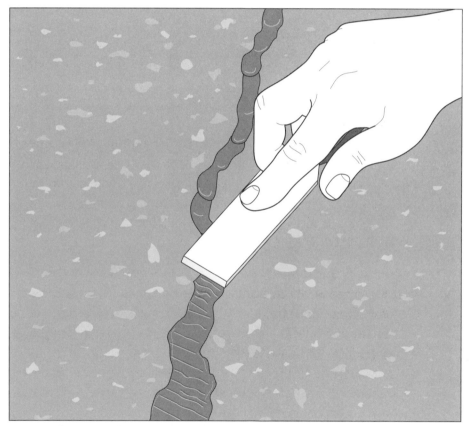

▲ Smoothing out the asphalt crack filler will help it adhere to and blend with the existing asphalt surface.

Stir or shake the sealer as described in the product instructions (and check to see if it requires a wet or dry surface on which to work). Your first coat should start from the house and work down the driveway or sidewalk. Pour on enough sealer to cover just a manageable area at a time; working a small area allows you to maintain a wet edge and avoid lap marks.

Immediately spread out the sealer with a long-handled applicator, working it into the asphalt and then smoothing it out. A second coat may be required, usually within twenty-four hours of the first (check product instructions). Apply the second coat perpendicular to the direction in which you spread the first.

To protect the sealer while it cures, block foot and vehicle traffic from the driveway for two days. Use brightly colored flags on tape or rope to ensure no one trips when it's dark.

Gravel

Periodically rake gravel driveways or sidewalks to redistribute the stones from high spots to low spots and to remove stones from nearby flowerbeds or grass. The stones will work themselves into the dirt surface, so you'll need to add another layer of gravel periodically. Gravel can be purchased through contractors or stone suppliers.

Brickwork and Pavers

The most important fix-it job for surfaces made of individual bricks or stones is to keep weeds from breaking up the material between the bricks. Many designs use sand to line these gaps, which may need to be renewed periodically. Spread coarse sand over the bricks or pavers, sweep it into the gaps (holding the broom at a 45-degree angle), and water it well. As the sand dries, it may settle; repeat the process as necessary.

Damaged bricks can be lifted up and flipped over to reveal an undamaged surface. If bricks are cracked or crumbling, try to replace them with similar-looking bricks. Chisel out the sand or mortar around the individual brick, pry it up, and replace the brick and the sand (or mortar) in the joints around it.

Decks, Steps, and Fences

Wooden decks, steps, and fences need to be kept free of stains, insects, and rot. Check regularly for warping, loose boards, rotten wood (especially on the underside of decks or steps), cracks, and popped nails. Small holes or cracks can be filled with wood putty. Replace any popped or loose nails with galvanized screws (use stainless steel for cedar or redwood decks). If you use the existing nail hole, use a screw slightly larger than the hole to ensure a tight fit. Wobbly railings and supports can be fixed by tightening any bolts that fasten them or by replacing loose nails with screws or bolts.

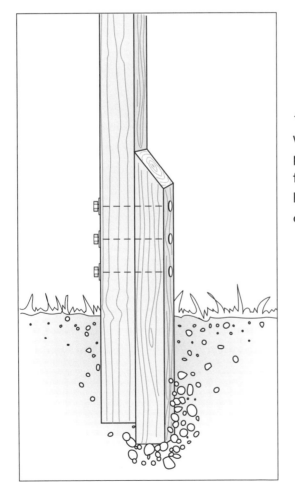

◀ Strengthening a wobbly fence post can prevent damage to the fence boards, such as loose nails or screws and cracked boards.

Replacing

If fence and deck posts have flat tops, add a slanted or rounded cap, or trim them into a slanted surface, to allow rain to run off instead of soaking in. You can strengthen wobbly fence posts by digging a hole on one side of the post and inserting another piece of post into the hole, slightly deeper than the existing post and extending about 12 inches above the ground. Drill several holes through the two posts and cinch them together with carriage bolts. Fill the new hole with concrete or tamped-down soil and gravel.

Boards

If a decking board is scratched or damaged, you may be able to remove its nails or screws, flip it over, and screw it back down, or simply replace the board. If this won't work, cut the damaged area out of the deck so that two edges of the cut are beside joists that support the boards (don't cut into the joists—leave good wood resting over the joists for support). Screw a piece of 2" × 4" to each exposed part of the joist, about 12 inches longer than the damaged area, to support the new boards. Cut new boards to fit, and screw them down into the 2" × 4"s.

This approach works for steps, too, if you cut away the damaged tread and screw new supports to the stringer (the board that supports each side of the treads).

For a damaged fence board, remove the whole board, cut a new one to fit, and screw it into place.

FACT

If the wood is splitting or cracking around the screws, predrill the screw holes. Use a drill bit slightly smaller than your screw so that the screw threads still cut into the wood, holding the screw in place.

Strengthening Joists

The joists that support the deck from the underside can sometimes crack, split, or sag. To repair a joist, cut two pieces of 2" × 6" (most joists are 2" × 6"; if yours isn't, cut the wood to match the width and depth of the joist) to a length that's about 6 feet longer than the damaged portion. Nail one 2" × 6" to each side of the damaged joist, centering the 2" × 6"s over the damaged area. Drill holes through all three pieces of wood so that you can insert and tighten bolts that will hold the repair firmly in place.

Gates

Gates are notorious for sagging, so that their hardware no longer closes the gate properly. To fix this, first determine what's causing the problem. Wobbly gateposts can be strengthened in the same way as fence posts, as described in the previous section. You can also try reseating one or both of the gate hinges to change the angle of the gate slightly. To do this, remove the hinge, and shim or chisel out the hinge mortise. If the gate itself is sagging, rather than one of the posts, remove the gate and try to bring it back into square by screwing two diagonal braces across it; use wood pieces that match the gate, or antisag rods, which you can buy at home centers. Alternatively, change the position of the latch hardware, or even the type of hardware, so that the latch can close again.

Cleaning, Sealing, and Preserving

Decks need to be cleaned periodically. Leaves and dirt can build up between boards, and the boards themselves can be damaged by ground-in dirt from footsteps. First, sweep the deck well, including between the boards. Commercial deck cleaners can then generally be rolled, mopped, or sprayed onto the deck, scrubbed in, and rinsed off.

The product you use to preserve, seal, and/or stain your wooden decks or fences depends on the material you're starting with (pressure-treated, raw, or stained wood), the look you prefer (natural wood or a color), and the use that the wood will see. (Avoid using paint on floors or steps, because it doesn't hold up well; stain is a better option, because it actually sinks into the wood.)

You can buy stains that combine preserving and sealing agents, for a one-step application. Just be sure that the product you purchase fits your needs—ask home center staff. Clean the deck, and let it dry (this takes about forty-eight hours). Check the weather forecast, and choose a time when the weather's warm and dry, but not hot (usually, above 50°F). Follow the product's instructions for application, drying time, and protection.

ALERT!

Protect vegetation from cleaning, preserving, and sealing agents by watering them well and covering them with plastic sheets (some cleaners can burn leaves). Protect yourself with long-sleeved clothing, gloves, a face mask, and safety glasses.

Building Fences

An entire chapter could be devoted to building different types of fences, but for now, it's enough to know that building your own fence, whether it's chainlink or wood, is certainly a job that you can handle. Regardless of the fence type, check with your municipality or county to find out what permits are required and to ensure that your fence design and placement fits local regulations. Talk to your neighbor if you want the fence to run on the property line; otherwise, run it at least 4 inches inside the property line, and be sure to phone your local "Call Before You Dig" number to have utility lines marked.

Plan your fence out on graph paper first, marking the location of all support posts. Eight-foot separations make good use of standard-sized fence components. Make a list of each component that you'll need, including the hardware to fix it all together. The fence outline and post locations can be marked on the ground with stakes or spray paint. Fence posts can be set in concrete or in metal anchor spikes (check them with a level to make sure they're standing straight).

Generally, once the posts are in place, you screw top and bottom rails into place for wooden fences, and then follow that with individual fence boards or preformed sections. For chainlink fences, you add a top rail and then stretch the chain mesh between the support posts. Use metal ties or wires to secure the mesh to the support posts and top rail, working in short sections at a time. Attach the gate, including hinges and latch hardware, and add fence post caps if needed.

Septic Systems

If you're not on a municipal sewer line, you need to keep a regular eye on your septic system. Basically, it consists of a tank that collects wastewater from your house. Inside the tank, solids settle to the bottom and bacterial action starts to break down the waste. Liquid waste flows out of the tank and into the ground through a series of perforated pipes (your septic field), which further filters the water (it may also flow into a second holding tank, where it's pumped out into the field). Eventually, the semisolid sludge at the bottom of the tank will need to be pumped out by a sewage contractor.

The key to maintaining a healthy septic system is to limit what goes into it. No products other than toilet paper should be flushed (even if they say they're flushable), kitchen scraps should be composted (not put through the garbage disposal), and chemicals or kitchen grease should never be put down the drain (not even drain cleaners; use augers instead). You should also be aware that bacterial "boosters" for the tank haven't been proved to work and, in fact, can throw off the bacterial balance.

ESSENTIAL

Depending on your septic system and how heavily it's used, you'll need to have the sludge pumped out of the tank every one to three years.

Too much water flowing through the system can take solid waste into the liquid waste pipes, so fix any running toilets or leaking faucets, and don't overload the system with too much water at any one time. For this reason, water from gutters and swimming pools should never be directed into the septic system.

You need to check the sludge level in the tank at least annually. Open the tank access and place a long stick or piece of thin lumber into the tank. When you bring out the stick, it will be wet up to the level of the liquid in the tank, but it will be stained up to the level of the sludge in the tank. If the sludge level is higher than one-third or halfway up the tank, call a contractor to pump it out.

If water isn't draining into the septic system properly, and an auger doesn't find any drain blockages, call in an expert immediately. The problem may be a blocked pipe, a full tank, or bacteria levels that have dropped too low. Fixing the problem right away might save you from cleaning up sewage backup.

To help your septic field stay healthy, keep trees and large shrubs away from it (their roots can break into the pipes), and don't allow heavy trucks to drive over it. If you notice a sewer odor in your yard, or unusual grass growth or murky water sitting in or near where the pipes drain into the septic field, call in an expert. Your field may have failed or become blocked, contaminating the ground with sewage.

Keeping your outdoor spaces well maintained, from driveways to decks, makes your house feel welcoming. Unfortunately, the great outdoors brings some unwanted guests, ranging from carpenter ants and termites to rodents and even deer. While this chapter helped you make your house and yard welcoming to people, Chapter 9 will help you make your house unwelcome to pests of the animal variety.

Chapter 9
Pest Control

The smallest of creatures can create the largest of problems for homeowners. The best solution is to prevent the pests from entering, followed by frequent inspections for signs of infestation. If that doesn't work, your best ally will be a humane, licensed extermination or animal removal company.

Pest Removal

You may need to call in an expert in pest removal, whether it's an exterminator for an insect problem or an animal removal expert for larger critters. Like any other service, you get what you pay for. A licensed, insured expert who comes recommended by friends or neighbors and holds membership in a recognized pest control association is a good start. Also, check with local government offices or wildlife conservation associations to find out what options are legal and recommended in your area.

Be sure that you understand all the details before signing any pest removal contracts. They should provide the following information:

- What the pest is
- How the pest will be removed
- What chemicals (if any) will be used and what their effects are
- Whether the work is guaranteed and for how long
- How animals will be treated (Some areas don't allow animals to be relocated; if they have to be destroyed, you should know that up front so that you can make an informed decision.)

A good pest control expert will not only assist you to get rid of any existing pests, but can also advise you on prevention measures. The key to animal removal, for example, is to prevent the animal (or another like it) from re-entering the house—which is why killing the animal won't necessarily solve your problem in the long term. For insect control, ensure that you understand your ongoing responsibilities (annual checks or resprays may be needed to keep the guarantee valid).

ESSENTIAL

Whatever pest or animal you're dealing with, remember that they're part of a bigger picture. However much you hate snakes, for example, they have the benefit of reducing mice populations. The trick is to keep the animals where they can go about their lives without interfering with yours.

General Pest Prevention Measures

Termites, mosquitoes, mice, squirrels . . . just a partial list of the critters that can crawl, fly, or scurry into your home is enough to make you think twice about opening your door. There are, however, a number of measures that will deter all manner of pests.

First, find out what insects and animals are problems in your area (local house inspectors, neighbors, and your municipality or county should be able to help); then determine what measures you need to take to keep them out. Regularly inspecting your home will also help to catch problems before they become widespread.

Seal Pests Out

Check your house exterior for gaps and cracks that could let in tiny (or larger) critters. Fix cracks in foundations and basement floors, and weather-strip or caulk around window and door frames and plumbing or electrical service entries. Fix any tears or holes in window screens. Also check attic, soffit, and bathroom/kitchen/dryer exhaust vents to ensure that they're well screened. If they're not, you can buy screens to fit most vents, or you can cut them out of screening material; the screen should be a little smaller than the outside frame of the vent. Remove the vent (usually by removing the screws that hold it in place). Place the screen over the opening, and replace the vent. Run a bead of caulking around the joint between the vent and the house for further protection.

Floor drains can also be screened, and chimneys can be capped. If you're sealing the house up against mice or other strong chewers, stuffing cracks or gaps with stainless steel wool or fine-mesh metal screens, and then caulking, will help.

Clean It Up

Cleanliness also helps. Keep surfaces clean, and avoid leaving food out where it can become attractive to pests. (Metal or glass containers with tight-fitting lids are better than plastic containers.) Check fresh produce for hangers-on as soon as it comes into the house, particularly if it comes in boxes or paper bags. Insects and mice like piles of newspapers or paper bags, so avoid keeping them around.

In the yard, store outdoor trash cans and compost piles away from the house, and remove trash from the house regularly. Harvest fruit and vegetables frequently, cleaning up fallen items right away. Bird feeders should be squirrel-proof, and any spilled seed should be cleaned up.

If insects are a problem inside the house, store birdseed and bulk pet food outside the house—but be aware that it could attract pests such as squirrels and mice. Wherever you choose to store it, ensure that the container's lid is tight fitting, and inspect the container regularly for signs of gnawing or disturbance.

Dry It Out

Insects are also drawn to water, so keep moisture levels in the house down; fix leaks, wipe up spills right away, and don't leave water sitting out (in plant trays, for example).

Rain barrels, wells, and other sources of standing water should be covered tightly.

Keep Wood Away

If you use firewood, set up your woodpile away from the house, several inches off the ground, and don't bring the wood inside until you're ready to burn it. Vegetation should be kept at least 18 inches away from foundations and walls if you have problems with insects, and old tree stumps, leaves, and dead wood around the house should be removed. Bark mulches attract insects such as termites, earwigs, and crickets, so keep them well away from any wood on your house.

Crawling and Jumping Insects

Insects such as ants, cockroaches, silverfish, and termites range from annoying to harmful, and they're small enough that even sealing off potential entrances may not be enough. Traps and sprays can be effective for small-scale problems, but for such potentially destructive insects as termites and carpenter ants, call an expert. The key to success is recognizing trouble signs as early as possible.

Although termites largely crawl (and eat), they form new colonies by sending special winged termites in search of new sites. Spotting these "swarmers," or their wings, inside your home may indicate that you have a colony that you don't know about. Another sign of termites at work is tunnels or lines of earth, about the diameter of a pen, that lead toward and inside the house (over foundation walls, for example). These shelter, or foraging, tubes provide the termites with a route from the ground to your wood. Soft or rotten wood may also indicate termite damage.

While termites actually eat wood, carpenter ants (which are big, dark-colored winged ants) damage wood by nesting in it. Like termites, they're attracted to rotten or decaying wood and to damp patches or water. You may see their small entry holes in wood, or sawdust piles below a wood surface.

FACT

Termite treatments should last about five years, but that will depend on the amount of chemical used in the treatment and how thoroughly it is applied. Always check that your pest control firm is experienced in termite treatments. Treating only specific spots isn't recommended, because termites can be operating where you can't see them.

Keep wood-loving insects away by ensuring that any wooden part of the house exterior is at least 6 inches above the soil surface (wooden steps and porch supports can act as highways into a house's framework). Also ensure that rainwater flows away from the house to prevent moisture from accumulating beside your foundation.

There is a limit to how much you can do, however. If termites or carpenter ants are present in your area, or you're seeing signs that they're in the house, talk to an exterminator about strategies. Chemical treatments provide a "firewall" around the house. Chemicals can also be injected into carpenter ant holes to kill them in the nests. Physical barriers, such as metal termite shields, can also be installed between a concrete or brick foundation and the wood above it.

Flying Insects

Insects that fly present even more challenges than those that crawl. It's almost impossible to keep your home entirely fly-free, although sealing it and maintaining door and window screens can help. Aside from the hygiene factor (flies love trash), some flying insects can be harmful. Mosquitoes are not only annoying; they can also carry disease. And wasps, bees, and hornets can deliver a nasty sting, especially if they're provoked or startled. Again, prevention is key.

Reduce mosquitoes around your home by eliminating or treating any sources of standing water in which they could lay their eggs. Pesticides are available, but talk to your municipality or county before considering them. First, get rid of water that's sitting in tires, toys, low-lying parts of your yard, tarpaulins, gutters, and other places that water isn't supposed to be collecting. For places where water is supposed to be, such as birdbaths and fountains, change the water at least weekly. Items such as rain barrels should be tightly sealed to prevent insects from entering. You may also need to protect yourself against bites by wearing long sleeves and using repellent outside, especially in the evening.

ALERT!

If any member of your household exhibits sensitivity to insect stings, talk to your doctor. Repeated exposure, such as second or third stings, can increase the sensitivity and even create life-threatening anaphylactic (allergic) reactions.

Your best defense against insects such as wasps is to check potential nest sites regularly; check for nests weekly in the spring, when the insects are building new nests. If you notice a large number of wasps in an area, carefully watch where they go, to locate their nest. Papery gray nests belong to wasps and are often found hanging below eaves, decks, or porches, or in attics. Wasps, bees, yellow jackets, and hornets also nest in holes in trees or the ground, and within house wall cavities.

If the nest is new and small, you may be able to handle it yourself. Choose a cool night, when the insects are at home and less mobile. A strong soaking from a garden hose spray nozzle may be enough to destroy the nest; commercial chemical sprays are also an option. Either way, ensure that you have a good escape plan in case the nest is not as docile as you expect. Hire an expert to handle larger nests.

Mice, Snakes, and Bats

Mice are a common problem in both rural and urban settings. They make themselves very comfortable in houses, actually preferring homes that are occupied (and therefore good sources of food), and can enter through holes as small as a dime. You may see one streak across the floor, but you're more likely to see their small, elongated droppings, or evidence of gnawing.

Whether you choose to trap and kill or relocate the mice, or simply try to drive them out of the house, the most important measure is to seal the house extremely well once they're gone. To convince them to leave, try leaving cat hair or peppermint-oiled rags around their entry holes (this also works for rats). Killing or removing the mice alone isn't a permanent solution, because they—or their rodent cousins—will simply find the access holes and move in again.

Mice can carry serious diseases, such as hantavirus. Clean mouse-contaminated areas with a solution of 1 part bleach to 4 parts water, and wear gloves, glasses, and a mask covering your nose and mouth while cleaning up.

Another problem with mice and other rodents is that they attract snakes—so getting rid of a mouse problem can actually help prevent a snake problem. It's important to know the types of snakes in your area (most are nonpoisonous, and all are helpful in keeping rodent populations under control), in the unlikely event that someone is bitten. The key to preventing snakes from entering a building is to seal all potential openings, from dryer vents to gaps around plumbing and electrical wiring. Also remove any attractive hiding places, such as brush or scrap lumber piles, from near the house.

Warm, damp compost attracts both rodents and snakes. You can place fine wire mesh under a compost bin or pile to prevent entry from below, or use a tumbling-style bin. Regularly forking the compost to air it out and turn it over will help the compost bin do its job, and it also makes the bin less comfortable for critters. Ammonia or a commercial repellent may also help.

If you notice bats flying around your eaves in the evenings, watch where they come from and where they go; they could be nesting in your attic. You can try to convince them to leave by switching on bright lights at night or by keeping the attic cool, but the best strategy is to wait until fall or winter, when they leave to find a hibernation site. Identify all the holes or cracks through which they're entering the attic (they can squeeze through cracks just $\frac{1}{4}$- to $\frac{1}{2}$-inch wide), and seal all but one of them. On this one, create a one-way exit-only barrier by securing netting or plastic strips to the exterior of the hole, leaving the bottom edge free. Once all the bats have left, seal the opening permanently.

FACT

Bats are one of the most effective mosquito control methods you'll find. You may not want them in your attic, but encourage them to nest nearby by building bat houses (instructions are available at home centers or at *www.batconservation.org*).

Larger Unwanted Visitors

Midsize pests include squirrels, groundhogs, skunks, porcupines, raccoons, and opossums, depending on your area, and can be a problem in both rural and urban areas. You're most likely to find them seeking shelter in attics, crawlspaces, decks, porches, and stairways. While they look cute, animals such as skunks and raccoons in particular can carry rabies, and any animal that's nesting in or close to the house brings insects and fecal matter with it.

The best option for getting rid of them is to call an exterminator, preferably one that has humane options for removal. You don't want to trap adult animals in the spring, for example, because you may be leaving babies inside the house—starvation is particularly inhumane.

If you're sure that there are no baby animals involved, watch for the animals leaving or entering the house. Once you've identified the access point, install a one-way door over it, or seal it up after the animal has left. If the animal is reluctant to leave, try using commercial repellents or rags soaked in ammonia close to the entryway. Bright lights, cayenne pepper, and radios playing all night also make your house less hospitable. Squirrels and skunks aren't fond of mothballs, either.

For burrowing animals like woodchucks and skunks, shield crawlspaces and areas below porches and decks. Fill any spaces that could become dens with dirt, and bury wire mesh fences at least 8 to 12 inches into the ground.

The Really Big Pests

Moving up the scale of problem animals, deer and even moose can be a challenge in rural and semirural areas, especially if you value your garden. Your best option is deer-proof fencing, but given that it needs to be 8 feet high, it's an expensive proposition. Talk to your local garden center about plants that don't attract deer or that can survive the occasional deer nibble, and about deer repellants. Vulnerable trees may need individual fencing or plastic sleeves for protection.

Scarecrows and other deer-frightening measures may help. Bright motion-sensor lights and water sprinklers, balloons, radios, and strips of aluminum foil are all options. Providing deer with an alternative attraction can also help—such as a salt lick, for example, far removed from your garden or tender trees.

Taking the time to protect your house from invasions by unwanted guests from the animal kingdom is essential—and it takes a lot less effort than trying to evict the guests once they've settled in. But there are also unwanted guests that walk on two legs. Chapter 10 deals with protecting your house against human pests. Ⓔ

Chapter 10
Security Watch

There's a great deal that you can do to make your home less attractive to uninvited guests of the human kind. Good visibility around the house, watchful neighbors, and strong locks are all part of the equation. In many areas of the country, a home alarm system that's obvious to burglars, but difficult for them to tamper with, is also essential.

Essential Lighting

Keeping your house and yard well lit is important, but too much illumination contributes to a phenomenon known as light pollution—where the night sky over a city is so bright that it obscures most stars and planets, and confuses migrating birds. You need to strike a balance that meets your lighting needs for safety and security without lighting your yard so brightly that you and your neighbors need blackout curtains in order to sleep.

First, determine which areas need to be lit. When you're inside the house, you need enough lighting at the entrances so that you can see anyone who's standing at the door. When you're approaching your house from the outside, you need enough lighting to make your way along walkways or sidewalks, from garages or sheds, to the house.

Installing photosensitive lights or adding light-sensing sockets to your existing lights at entrances means that you'll never again have to remember to turn on the lights: They'll turn on automatically at dusk. Motion-sensitive lights, meanwhile, turn on when they sense movement within their range, and then turn off automatically after a time delay. These can be great near garages, automatically switching on when you approach, and are also ideal for lighting potentially vulnerable areas of your house or yard.

Low-voltage outdoor lighting is another solution that illuminates specific areas without being too bright, and it is particularly effective for lighting walkways.

FACT

Solar lights are another garden alternative, but they tend to provide very low levels of light. Since they depend on sunlight, they're not the best alternative for security uses.

The Most Secure Doors

Doors are a natural entry point for burglars. Make it more difficult for them by keeping your doors locked at all times—whether you're away from home, inside the house, or in the yard. (Your insurance company may be less than impressed to hear that the burglar was able to simply turn the door handle and walk in.)

Solid Wood or Metal Doors

Burglar-resistant doors consist of solid wood, or of wood filled with insulation and clad with metal. Hinges should always be placed on the inside of the door, not the outside, so that the hinge pin can't be removed from outside the house. If the door has windows, they should be small enough, or far enough away from the lock, that a burglar can't break them and reach through to operate the lock from the inside.

If your older house has a bulkhead entrance into the basement (where wooden doors swing up to open to the exterior), secure the doors with two crossbars that sit across the inside width of the doors and fit into slots on either side of the doors that are reinforced with either concrete or solid wood.

Sliding Glass Doors

Patio doors that slide closed are particularly vulnerable to break-ins. One security option is to install a locking bar, which is a metal bar that fits across from the edge of the sliding door to the door frame. Screw the hinged bracket to the door frame at the midpoint height of the frame, and screw the locking bracket to the corresponding midpoint height of the door (predrill your holes, and ensure that you don't screw so far into the door that you risk breaking the glass). The bar fits onto the hinge bracket, and swings down into place over the locking bracket.

To prevent the door from being lifted out of its track, insert two or three screws, evenly spaced, along the upper track. Predrill the holes, and leave the screws protruding just a little less than the point at which they would interfere with the movement of the door.

Another security measure is to install a lock that inserts a pin into the door frame at the bottom edge of the inside sliding door. You screw the lock to the edge of the door and drill a hole through the frame for the locking pin to fit into.

If the drill is bouncing off the surface rather than drilling into it, make a starter hole by tapping an awl with a hammer. This creates enough of an indentation to hold the drill bit in place while it starts cutting.

Making Use of Locks

Exterior doors should be equipped with deadbolt locks, which use a bolt that extends out of the door and into the door frame by at least 1 inch. You'll find two basic types: single-cylinder deadbolts, which use a key to lock them from outside and a knob or latch to lock them from inside; and double-cylinder deadbolts, which need a key to lock them from inside or outside. Although double-cylinder locks are more secure, they do present a quick-escape problem for anyone inside the house and may be restricted by fire codes. If you have one of these locks, keep the key nearby at all times, but place it out of reach of a window that could be broken into.

Installing a Deadbolt

To install a single-cylinder deadbolt, first choose one that fits the way your door opens (right-handed or left-handed). Tape the template that comes with the lock to the door at a convenient height (matching existing holes if possible, to eliminate the need to drill new ones), and mark the center of the two required holes as necessary: one through the door for the lock (the keyhole) and its knob/latch; and one into the door edge for the deadbolt and the locking mechanism. Use a hole saw bit on your power drill to cut the hole through the door (drill part of the way through from both sides of the door to avoid splitting the wood on the finished surface), and a spade bit to drill the hole through the door edge for the deadbolt. Insert the locking mechanism through the hole you drilled for the deadbolt; then insert the two halves of the lock (keyhole and latch) into the main hole, through the locking mechanism, and screw them together.

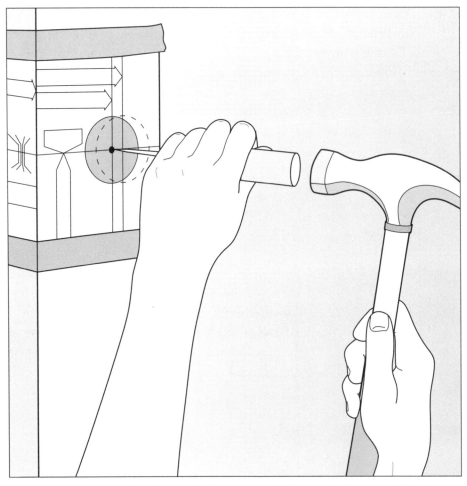

▲ Use a hammer and awl to mark the center of the two holes needed in the door, as shown by the lockset's template.

Close the door, and place the strike plate (the metal plate on the door frame that the deadbolt passes through) beside the door frame at the right height to meet the deadbolt, marking its position with a pencil on the frame. To create the mortise (depression) in which the strike plate will sit, open the door, place the strike plate in the position you marked, and trace around it with a pencil. Use a utility knife to score just on the inside of the pencil markings (this ensures that the mortise won't be too large). Then make a series of cuts across the mortise with a chisel (held at a 45-degree angle) and hammer. Chisel out the material between these cuts to the depth of the strike plate, holding the chisel at a 15- to 20-degree angle.

Use a spade bit to drill the hole in the door frame/wall for the deadbolt to go into. Screw the strike plate over the mortise and deadbolt hole using 3-inch screws, which will pass through the door frame and into the wall structure.

▲ When you're chiseling out the mortise for the deadbolt's strike plate, it's best to err on the side of caution. Take out as little material as possible—you can always go over the mortise again if it's not deep enough.

Strike Plates

Strike plates can be reinforced to reduce the risk that the wood underneath them will splinter and give way if someone attempts to kick in the door. Options include stronger strike plates that use six screws instead of the usual two, or that have a metal box for the deadbolt to slide into. Metal plates are also available that fit on the door and the frame, to strengthen the wood's resistance.

QUESTION?

How do I strengthen the door frame itself?
Remove the existing strike plate and hinges, along with the corresponding trim pieces around the door frame. There's likely a gap between the frame and the wall structure. Insert strips of solid wood into the gaps, then replace the trim, the strike plate, and the hinges.

Peepholes

Peepholes allow you to see who's outside before you make yourself vulnerable by opening the door. When choosing a peephole, ensure that it will fit your door's depth, and opt for the higher-quality glass peepholes (with at least a 180-degree field of vision), rather than plastic peepholes. To install, drill a hole in the center of the door at about eye level. Drilling halfway into the door from both the inside and the outside will create a neater edge than if you drill all the way through it from one side. Be sure to keep the drill level.

Take the peephole apart by unscrewing the lens from the base. The lens half goes into the hole from the exterior side of the door; the base goes in from the interior. Screw the two halves back together.

Windows

Most windows need serious security help, which is available in a variety of lock styles. Some sliding-window locks screw into the window frame and flip over the edge of the windowpane to hold it in place. Other types include a pressure screw that's clipped onto the sliding-window track behind the window, preventing the window from being opened at all. (This may only be appropriate for windows you don't use very often and where quick escape isn't an issue.) A length of dowelling inserted into the bottom track between the edge of the sliding window and the window frame can also prevent the window from being opened.

For casement or awning windows that are operated by a crank handle, remove the cranks and place them nearby (but not within reach of a broken window). For basement windows with a latch fastener, try a lock that screws onto the wall above the latch and flips down over the latch, to prevent it from being tampered with.

Pins

The latch that closes most double-hung or sash windows is no substitute for a lock. To effectively secure the windows, install window pins (or screw eyes, which are easier to insert and remove) that prevent the windows from being raised or lowered. Drill a hole just slightly larger than the pin through each top corner of the lower window frame, into the bottom corners of the upper window frame (don't drill all the way through the upper window frame). The pin sits inside the hole (protruding slightly so that it's easy to remove from inside the house) and holds the windows together so that they can't be opened.

To prevent the drill from going too far into the upper window frame, wrap the drill bit with a piece of masking tape at the maximum depth you need. When the edge of the tape meets the window frame, you've drilled as far as you need to go.

You can lock the windows in a partially open position (for air circulation) by drilling another set of holes in the upper window frame an inch or so above the first set.

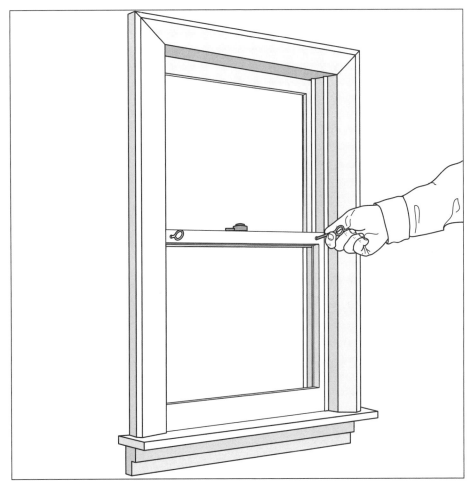

▲ Window pins or screw eyes lock the upper and lower window sashes together so that they can't be moved up or down from outside the house.

Security Film

A high-strength safety film for glass is available that prevents the glass from shattering apart on impact. The glass might crack, but it remains intact on the film. The film needs to be installed by a professional (this is not the same as window film available at home centers that only screens out the sun's ultraviolet rays). Small window stickers that identify the film let potential burglars know that they can't break through the window, even if they try.

Window Bars and Grates

Basement windows are another weak point for break-ins. Window bars or grates are one of the most secure ways to protect them, and their design has improved considerably over the years, so that they no longer look quite so prisonlike. You don't, however, want to make the windows so secure that they can't be used as an escape route in an emergency, especially if the basement has bedrooms or playrooms. Opt for a system that has a quick-release device that's operated from the inside without the need for a key (check local building codes or regulations to find out if they specify a system that's either permitted or prohibited).

Generally, these quick-release window bar designs are attached by screwing the guide rail to one edge of the window frame, sliding the grill (the bars) onto the rail, positioning the other guide rail, and securing it. Ensure that the screws are long enough (at least 3 inches) to fasten into the studs on either side of the window frame.

Choosing a Home Alarm System

There are two types of alarm systems: wired systems, where electrical contacts on doors and windows sound the alarm when the window or door is opened and contact is broken; and wireless systems, which use infrared, ultrasonic, or microwave technology to sense movement. Wired systems require less in terms of both cost and maintenance, but are more easily tampered with than wireless systems.

FACT

A truly effective home alarm system should be professionally installed, but there are some stopgap measures that you can take. Portable alarms can be hung on doorknobs or placed across from the door to sense movement, for example.

You also need to decide whether to have your alarm system monitored. While central monitoring is an ongoing expense, it can be worthwhile, especially if the house is left vacant frequently. Whether or not your alarm is monitored, check with your municipality, county, or police department about false alarms. These have become a serious nuisance in many areas, and some local governments have instituted fines for frequent offenders.

A professional alarm system that's centrally monitored has several advantages. It can be wired into smoke and carbon monoxide detectors, and temperature sensors, so that the monitoring company will be able to detect fires and malfunctioning furnaces. This can reduce your insurance costs.

If you're looking for a professional home alarm company, seek out recommendations from friends or colleagues. The installation company should carry a license, liability insurance, and membership in a national trade association, and its employees should be bonded.

You've now approached the exterior of your house from every angle, from the materials that encase it to the threats posed by weather, pests, and break-ins. It's now time (finally!) to head inside to find interior fix-it jobs, starting with the basement in Chapter 11.

Chapter 11
Down in the Basement

The most common problem in basements is excess moisture, caused either by water leaks or condensation. You've already handled many of the causes of water seepage into the basement, including blocked gutters, leaking pipes, unprotected basement window wells, and incorrectly sloped ground. In this chapter, you'll learn about other common moisture problems down under—including the potential for sewer backups from municipal sewer lines—and how to tackle them.

Basement Moisture

Problems in basements are much easier to see—and to solve—if the area remains unfinished. Particularly if you have a damp basement, you need to fix the moisture source before attempting any renovations or finishes, such as insulating or painting. Most of the following fix-it projects therefore deal with an unfinished basement. If yours has already been renovated, you may need to call in a contractor, because it's difficult to know how or where to access the areas needed to solve the problems. This chapter may, however, provide valuable clues as to the source of the moisture.

If your basement is used for storage, avoid keeping anything down there that could absorb moisture (such as clothes and old newspapers), and store items well off the floor. Where frequent flooding is an issue, protect the legs of wooden or metal shelving units from rot or rust by placing them in empty plastic containers, such as margarine or ice cream tubs, until you can solve the problem.

FACT

A white powdery substance on concrete walls or floors is actually mineral crystals left there when water evaporated away from the surface. It's called efflorescence and is a sign of moisture problems. Scrub it away with a stiff brush, regular household cleaner, and hot water.

Moisture that forms on a concrete basement wall may be coming from two sources—water seeping through the concrete wall or condensation. If you're not sure which it is, dry several small areas on the walls and floor with a hair dryer, and duct-tape a piece of aluminum foil or plastic wrap securely to the wall. Wait about three days, and check the surface again. If the foil or plastic is wet on its outer surface, your problem is condensation. If the moisture is between the foil/plastic and the wall, the water is coming in through the wall. (If you're really unlucky, you'll find both problems.)

Dirt Floors

Older homes may still have dirt floors in basements or crawlspaces, which can be an entry point for moisture, insects, and radon gas—none of which you want in your home. Your first line of defense is to lay a thick sheet of plastic over any bare dirt, carrying the plastic up the walls to a height that's just above ground level. To join two pieces of plastic, overlap the seams by about 12 inches, and duct-tape them together.

When you're doing this, be careful not to cover any ventilation openings. A crawlspace should have a vent on each wall so that air can move about under the house. (Check that the openings are screened so that they don't become an entry point for mice or other wandering critters.)

A more permanent solution is to talk to a professional contractor or house inspector about whether pouring a concrete slab over the dirt is a practical measure.

Cracks in Concrete Floors and Walls

Don't panic if you see hairline cracks in your concrete. You will want to call in a house inspector or contractor, however, if the cracks are wider than $\frac{1}{8}$ inch, the two edges of the crack don't match each other, the cracks are changing direction over time, or they're widespread. These might signal a settling or heaving problem that needs expert help.

Small cracks in concrete walls and floors or in the mortar between concrete blocks can be patched in the same way as described in Chapter 7 (for mortar cracks, clean out any loose or water-damaged mortar around the crack). Hydraulic cement is a good solution, because it expands when it comes into contact with water, thus helping to seal the crack against water leaks. If you're dealing with a crack on the inside of a wall, check out the corresponding area on the outside of the wall (digging down as necessary). You may need to seal the crack from both sides of the wall. After you've fixed the crack so that it no longer leaks, seal the wall or floor with concrete sealer to further prevent moisture seeping through the wall.

Floor Coverings

If you have a wet or damp basement, the worst thing that you could put on the floor is a carpet, which will soak up the moisture. Painting a problem basement floor is also a waste of time, because the paint will peel. Instead, solve your moisture problems, and then consider floor coverings—including simply sealing the floor with several coats of sealer.

Appliances such as furnaces, hot-water heaters, washers, and dryers are often placed on basement floors, where they can be vulnerable to even minor flooding. It's best to raise them up above the floor by about 4 inches, using either a poured concrete or brick platform. This is a fairly ambitious project if you've never worked with mixing concrete before, so seek expert advice or help.

Condensation

To solve a condensation problem, where the basement is damp in general, try using a dehumidifier to take out the extra moisture in the air. Empty the water tray frequently to prevent mold from building up in the dehumidifier. Also assess the house's ventilation system (a house inspector can help you with this). Is the house too airtight, so that moisture building up in kitchens and bathrooms isn't being exhausted properly?

Condensation can also form on cold surfaces, such as cold-water pipes when the air around the surface is warmer (think of icy lemonade in a glass on a hot day—the outside surface of the glass quickly gathers a coating of water). To solve this, insulate cold-water pipes or air-conditioning ducts following the instruction for insulating hot-water pipes and furnace ducts in Chapter 6.

Dealing with Leaks

Water leaking into basements may enter through window frames, cracks in walls or floors, and the seam between the wall and the floor. To solve a leak problem around windows, check the frames. If they're wood, they may need to be repaired (see Chapter 17) or even replaced. Caulking around the exterior window frame where it meets the house, and replacing any broken or crumbling putty where the glass meets the frame, can also help.

Cracks in concrete walls and floors can be fixed as described in the previous section and in Chapter 7. You can also caulk the seams where the outside basement wall meets sidewalks, steps, and driveways with concrete caulking.

If water is entering the seam between the wall and the floor, or through floor cracks, you should call for expert help. Most houses drain water away from their basements with a system of weeping tiles, or perforated pipes, that collect water from around the exterior of the basement wall and redirect it safely away from the basement. If this system fails, the water can seep into the basement, often through the wall/floor seam. A high water table, where the ground water is approaching the level of the basement, can also create water seepage through floor cracks and the wall/floor seam.

To permanently solve these moisture problems, the weeping tile or pipe system needs to be repaired. This involves digging up the earth around the basement and relaying the gravel surface under the pipes, and the pipes themselves. The contractor should also fix any cracks in the exterior wall and coat the whole wall with a concrete sealer before replacing the dirt. This is also a good time to tackle problems with leaky basement windows, while they're easier to get at.

QUESTION?

How do you stop water from entering through the wall/floor seam when there's already a sump pump system installed? Assuming that the system is collecting water properly (something that an expert needs to check), a drain system can be installed that covers the basement's wall/floor seam, so that any water that seeps in is redirected to the sump pump.

A high water table isn't something that even an expert can change. However, a sump pump system can control the water seeping into your basement by pumping water away once it rises high enough to enter the basement. These systems should be installed by professionals who know how to effectively collect and redirect the water so that it doesn't cause you, or your neighbors, any additional problems.

Maintaining Sump Pumps

Most sump pump systems consist of a pit into which the pump (either a pedestal type, which sits above the water, or a submersible type) is placed. A drainage pipe takes the water away to where it can be distributed safely into the ground (sump pump drains shouldn't be connected to sewer lines, because a severe rainstorm can overload the sewers, possibly causing the water to back up into the house).

Most pumps run on house electricity (they should be plugged into a GFCI-protected outlet), but since severe weather can cut power supplies just when they're needed the most, choose a pump with a battery backup. A submersible pump may also be wise if the risk of flooding the basement is high, because if a pedestal pump's motor ends up sitting in water, you'll need to replace it.

To check the system (which you should do in spring and fall, and before leaving the house on vacation), lift off any covers that fit over the pump and pit. The pit can accumulate sand, dirt, and other debris, so you'll need to clean it out. If the water in the pit has a bad odor (which happens if it sits for a long period without being flushed out), gradually pour about 5 gallons of water into the pit. This should force the pump to come on, flushing out the old, smelly water.

Pouring water into the pit is also a good way to check that the pump is switching on when it should. If it's not, check the circuit breaker to make sure that the circuit is working. Also check that the floats that operate the on/off switches are moving freely. If neither of these efforts fixes the pump, call a plumber.

Examine the drainage pipe to make sure that it's in good condition, and check outside, where it empties, to make sure that water is draining through it properly. Similarly, check the screen that covers the pump's water intake to make sure it's clean (if the pump comes on regularly, you

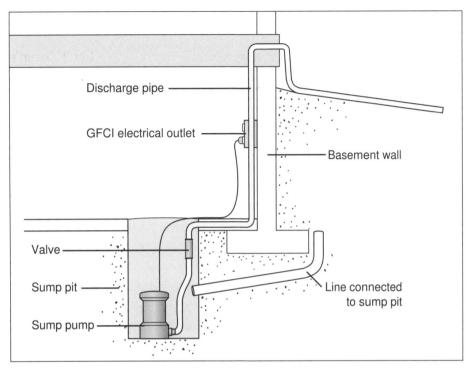

Discharge pipe

GFCI electrical outlet

Basement wall

Valve

Sump pit

Sump pump

Line connected
to sump pit

▲ A typical sump pump system takes water from around the house foundation
and redirects it far enough away that it won't enter the basement.

may need to check this screen monthly). If you're not familiar with your
sump pump system (you've just moved in, for example), have it inspected
by a plumber.

- Have the plumber explain the pump system to you, along with any
  required maintenance.
- Ensure that the system is pumping water well away from the house
  (and not into sewer lines or septic systems).
- Ensure that drainage pipe has a backwater valve on it to prevent
  water from flowing back toward the pump.

Backwater Valves

If you've ever had water from the sewage system back up into your basement, you already know how much time and trouble backwater valves can save you. Municipal sewer lines can become blocked or overwhelmed. When this happens, the water backs up along the system into the houses that are connected to it, through floor drains, toilets, and bathtubs—which can be a nasty surprise.

This problem often occurs in low-lying areas where the plumbing in the basement sits at a lower level than the sewer line in the street. Many areas now mandate backwater valves in vulnerable areas, to stop the damage caused by several inches of sewer water in house basements. These valves have a flap inside them that lets water flow out unheeded, but snaps closed if water attempts to flow back the other way. They need to be installed in the house's main sewer line or a drain line, in a position to block sewage from entering the basement plumbing.

This is a complicated job, especially if the right location for the valve lies under a concrete basement floor. You should call in a plumber to set the right location for the valve and to install it. (If it's installed in the wrong place, it might stop sewage from coming out through a floor drain, but reroute it into a toilet or washing machine.)

E ALERT! Check with your county or municipality to find out what its policy is regarding backwater valves. In some areas, backwater valves are required by building codes, but in others, their use might be restricted or bound by building permits.

Backwater valves are also available to protect individual drain lines within the house, and they can be useful if you can't install a valve on the main line. You need to understand, though, that blocking the flow of sewer water into one area will force it out of another. You may, for example, choose to protect a floor drain in a utility room that contains your furnace, or to protect the drain pipe that leads out of your washing machine, but you'll have to realize that the wastewater will then likely appear in a downstairs bathtub, or back up through a toilet. It's a good idea to consult a plumber or house inspector before installing backwater valves anywhere so that you understand potential consequences.

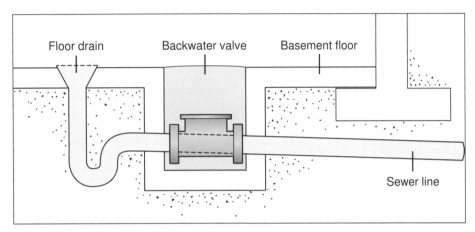

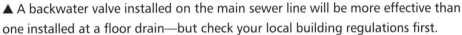

▲ A backwater valve installed on the main sewer line will be more effective than one installed at a floor drain—but check your local building regulations first.

Most basements will have a floor drain somewhere—usually in a furnace or utility room. The drain is there to handle floods from within the house, such as a broken hot-water heater or washing machine, so a backwater valve installed in the drain needs to operate properly, letting water out but not in.

Valves are available in a range of sizes, so measure the interior diameter of the drain pipe that you want to seal, and buy the right valve for the type of installation (in this case, a floor drain). If the drain is an odd size, you may need to buy a sleeve that fits into the pipe and forms the right size opening for the valve. Lift up the grate from the drain, and clean the top of the drain line. One common backwater valve uses a rubber gasket to seal the gap between the valve and the pipe. Drop the valve into place and tighten the screws on its top until the rubber gasket presses out to meet the pipe. Hold the valve in place and level while you're tightening the screws.

Check that the valve flapper is working freely before pouring some water through the valve to test that it's draining properly. You'll also need to check the valve periodically, to clean out any debris that might have fallen onto it.

Insulating Basements

Insulating a basement isn't a difficult job, and it can make a significant difference in your heating and cooling bills. Just make sure that any water leaks or seepage problems are solved before you start insulating. You should also check local building codes or talk to local house inspectors or contractors before you start to find out if there are any specific materials or techniques called for (or prohibited) in your area. Some codes require insulation to be covered up with a wall surface, such as wallboard, for fire safety.

Where you're insulating for cold climates, vapor barrier should be installed on the inside surface (the heated side) of the insulation. In warmer areas, vapor barrier might not be required or may be suggested for the outside surface (uncooled side) of insulation. Always check your local codes.

Insulating Basement Walls

Concrete basement walls can be insulated with rigid insulation boards. This is a straightforward fix-it job that would probably take you just a weekend to finish, depending on how large your basement is. You can buy 2-inch-thick foam insulation boards in 2' × 8' sheets.

Your first step is to install 2" × 2" furring strips (long strips of wood) vertically on your basement walls, placing them 2 feet apart from one another (the width of the insulation sheets) to reduce the number of cuts to the insulation boards. The insulation boards will fit between the strips, which will then provide a surface for installing vapor barrier and wallboard. Mark a vertical line on the wall, using a plumb line to ensure that the line is straight up and down. Glue a furring strip to the line with construction adhesive designed for wood and concrete surfaces. (If you want to install wallboard after insulating the basement, be sure to glue furring strips to the wall between the bottom and top edges of the vertical furring strips as well, so that they form a framework to attach the wallboard to.)

FACT

Basements often have exposed joists at the top of their concrete wall, where the wall meets the first floor. You can insulate these by stuffing pieces of fiberglass batts into them. The fit should be snug, to avoid gaps around the insulation and the joists, but not so tight that the insulation is compressed.

Use a utility knife and level or long ruler to cut the insulation boards to the height you need. Measure the location of any electrical outlets, switches, or other obstacles, and transfer them to the insulation board so that you can cut appropriate holes for them. Glue the boards to the concrete wall with panel adhesive that's designed for the insulation and concrete.

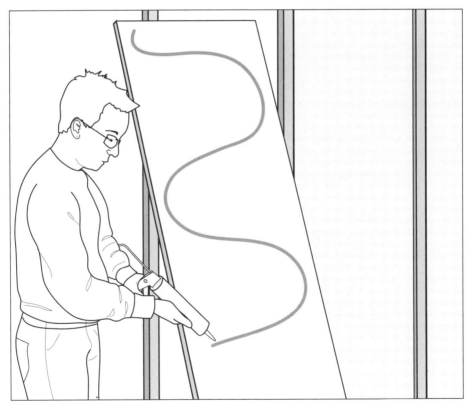

▲ Panel adhesive that's designed to bond between concrete basement walls and rigid insulation boards makes installation of the boards a quick job.

Attach the vapor barrier (clear polyethylene sheeting available at home centers) over the insulation by stapling it to the furring strips. You can seal any seams with wide plastic tape.

Insulating Unheated Crawlspaces

To help protect the floors above unheated crawlspaces, the crawlspace ceiling should be insulated. The easiest way to handle this is to use fiberglass batt insulation that has a vapor barrier or foil facing already installed on one side. Cut the batts to fit between the joists (snugly, but without squeezing the insulation too tightly), and lay them, vapor-barrier/foil-side up, between the joists. (To cut fiberglass batts, compress the fiberglass with a piece of 2" × 4", and use the wood as a guide to run your utility knife through the compressed insulation.)

Cut the insulation so that it fits around plumbing pipes and electrical wires, but be sure to cut an extra 3 inches of material away around anything that could heat up, such as chimney flues. Use furring strips nailed to the underside of the joists to prevent the insulation from sagging or falling down.

ALERT!

Be sure to protect yourself from loose fibers when handling fiberglass insulation. Wear a breathing mask and safety goggles, a hood, gloves, long pants, and a long-sleeved shirt (coveralls work best).

Now that the basement is dry and weatherproof, you might be thinking that you could head upstairs. Stay put, however. The next chapter deals with floors, and the first fix-it job is eliminating those annoying squeaky floorboards. The best place to start that task is—you guessed right—the basement. Ⓔ

Chapter 12
Fixable Floors

If your floors are squeaky and creaky, or your floor covering has sprung a hole or tear, don't despair—there are fix-it solutions for all of these problems. Of course, if the problem is structural, such as a sagging floor, skip fix-it and go right to the professionals. Otherwise, check out these options for silencing floors, tightening stair components, and repairing floor coverings such as hardwood, ceramic tile, resilient flooring, and carpet.

Solutions for Squeaks

It's a fact of fix-it life: Wood floors will eventually squeak wherever two pieces of wood rub together, including floorboards, joists, and the bracing pieces that bridge the joists. As a first defense, check the humidity in your house using a hygrometer; it should read between 30 and 50 percent. If the house is too dry, increase the humidity to see if that reduces the squeaking.

If it doesn't, and you can see the underside of the floor that's squeaking, have someone walk over the floor. Watch for movement in the wood whenever you hear a squeak, and mark the area with chalk so that you'll remember where the fix is needed.

Squeaky Floors

For hardwood floors that squeak, clean out any dust or debris in the joints between the boards, and lubricate the joints with a squeezable tube or bottle of powdered graphite or talc—just blow it in. Another option is to insert finishing nails (with very small heads) between the floorboards, at a slight angle to make them less likely to pop back out.

FACT

Flooring repairs often involve drilling pilot holes in which screws need to be countersunk (sinking the screw head slightly below the surface). Although you can use a combination of bits in sequence to create a countersunk pilot hole, it's much easier and quicker to use a combination drill bit to shape the entire hole the first time.

If this doesn't work, and you can access your floor from below, tap a glue-coated wedge between the joist and the subflooring wherever the floor is squeaking. If there's no room for a wedge, screw angle irons or glue-coated blocks of wood against the bottom of the floor and the side of the joist.

To deal with squeaky floors covered with carpet, you can buy or rent a tool that drives a special screw through the carpet and into the subflooring and joists, breaking off the screw's head at the surface of the subflooring.

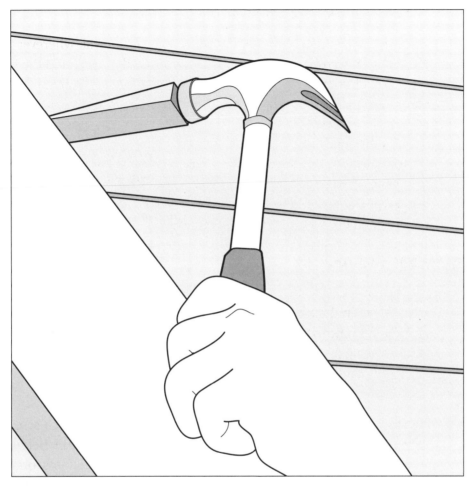

▲ Coating the wedge with wood glue will prevent it from working loose over time as the floor is walked on.

Squeaky Stairs

Like floors, squeaky stairs are easiest to fix from the underside, if they're accessible. Coat thin wedges with wood glue, and tap them into the joints where the tread meets the risers. If there's no room for wedges, two shelf brackets or angle irons, or several glue-coated wood blocks, can be screwed to the back of the riser and the bottom of the tread (drill pilot holes, and keep the screws at least ¼ inch away from finished surfaces). For added stability, also wedge or connect the edge of the riser against the edge of the stringer that runs up each side of the stairway.

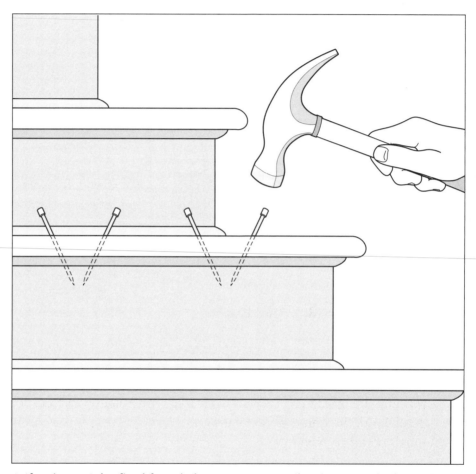

▲ If stairs can't be fixed from below, you can try silencing squeaks from above. A noisy tread can be wedged where it meets the rear riser, or nailed where it meets the front riser.

If you can't get under your stairs, you'll have to work from the finished side. Try the powdered graphite or talc fixes first, blowing it into the joints, including the one where the tread meets the riser. (You may need to remove any molding that sits over that joint to access it.) If there's even a small gap between the tread and the riser, tap thin wedges into it with a hammer, being careful not to hit the tread. You can hide the wedges and gap by nailing a strip of molding over the tread/riser joint.

Another option is to drill pairs of nail holes through the top of the tread into the riser below it, angling the nail holes in each pair toward each other. Insert the nails with a nail set so that you can cover their heads with wood putty. You may be able to see from the gaps between the tread and the riser that nails won't be sufficient to cinch together the two components. In this case, use screws, angled straight down into the riser through the tread. For added stability, nail or screw through the tread into the stringer on either side of the stairway.

Whenever you're using screws, drill counterbored pilot holes first so that you'll be able to sink the screw head, and then hide it with a wood plug or putty.

Patching Subflooring

You may need to replace a piece of the subflooring that sits under your floor covering, most often due to water damage (under a toilet, for example). First, mark straight lines around the damaged area, trying to position them next to or near joists (to provide nailing surfaces for the patch). Cut the damaged area away, and use it as a template to cut a patch out of plywood the same thickness as the floor. The patch should be just a touch ($\frac{1}{16}$ inch) smaller than the damaged area, to allow for expansion and contraction of the flooring.

Nail strips of 2" × 4" to the joists that you've revealed. The patch will sit on top of these strips and be screwed into them. If the patched area needs to bear extra weight, such as that of a toilet, you can use 2" × 6"s instead, nailing them to the joists on either side of the cut area, and also across the cut area between the joists.

Lay a bead of glue along the nailing strips and between the nailing strips and the joists. Screw the patch into place.

Carpet

The kindest thing you can do for carpet is to vacuum it at least weekly. Dust and dirt accumulates over time and can grind down the fibers. Small burns or stains can be fixed quite easily if you have a scrap piece of the same carpet (take it out of a closet, for example). Use a carpet-cutting tool (it looks like a cookie cutter) that's big enough to fit over the damaged area. Place the tool over the area, press down, and twist. Use the same technique to cut a patch of the same size out of the scrap carpet, matching any patterns as much as possible. (Larger patches can be cut with a utility knife.)

Lay double-sided carpet tape in the hole, extending below the edges of the good carpet. Place the patch in the hole, matching the pattern. Apply seam adhesive to the seam between the patch and the good carpet.

Sealing Carpet Seams

Carpet can indeed come apart at the seams. To fix this, remove any of the old carpet tape under the seam and replace it with a length of either double-sided adhesive carpet tape or heat-activated carpet tape along the entire seam. Be sure to center the tape so that it fits under both of the carpet edges. For the adhesive tape, press the seam edges down onto it firmly. For heat-activated tape, run a seam iron (which can be rented) over the tape (under the carpet edges) to heat it. Follow along with one hand behind the iron, pressing the carpet edges down firmly against the tape.

Restretching Carpet

If the carpet is coming loose from the walls, it can be restretched. You'll need to buy or rent a carpet kicker (a long bar with a pronged head). First, remove the baseboards from the wall where the carpet is loose. Take a look at the carpet strips (the long metal strips with sharp prongs that stick up to hold the carpet in place). If they're loose, screw them back down. If they're damaged, replace them.

Hook the carpet back over the metal prongs, starting in the middle of the loose area and working out toward the sides. To do this, press the carpet kicker into the carpet a few inches away from the wall. Press your knee firmly into the carpet kicker's support, giving it a sharp kick if necessary. This should insert the underside of the carpet over the carpet strip prongs. Once the carpet is back over the carpet strip, replace the baseboards (trimming any excess carpet with a utility knife as necessary).

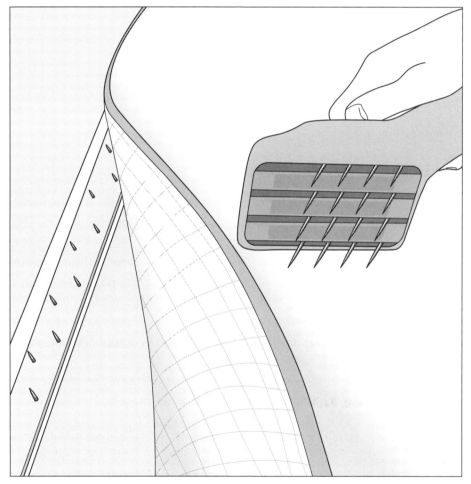

▲ Insert the prongs of the carpet stretcher into the carpet about 2 inches from the carpet strip—this should stretch the carpet enough to hook over and remain fastened on the carpet strip.

Ceramic Tile

Ceramic tile does need occasional maintenance, to replace broken tiles or to regrout the joints between the tiles. Before tackling a fix-it job, however, assess any underlying problems. If you find any of the following, you may be dealing with adhesive that's failing, a floor surface under the tile that's not level or that's flexing too much, or water that's seeping under the tiles and into the flooring. You'll likely need to replace the tiles, and possibly the subflooring.

- Many tiles are loose or cracked.
- The grout is deteriorating over the whole area.
- The floor feels spongy when it's pressed.
- The tiles have a cloudy discoloring.

Replacing a Broken Tile

First, you need to remove the damaged tile. Use a grout knife (a jagged metal blade in a holder) to carve out the grout around the tile, being careful not to scratch the surrounding tiles. Save some of the old grout chips to make it easier to buy the right color replacement grout.

You may be able to pry the damaged tile up off the floor by inserting a small pry bar or cold chisel under it and tapping the bar or chisel with a hammer. If not, strike the tile at its center, breaking it into pieces that should then come off more easily. Scrape off any old tile adhesive or loose grout to provide a smooth surface.

Spread tile adhesive onto the back of the new tile with a notched trowel. Press the new tile into place, centering it in the gap. If it's not sitting down far enough, lay a piece of carpet or foam over it, and tap it into place with a block of wood. Hold it in place with masking tape or tile spacers. Clean out any adhesive that has seeped into the joint around the tile. When the adhesive is dry, grout around the tile (as described in the next section).

Regrouting Tiles

Ceramic tiles can last a long time—longer, in fact, than the grout around them, which can crumble or become discolored. Eventually, you'll need to regrout the tiles, which is a job that will take at least a day, and probably a weekend, for a typical bathroom floor. (Before you start, check that the ceramic tiles and the wall behind them are in good shape.)

Grout is a powder made of cement and pigments and comes in a variety of colors. Floor grout usually contains sand, while wall grout generally doesn't, although you'll also find all-purpose grouts. When mixed with water or a grout additive, the powder becomes a strong and flexible joint filler. (Using grout additives can improve grout performance and color retention.)

Start by removing any silicone caulking in the area to be regrouted and raking out the old grout from the joints with a grout knife. Use a stiff brush or vacuum to clean out any loose pieces or dust, giving you a clean surface to work on.

Add the grout powder to the water or additive, as per your grout's instructions. Apply grout to the tiles with a rubber-bottom float, packing it into the joints. Work diagonally across the tiles, in a figure-eight motion, to avoid pulling grout out of the joints you've just filled.

ESSENTIAL

Wear gloves during this fix-it job, first to protect your hands when you're chipping out the old grout (tile edges can be sharp), and then to protect your hands from the new grout, which can be caustic.

Remove excess grout by holding the float at a right angle to the tiles and running it diagonally across the joints; then use a water-dampened sponge to clean any remaining grout off the tile surfaces, always moving diagonally (work on an area about 2 feet square at a time). Rinse the sponge after each pass to ensure that as little grout as possible remains on tiles. (If you use a grout cleanup solution instead of water, you may need to allow the grout to set in the joints before doing this. Check the package instructions for suggested times.)

Level out the grout in the joints by pressing the joints lightly with a damp sponge. Any remaining grout haze that forms on the tiles can be wiped away the following day. Let the grout cure according to package directions (usually twenty-four to forty-eight hours).

Once the grout is cured, run a bead of silicone caulking in the space wherever the tiles meet another material, such as a bathtub (fill the bathtub with water first, to help prevent the caulk from cracking). Smooth the bead out with a moistened caulking tool, curved spoon, or sponge, and allow it to cure.

▲ Regrouting ceramic tiles is messy, and it can be time consuming—but the end result is a clean new finish for your tiles, and it's a lot faster than replacing the tiles themselves.

Sealing Grout

Grout will last longer if it's sealed against water and dirt. You can buy grout sealer at home centers—just follow the instructions on your product. In general, you'll first clean the grout and the tiles (if you've just regrouted the seams, you'll need to let the grout cure for at least three weeks before sealing). Paint the sealer onto the grout seams, trying to avoid getting too much on the tiles themselves, unless your product is designed to seal tiles as well. You may need to apply two to three coats. Let the sealer dry as per your product instructions. You can expect to reseal the grout every year or so, depending on how much use or water splashes the area receives.

Hardwood

A variety of kits is available to help you fix or refinish hardwood floors. For small scratches, buy a scratch kit or shellac crayon, and fill in the depression, buffing any excess material away with a soft cloth. For larger holes, use a wood-patching material. Apply it with a putty knife and let it dry; then sand it, and apply wood restorer (check your wood-patching material instructions for the right product to use).

Fixing Floorboards

To repair cracked or split wooden floorboards, first drill pilot holes on either side of the crack, about every 2 inches along its length. The holes should be angled so that the nails will be driven toward the bottom of the crack (this will cinch the two sides of the crack together). Inject the crack with wood glue, and insert the nails with a nail set so that their heads are below the board's finished surface. Fill the holes with wood filler.

A buckled floorboard can be brought back into place from below by inserting a screw through the subflooring and up into the floorboard (stopping ¼ inch short of the finished surface). Drill a pilot hole first, and use a washer between the screw and the subflooring to provide a solid surface for the screw to tighten against. As it tightens, the screw will pull the floorboard back into place. This technique also tightens loose floorboards.

If you can't access the underside of your floor, you'll have to tighten loose boards by nailing through them into the subflooring from above. Drill pilot holes through the centers of the boards, to avoid splitting the wood. Use a nail set to punch the nails slightly below the surface of the boards. Fill the holes with wood filler, and finish to match the boards.

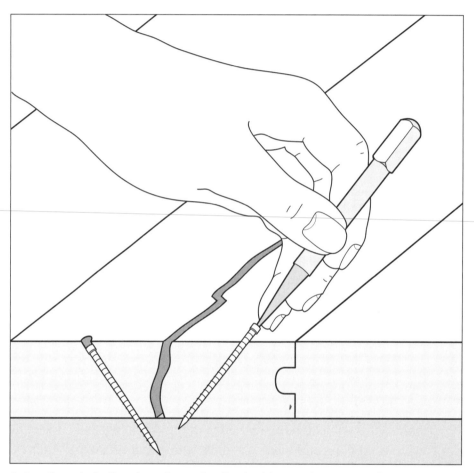

▲ Small cracks in floorboards can be fixed with wood putty and flooring nails.

Refinishing Floors

Products are now on the market that will renew the finish on the floor and hide minor scratches without the need to sand. Generally, the products work in three steps. A chemical solution roughens the existing finish, a bonding solution creates a bond between the existing finish and the finish that's about to be applied, and the finish coat is then brushed or rolled on.

These work well for wood that is worn, scuffed, or lightly scratched, but for badly damaged floors, you need to sand off the existing finish and recoat it. Although a handy homeowner can do this, it's a big, messy, time-consuming job that can easily go wrong if you don't sand the floor properly—and the power sanders can be a challenge to operate. Consider calling in the professionals for this one. They'll do the job much more quickly than you can, and with a lot less stress and mess.

Resilient Flooring

Resilient flooring such as vinyl tiles and sheet flooring are relatively easy to burn, scratch, or tear, so knowing how to fix them can save replacing the entire floor. In some cases, however, replacement will be called for. If many of the tile edges lift up easily (slide a putty knife under the edges to check this), or if the floor is showing lots of air bubbles, the glue that holds the flooring down has probably failed, and the flooring needs to be replaced.

E ALERT!

How old is your resilient flooring? If it was made before 1986, it could contain asbestos (see Chapter 4). The asbestos isn't a problem unless the flooring is deteriorating, or you want to cut through it or remove it. Call in a contractor who specializes in asbestos to advise you on the best action.

Fixing Tears or Scratches in Resilient Flooring

Small holes can be fixed so that you'll hardly notice them. Use a razor to peel off the very top layer of a piece of flooring from a hidden area. Cut up the layer into tiny pieces, and mix them with clear varnish to make a thick paste. Spread the paste into the hole with a putty knife, smooth it down, and let it dry.

Replacing a Resilient Floor Tile

To remove the damaged tile, lay a cloth such as an old dishtowel over the tile, and run a heated iron over it for several minutes. This should warm the tile adhesive so that it becomes pliable. Insert a putty knife under the edge of the tile, and pry it up. Scrape off any glue that remains on the floor.

If the replacement tile is self-adhesive, remove its backing. If not, coat the floor with tile adhesive, using a notched trowel to create "rows" of glue. Lay the new tile down, butting it up against one edge of the existing tile, and pressing it down firmly into place. Wipe off any excess glue that squeezes out.

Regluing Edges

If the tiles or flooring are starting to lift up at the edges (especially in just a small area), pry up the edges a little, clean out any debris or dirt, and spread adhesive under them. Press the flooring into place, wipe away excess glue, and weight the repair with heavy books or bricks while the adhesive dries.

You can use the same technique to fix air bubbles in resilient flooring; slit the bubble with a utility knife, and glue down the edges.

Patching Resilient Flooring

For larger areas of damage, try to find a scrap piece of flooring (such as in a closet) to use as a patch. Lay the patch over the damaged area, taping it in place to match the pattern. Cut through the patch and the damaged flooring at the same time with a utility knife (use a metal ruler as a straightedge). Remove the damaged piece, and scrape off any old glue from the floor. Apply new adhesive to the floor using a notched trowel, and press the patch into place, immediately wiping up any excess glue. Weight down the patch while the glue dries.

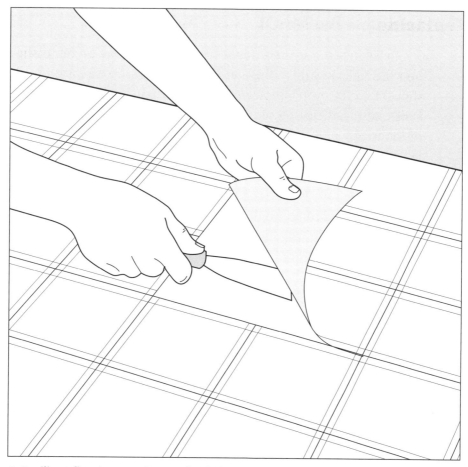

▲ Resilient flooring can be patched almost seamlessly if you follow the pattern in the floor design to cut around the damaged area.

Stairs

With time and handling, the individual components that make up a set of stairs can loosen, crack, and even break. Fixing the problem as soon as you notice a slight wobble can save you a major repair later.

Stairs covered with resilient flooring can be slippery on the tread's nosing, or front edge. To prevent falls, install nosing guards. Cut these ridged vinyl covers to fit the tread, and then glue them over the nosing with contact cement. (Metal nose guards are also available; they are screwed on, rather than glued.)

Tightening a Handrail

Gently tap glue-coated wedges into any gaps that are appearing between balusters (spindles) and the handrail. If you're too aggressive with the wedge, you can actually loosen the handrail even further, so go slowly, testing the handrail frequently to check your progress. Visible parts of the wedge can be trimmed carefully with a utility knife—just avoid cutting into the underside of the handrail.

Alternatively, angle a screw through the top of the baluster up and into the handrail. You'll need to counterbore a pilot hole for the screw so that you can patch and hide the screw head. A squeeze of wood glue into the pilot hole will strengthen this repair, but be sure to wipe off any excess glue right away.

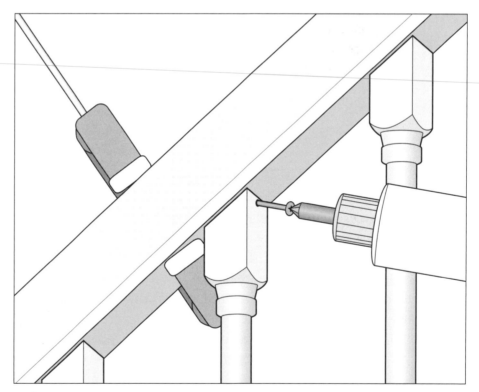

▲ If there's no room to insert a wedge between the handrail and the baluster, tighten the handrail against the baluster by inserting a screw through a predrilled hole into the handrail.

Tightening Balusters (Spindles) and Newel Posts

If your balusters are nailed to your treads, inserting an angled, countersunk screw through the bottom of the baluster into the tread will tighten the baluster. (Don't forget to predrill screw holes.) The same technique can be used to tighten a newel post; insert several screws through the post and into the floor. (If the newel post is accessible from under the stairs, first tighten the bolts that hold it to the joist—this may be all the repair that's needed.)

For balusters that are dovetailed into the tread, first remove the molding that hides the dovetail. Insert a screw straight through the dovetail and into the tread, and inject wood glue into the dovetailed joint. Nail the molding back on.

QUESTION?

My baluster is cracked. Can I fix it without removing it?
Small cracks can be fixed in place by filling them with wood glue and clamping the crack closed while the glue dries. For larger cracks, however, you'll probably need to replace the baluster with one from your home center, used building store (great for older styles), or custom-maker.

You now know how to fix almost any kind of flooring that you're likely to find in your house, from hardwood floorboards to resilient flooring such as vinyl tiles. Anything more complicated (such as laying flooring) is more a renovation than a fix-it job, but do your research—many of these jobs are time consuming but entirely manageable. For now, stop looking down at your floor, and start looking up at your walls. Chapter 13 deals with wall fix-it projects.

Chapter 13

Winning Walls

Walls tend to get taken for granted once the decorating has been decided upon—that is, until a doorknob punches through them, or nails start popping circles of paint off them. While prevention is always best, there's a range of wall repairs that are reasonably straightforward. In fact, most just require lightweight joint compound and putty (or taping) knives of varying widths.

Washing Walls

Washing walls might not sound like a fix-it job, but it is. Over time, walls become coated with grime, kitchen grease, and particularly cigarette smoke. Regular household cleaners designed for painted or wallpapered surfaces work well, but only use them if you're not preparing the wall for painting. Some of their ingredients may leave a residue that will prevent new paint from adhering properly.

If you do plan to paint, invest in a cleaner such as TSP. (You'll need gloves and safety glasses for this one.) Mix it according to the package directions, stir it well, and wash the walls with a large sponge, working from the bottom to the top of the walls (if you work down, the cleaning solution runs down the dirty part of the wall in drips, leaving tracks behind that are difficult to remove). Rinse the walls extremely well, changing the rinse water frequently.

If you're dealing with mildew, try a solution of 1 part bleach to 4 parts water. Rinse the walls with clean water, changing the water as necessary so that you're not applying dirty water to the walls.

Beware of brown or gray stains on walls and ceilings; they often indicate that water is soaking into the wallboard or plaster. Always find and fix the leak. You can try cleaning the stain with a 1-to-4 solution of bleach and water, but it probably won't come out. To hide it, look for a stain-blocking primer at your paint store, over which you can apply the wall's finish color. If you don't have any of the existing finish color, take a small paint chip to the store and ask the staff to match it.

ALERT!

Use caution when washing around light switches and electrical outlets to avoid giving yourself a shock. A damp rag, carefully used, is better there than a wet sponge. For extra safety, turn off the circuit breaker(s) to the switches or outlets in question.

If your walls are in bad shape, with peeling paint or deteriorating plaster, check for and fix any underlying problems, such as water leaks, and consider applying a wall liner over the wall. This special paper surface will seal the wall (which might be helpful if the wall's paint contains lead) and provide a clean new surface on which to paint or hang wallpaper.

Anchoring Nails and Screws

The best way to anchor nails and screws is to find a stud behind the wallboard or plaster wall surface and drive the nail or screw into the stud. In an ideal world, there would always be a wall stud where you need to hang a picture or a shelf. In the real world, however, there rarely is, which is why there's such a variety of winged, ribbed, and pointed hangers available. No matter how they look, they're all designed to spread the weight of whatever's hanging on them over or into a wider area of wallboard or plaster than a nail or screw alone could.

To support lightweight to medium loads on a wallboard surface, such as mirrors and curtain rods, you should be able to use plastic anchors for the screws, "molly" bolts, or Grip-It screw anchors. These work by creating an anchor that squeezes against the wallboard. Some types can be hammered into place, but others require predrilling a hole. For plastic anchors, the hole needs to be the same size as the anchor.

For heavier loads, look for toggle bolts. When these are inserted through a drilled hole in the wall, their spring-loaded "wings" expand against the back side of the wall, reinforcing the wallboard. The hole needs to be the same size as the toggle bolt with its wings collapsed.

Plaster is much more likely than wallboard to crack or crumble when a nail or screw is inserted through it, and studs are more of a challenge to find because plaster is thicker than wallboard and doesn't use screws or nails when it's installed. Avoid using nails in plaster. Instead, predrill holes for screw-holding anchors similar to those used for wallboard.

When you're drilling the holes for the anchors, stick a piece of masking or painter's (low-tack) tape over the spot. This will help to reinforce the plaster surface, making it less likely to crumble as you drill. Taping a plastic sandwich bag under the hole will catch a lot of the plaster dust that will fall.

For inserting screws into ceramic tile surfaces, you'll need plastic screw anchors. Predrill a hole the same size as your plastic anchor, using a masonry bit. Putting masking tape over the spot where you drill, and operating the drill slowly, will help prevent the tile from splintering.

What's the easiest way to find studs behind a wall?
Nails in baseboards, slight indentations in a line on the wall (indicating where nails or screws hold wallboard to studs), and electrical outlet or switch boxes are all excellent stud markers. You can also try inexpensive magnetic stud finders (which find hidden nails or screws) or more expensive electronic stud finders.

Dealing with Wallboard

Wallboard, also known as drywall or gypsum board, is one of the most common wall materials. Panels—generally 4' × 8' in size—consist of an inner layer of gypsum plaster that's covered on both sides by strong paper. The panels are nailed, screwed, or glued to the wood studs that form the inner framework of the wall, and their seams are sealed with tape and joint compound, so that when you look at a wallboard wall, you shouldn't be able to tell where the panels meet. If you're using wallboard in a damp location, such as a bathroom, it should be water-resistant (often referred to as greenboard, for its color), as should the joint compound you use.

Repairing Wallboard

Very small holes or shallow gouges that aren't cracked can be fixed with a quick layer of lightweight joint compound (sold as a powder that you mix with water, or as an easier-to-use ready-mixed product) applied with a putty or taping knife that's slightly wider than the area you're working with (generally 4 inches wide). Let the compound dry, sand it level with the wall surface, and prime/paint to match the wall.

Small cracks and medium-sized holes (like those created by a door handle) can be fixed with self-adhesive mesh tape or screening and joint compound. Bigger holes—those larger than 5 inches across—may need the added strength of a wallboard patch. Your first step in both cases is to clean up the crack or hole by removing loose pieces of wallboard and brushing away any grit or dust particles.

For the tape/screen method, cut the tape/screen to fit, allowing about 2 inches of extra material on all four sides. Peel the backing away from the adhesive surface, and stick the tape or mesh screening over the hole or crack, pressing it down firmly and smoothing it out to keep it free of creases or bubbles. Using a 4-inch putty or taping knife, apply a layer of joint compound to the wall over the tape or screening, spreading it downward and diagonally as you cover the area. Let it dry (usually eight to twenty-four hours, but check your product instructions).

Once the joint compound is dry, sand it lightly with 100-grit sandpaper, being careful to sand only the compound, not the wallboard itself. Apply a thin coat of compound with a 6-inch putty or taping knife, feathering it out on the edges to form a smooth transition to the wall. When that's dry, sand it lightly with 150-grit sandpaper and apply a very thin finish coat of compound with a 10-inch knife. The compound should extend to two or three times the size of the original hole or patch. Let it dry, sand again with the 150-grit sandpaper, and then paint with primer and a finish coat to match the wall. (You may be able to get away with two, rather than three, coats of joint compound, but keep in mind that three thin coats of compound will provide a much cleaner repair than one or two thicker coats.)

FACT

Sanding the joint compound when it's dry creates a lot of fine, messy dust. Using a dampened sanding sponge will give you a smooth finish while significantly reducing the dust flying around. Always use a dust mask while sanding, to avoid inhaling the dust, and wear eye protection.

For holes larger than 5 inches across, use 1- to 2-inch-wide strips of scrap wood or wallboard as a backing plate for a wallboard patch. Insert them through the hole, and fasten them with wallboard screws or glue so that they span the back of the hole.

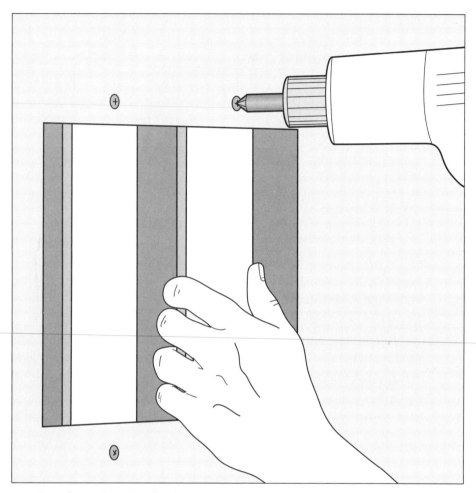

▲ Strips of wood used as backing plates behind a wallboard patch give it stability.

If you're lucky enough to still have the piece of wallboard that came out of the hole, you can use it as a patch. Brush off loose particles, coat the edges and back with joint compound, and insert it into the hole against the backing plate. You can also glue the patch against the backing plate with a hot-glue gun, if you find that's easier.

If you don't have the missing wallboard—it often falls into the wall—cut the hole into a square or rectangle using a wallboard saw or sturdy utility knife before inserting the backing plates. Cut a piece of scrap wallboard into a patch that is slightly smaller than the piece you removed. Coat and insert as previously described.

Once the patch is in place, apply joint compound as you would for a tape or mesh screen repair. When you're smoothing the first coat of joint compound into the patch's seams, hold the putty knife at a 45-degree angle to the wall. This helps to force the compound into the seam.

If the hole was caused by a doorknob, don't forget to install a doorstop to prevent it from happening again. The type that slips over a hinge pin is effective, and it's usually less intrusive than the spring-type that screws onto a baseboard (toddlers and puppies love playing with the latter).

Nail Pops

Wallboard installed with screws will reduce the incidence of "nail pops" appearing in the wallboard's painted or wallpapered surface later on. Because screws are more time consuming to install than nails, however, nails are often used, leaving homeowners to deal with the annoying little paint cracks or circles coming off over the top of the nails.

To fix nail pops, drive the nail back into the wallboard if it's still snug in its nail hole. If it's not, remove it. In either case, insert a screw through the wallboard and into the same stud that the nail went into, about 2 inches from the popped nail. The screw should create a "dimple" in the wallboard, so that its head is slightly lower than the wallboard surface, without tearing the wallboard paper.

Cover the popped nail's head or hole and the screw head with three layers of joint compound, as detailed previously for repairing wallboard.

Replacing Wallboard

Repairing wallboard sometimes isn't enough, especially if you have an area of water damage—in a flooded basement, for example—that has to be cut out. In this case, you'll need to replace the wallboard. This isn't a difficult job, but it's time consuming because you have to wait for the joint compound to dry, and it can be messy when you're sanding; the joint compound dust is so fine that it seems to go everywhere.

Here's how to calculate the quantity of materials you'll need for a small area:

- Wallboard: measure the wall surfaces to find the area in square feet, add 15 percent for mistakes and cuts, and if you're using 4' × 8' sheets of wallboard, divide your total by 32 (the area of the wallboard sheets)
- Screws: about $\frac{1}{2}$ pound for each 100 square feet of wallboard
- Joint compound: 15 pounds for a 10' × 8' area
- Joint tape: 60 to 75 feet for a 10' × 8' area

To cut new wallboard, mark the cutting line on the face of the wallboard, then score the paper along the line with a utility knife (running the knife blade against a level or straightedge makes this easier). Lift the board up, and snap it by sharply banging the reverse side of the board so it breaks along the line that you've cut and folds toward its reverse side. Cut through the paper on the reverse side along the fold to prevent the paper from tearing. (This should form a clean edge, but you can also sand any rough edges to create smoother joints if necessary.)

To install the wallboard, work from the ceiling downward. Use nails to tack up the sheets, and then fasten them securely with screws every 6 inches. (A dimpler drill attachment inserts screws without cutting the paper.) A board lifter or pry bar will keep the bottom piece of wallboard the required ¼ inch off the floor while you fasten it in place. Use L-shaped wallboard pieces around window and door frames; a wallboard joint at the frame corners can crack.

FACT

When feathering out the joint compound, apply greater pressure to the outside edge of the knife, spreading the compound more thinly. This results in a seamless finish between joint tape and wallboard.

There are two types of wallboard joints: butt, where the boards' short or cut sides meet; and tapered, where the long sides meet. Butt joints require thin coats of compound; tapered joints need a slightly more generous first coat to build a level surface. For corners, try products such as paper-laminated steel corner bead, which installs with joint compound and is less likely to crack or chip than a regular steel corner bead. You can also buy special taping knives to handle inside and outside corners, which make the process not only easier, but more professional looking as well. Normally, you need three coats of joint compound to effectively coat the joints, but two coats often are enough for inside and outside corners.

Use three progressively larger knives to apply compound, starting with one that's about 4 inches wide. Apply compound to the joint with this narrowest putty knife, covering only as much area as can be worked in three to four minutes (the compound loses adhesion as it dries). Embed a length of joint tape in the compound along the joints using a putty knife. Hold the knife at a 45-degree angle, and draw it along the joint, over the tape, to remove excess compound and eliminate air bubbles. The tape should be level with the face of the wallboard, fully embedded in the compound, with enough compound between the tape and the wallboard to ensure adhesion. Let it dry for eight to twenty-four hours as required, and then sand to a relatively smooth finish with 100-grit sandpaper.

Using a medium-width knife (about 6 inches), apply a second coat of compound to the joint, covering the tape. Feather the edges of the compound about 2 inches beyond the first coat. Let it dry, then sand with 150-grit sandpaper. Use the largest putty knife (about 10 inches) to apply a third coat, again feathering out 2 inches beyond the second coat on each side. Let it dry, then sand with 150-grit sandpaper to a smooth finish. (Note that your nail/screw dimples must also be filled using three coats of compound, but they don't require joint tape.)

Dealing with Plaster

Older houses are much more likely to have plaster walls than wallboard. Generally, coats of plaster are applied to some kind of backing material, or lath, such as thin strips of wood or metal mesh screens. Although plaster has some advantages over wallboard, such as better soundproofing and insulation values, it can be a pain to work with, as it cracks and crumbles quite easily. As always in home fix-it, repairing a hole or crack while it's still small may help you avoid calling in a repair expert later on.

If you're painting plaster walls, keep in mind that a no- or low-gloss (matte, satin, or eggshell) finish is better at masking the inevitable uneven areas, while a glossy finish will highlight any flaws.

Patching Plaster Cracks

Apply wallboard tape over hairline cracks in plaster to reinforce the crack and to prevent the crack from spreading or recurring. Seal with joint compound as you would for wallboard.

For narrow (but not hairline) cracks, you can use an acrylic paintable caulk. Short cracks may just need a squeezable tube of caulking; longer cracks are more easily filled using a caulking gun. Smooth the caulk level with the wall surface using a moistened straightedge such as a putty knife. Cracks that are wider than ½ inch should be filled with patching plaster (follow the directions for patching large plaster holes, following).

Patching Small Plaster Holes

For holes less than 5 or 6 inches across, first brush out any loose plaster or dust from the crack or hole. With a utility knife, widen the underside of the crack or hole so that it's slightly wider at the back than it is at the wall surface. This helps the patch stay in place.

Apply joint compound (the same kind used for wallboard) or spackling compound to the area with a putty or taping knife, and smooth it so that it's level with the wall surface.

FACT

You'll find three types of patching compound for plaster: joint compound, spackling compound, and patching plaster. Joint compound is easiest to use, but it tends to shrink and takes eight to twenty-four hours to dry. Spackling dries faster, but it's harder to sand. Patching plaster dries quickly and doesn't shrink, but it is harder to work with.

If the crack or hole is deeper than 1 inch, apply the compound in layers rather than completely filling the hole with compound all at once.

Let each layer dry before applying the next one, to reduce the chance of the repair cracking or pulling away from the edges, and sand as you would for a wallboard repair.

Patching Larger Plaster Holes

If the hole in the plaster is substantial, such as 6 inches across, consider using a wallboard patch, just as you would for a hole in a wallboard wall. Insert a backing plate into the hole (unless the lath is still in place, in which case it takes the place of a backing plate), glue the patch to it, and seal the edges with joint compound, sanding successive layers until it's smooth.

An alternative to a wallboard patch is to use patching plaster (in this case, a better choice than joint compound, because it's much less likely to shrink and crack while drying). First, brush out any loose plaster or dust from the hole, and widen the underside of the hole so that it's slightly wider at the back than it is at the wall surface. If the lath backing for the plaster is missing, create new lath by gluing wood strips (paint stirrers work well) against the back of the hole, following the lath pattern in the surrounding plaster, or inserting mesh screen behind the hole.

Brush on a latex bonding liquid. This product helps the patch adhere to the existing plaster and usually eliminates the need to moisten the existing plaster before patching it. Mix the patching plaster according to its instructions, and apply it in three layers: one that you force through the lath; one that takes the finish to within about ¼ inch of the surface; and one that finishes the repair. Draw a crosshatch pattern in the surface of the bottom two layers to help the next layer adhere to it, and let it dry. On the final layer, smooth out the surface with a straightedge or putty knife to match the surrounding surface.

Plaster is often textured. If this is the case, examine the texture to determine how to reproduce it. You may be able to use brushes or sponges to create a stippled or ridged effect. Be warned that this takes practice. If the repair is in a highly visible area, you may want to bring in a professional who'll be able to blend the new surface with the old much more effectively.

Wallpaper Fixes

Over time, the seams between sheets of wallpaper can lift up, bubbles in the surface can appear, and the paper itself can tear. If the damage is limited to a small area, try repairing it using a squeezable bottle of wallpaper glue (available at paint and wallpaper stores), or a glue syringe, and a small roller. However, the presence of many bubbles or lifted seams, or damage over a large area, probably requires stripping off the old wallpaper and either painting or repapering the walls, as it may indicate that the wallpaper adhesive has failed.

QUESTION?

How do I clean stains on wallpaper?
Many types of wallpaper can be washed, but you should test-wash an inconspicuous area first, and avoid soaking the paper. If your wallpaper can't be washed, check for special wallpaper erasers at paint stores. They work well, particularly on small areas.

Regluing Wallpaper Seams

Lift the loose edges of the wallpaper seam and run the nozzle of the glue bottle under them, leaving a bead of glue behind. Press the edges down into the glue using a small roller. Carefully remove any excess glue that has squeezed out of the seam with a damp sponge.

Removing Bubbles

Cut a slit through the bubble with a utility knife, preferably following a straight line in the wallpaper pattern (this helps to hide the seam). Insert the glue nozzle or syringe under the paper, and squeeze a small amount of glue under the bubble area. Use a roller to carefully press the paper back down, working from the edges of the bubble toward the slit. Remove any excess glue that has squeezed out of the seam with a damp sponge.

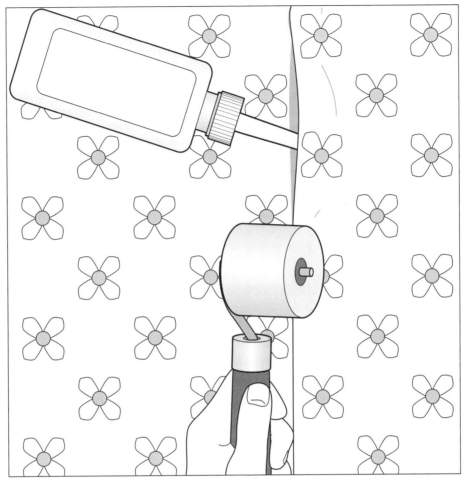

▲ Wallpaper seams can be resealed quickly and easily, but it's best to catch them before the paper begins to tear.

Patching Wallpaper

A torn area of wallpaper can be patched effectively if you have scraps of the paper, or if you can still buy the pattern. If not, consider carefully soaking or steaming off a piece of wallpaper from an inconspicuous area, such as inside a closet. The patch should be slightly larger on all sides than the damaged area.

Position the patch over the torn area, using low-tack masking tape on each corner and matching the pattern exactly. Use a utility knife to cut through both layers of paper at the same time, and remove the patch. This creates an exact pattern match for the patch.

Spray the damaged area with warm water or soak it with a sponge, trying not to get the surrounding paper wet. Let the water soak in, loosening the adhesive to the point where you can scrape or peel the torn area off. (A putty knife can help the process along, but be careful not to damage the surrounding paper.)

Squeeze glue onto the wallpaper patch and under any edges of the surrounding paper that might have loosened. Press the patch in place, and then go over it with a roller to create a good bond with the surface. Use a damp sponge to clean off any glue that squeezes out from under the seam.

Moldings and Panels

From a practical point of view, molding is used to hide the gaps between joints, such as where the floor meets a wall (baseboard or shoe molding), where a door frame joins a wall (casing), at the ceiling (crown molding) or to protect walls from being damaged by chair backs (chair rail). Panels such as wainscoting (which generally extend up to chair-rail height) are used mainly for decor, although they may well be hiding unsightly wall damage.

Repairing Wooden Moldings and Panels

Moldings, trim pieces, and panels can get gouged or damaged, and they can warp. To fix scratches, holes, or gouges, buy a wood pencil that matches your finish, or wood putty that can be refinished. Color in the scratch with the pencil, or apply the putty with a putty knife, smoothing it to match the wood surface. Finish to match the existing wood. For large gouges, you can also use wood epoxy paste, which you can shape and finish to match the existing wood surface.

To fix a warped molding strip or panel, try driving screws into studs along its length. The screw threads should tighten the wood against the underlying studs, fixing the warp. Countersink the screws so that you'll be able to cover their heads with wood putty and finish it to match the existing wood.

If your wall is not entirely plumb, there may be a gap between the molding and the wall. Insert a bead of wood glue into the gap, and brace the molding against the wall while the glue dries. Another option is to add shoe molding to cover the gap, or you can caulk it with paintable caulking.

Replacing Moldings and Panels

If the damaged area can't be filled, or the warp can't be fixed, you may need to replace the molding or the panels (or one or more tongue-and-groove planks that form wainscoting). The first step is to remove the existing piece. Molding can often be pried off the wall with a pry bar, but be sure to protect the floor or wall surface that you're using for leverage with a block or strip of wood.

Buy a length of molding to match the profile of the piece you've removed, and cut it to fit. (You may need to miter, or cut the ends at a 45-degree angle, to fit the new piece; use the piece you've removed as a pattern.)

Panels can be pried off and replaced with new sheets, but if they were glued on, taking them off can be a time-consuming hassle. For tongue-and-groove boards or panels, you may need to cut through the center of the damaged board lengthwise with a jigsaw or chisel to enable you to lift each side of the board away from the tongue or groove that it fits into. Depending on the style of the paneling, you may also need to remove the base or shoe molding that runs along the bottom of the paneling.

On the replacement board, cut the back edge of the board's groove away. Insert it into the space so that its tongue fits into the existing wood's groove. Nail the new board in place through its groove, and replace the base molding.

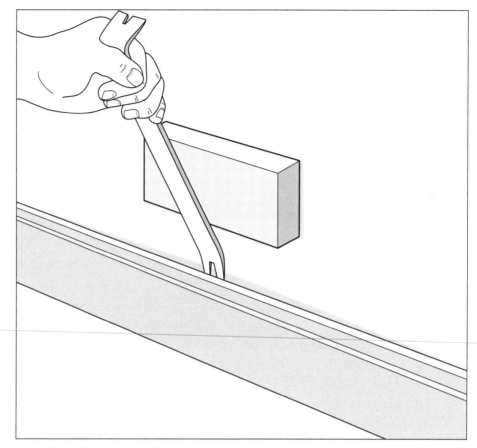

▲ A piece of 2" × 4" lumber or even a strip of plywood placed under the leverage point of the pry bar protects the finished wall surface.

You've now worked your way through the wall coverings that you're likely to find in most homes, from wallboard and plaster to wallpaper and paneling. Now that your walls are in good shape, turn your attention to your fifth wall: the ceiling. You'll find similar problems and solutions up there, with a few quirks that come courtesy of gravity. Check out Chapter 14 to find out more.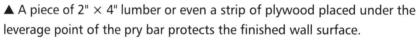

Chapter 14
Simply Ceilings

You might not think of ceilings as needing maintenance—but indeed, they do need occasional attention. First, they need to be kept clean and, in particular, free of cobwebs, which can trap dust and grease particles. You should also watch for any sign of sags, cracks, or water stains. Finally, examine lights, fans, and hooks or hangers. They should hang securely from the ceiling, and there should be no cracks expanding around them.

Brightening Dull Ceilings

Ceilings need to be cleaned just as walls do. They provide some extra challenges, however, not the least of which is fancy finishes such as stippling or orange-peel textures. In these cases, your only choice to brighten a dull ceiling might be to use a spray gun or deep-napped roller to prime and paint the surface with a stain-blocking primer and paint.

If you're working with a smooth surface, however, try cleaning it with a TSP solution (as for walls in Chapter 13). You can try cleaning water stains with a solution of 1 part bleach to 4 parts water, but it's likely that the brown or gray water ring at the edge of the stain will linger. In this case, again, you'll need to apply a stain-blocking primer under a finish coat (or two) of paint.

Ceiling Cracks

Cracks in ceilings are fairly common, and may be quite harmless. In a wallboard ceiling, they'll often show up along the joints between boards. In any ceiling, they may occur when a house goes through an entirely normal settling period. If, however, the cracks appear suddenly, are wider than $1/8$ to $1/4$ of an inch, or run at odd angles, you should consult a house inspector or contractor to find out if they're signaling a more serious problem with the foundation.

To fix the cracks, fill them with paintable caulking, smoothing the surface of the caulking with a putty or taping knife to blend in the crack with the rest of the ceiling surface. You can also use self-adhesive wallboard tape to cover the cracks to help stop them from spreading or recurring, just as you would for walls (see Chapter 13). Once the fix is dry, prime and paint the patched area to match the rest of the ceiling.

Leaking Ceilings

A sagging, bubbling, or brown/gray-stained ceiling is a sign that water is leaking onto and soaking the ceiling. To release the water before the combination of weight and gravity collapse part of the ceiling, prepare to drill a small hole in the center of the stain. Move any furniture away from the area, line the floor with plastic, and set a bucket under where you're drilling.

ALERT!

Ceilings can be awkward to work on, because you're constantly reaching up above your head and balancing on ladders. Some cathedral ceilings can be too high for comfort (or regular household ladders), in which case you may want to call in an expert with the right equipment.

Because water and electricity don't mix, it's best to use a hand drill to release the water, rather than an electric drill. Stand slightly to the side of the hole, to stay as dry as possible when the water is released (and in case any part of the wallboard or plaster comes down as you drill). Once you've drilled the hole, mop or soak up any water right away to avoid damaging floor coverings such as hardwood or carpet. If the ceiling is sagging, prop it up by making a T-brace from a long and a short piece of wood (such as 2" × 4"s). Screw the middle of the short piece to the end of the long piece, creating a T. Place the top of the T against the ceiling, bracing the bottom on a nonskid surface (masking tape on the floor works well).

Now you need to find the source of the leak, which could come from a variety of places: a leaking air conditioner in an attic, a roof leak, faulty caulking or sealing in a bathroom, or leaking pipes. Since water can travel a long way from the actual leak, try to trace the water's path back from the ceiling; you should be able to see damp areas or water tracks along joists, for example.

You may need expert help here, both to find the leak and to repair the ceiling. Don't hesitate to call for it. A plaster or wallboard ceiling that has been soaked with water will likely need to be replaced.

▲ A sagging ceiling can be supported with a T-brace while you investigate the problem.

Sagging Ceilings

If water isn't the problem behind a sagging ceiling, it may be that the wallboard's nails or screws are coming loose from the joists that they've been driven into, or that the wallboard is dropping down over the nails or screws. Brace the ceiling material with a T-brace (as described previously), carefully easing the wallboard back up to touch the joists. (For a plaster ceiling, you just want to take the weight off the plaster with the brace while you call in an expert. Sagging plaster is not a do-it-yourself fix.)

Locate the joists; you should be able to see a line of indentations or nail pops where the original fastenings were driven into the joists. The original fasteners were probably nails, which by now have likely worked loose. If that's the case, remove them after you've driven screws through the wallboard along the joists at 6-inch intervals (if the nails are still snug, however, you can just hammer them back in after you insert the screws). Countersink the screws slightly (without breaking the wallboard paper) with a dimpler attachment for your drill. Cover the screw heads with three layers of joint compound, sanding between coats, to create a smooth surface (see Chapter 13) that you can then finish to match the rest of the ceiling.

You may find that the tape that seals the wallboard joints has loosened as a result of the sagging. If so, remove the tape, and check the nails or screws on either side of the joint. They'll likely need to be replaced with new screws, to which you can add washers to help support the vulnerable edges of the wallboard. You'll then need to seal the joints with tape and joint compound (as you would for replacing wallboard in Chapter 13).

Damaged Wallboard Ceilings

To fix cracks or holes in wallboard ceilings, follow the same basic procedures as for walls (Chapter 13). Cracks can be reinforced with self-adhesive wallboard tape, then sealed with joint compound. Small holes can be patched with self-adhesive mesh screen and covered with two to three successively larger and thinner layers of joint compound.

To fix ceiling holes larger than 5 to 6 inches wide, however, it's best to use a large backing plate made out of plywood (rather than the strips of wallboard or lighter wood that you could use for a hole in a wall), which will make the repair sturdy enough for a ceiling, where gravity will be acting against it. First, clean up the hole or crack by removing loose pieces of wallboard and brushing away any grit or dust particles. Then, cut a piece of plywood that will fit through the hole and extend past the hole's width by about 2 inches on two sides, to use as a backing plate. Fasten it to the wallboard using screws. Attach the wallboard patch to the plywood, again using screws.

You can then apply joint compound over the patch's seams and the screw heads. Start with a 4-inch putty or taping knife. When you draw the knife along the seams for the first time, hold it at a 45-degree angle to force the compound into the seam. Let it dry (usually eight to twenty-four hours, but check the product's instructions).

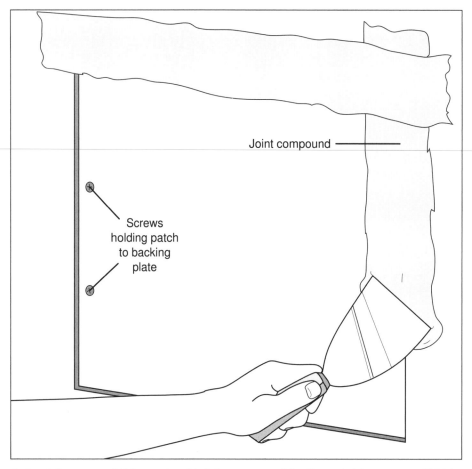

Joint compound

Screws
holding patch
to backing
plate

▲ Applying several thin coats of joint compound to the patch's seams will hide the repair more effectively than one or two thicker coats.

Once the joint compound is dry, lightly sand it with 100-grit sandpaper; then apply a thin coat of compound with a 6-inch putty or taping knife, feathering it out on the edges to form a smooth transition to the existing ceiling surface. The compound should extend beyond the original patch by about 6 inches on all sides so that it blends gradually into the ceiling. When that's dry, lightly sand it with 150-grit sandpaper; apply another coat of compound, this time with a 10-inch knife, again feathering it out (by this time, you may be covering the entire patch with a light coat of compound). Sand with 150-grit sandpaper, and paint with primer and a finishing coat to match the ceiling.

If your ceiling is plaster, before you try to repair cracks or small holes, assess the state of the plaster. If it's soft or spongy, call in an expert. The plaster has likely absorbed enough water that it should be replaced with new plaster or with wallboard, rather than repaired. While small holes or cracks in plaster can be fixed as for walls in Chapter 13, larger areas should be repaired by a professional.

Ceiling Tiles

Ceiling tiles can form a ceiling in several ways. They might be glued directly to the ceiling material, or they might be glued and/or nailed or stapled to furring strips that are attached to the ceiling. They could also be suspended on a framework that hangs from the ceiling.

A common problem with ceiling tiles is staining, usually from water, because they tend to be absorbent. The stains are difficult to remove, so either replace the stained tiles, or apply a stain-blocking primer and paint finish to them (ensure that you use a paint designed for these porous surfaces). If you're dealing with mold or mildew stains, first treat them with a 1-to-4 bleach and water solution, and then use a stain-blocking primer that is rated for use over mildew stains.

Suspended Ceilings

A suspended ceiling is the easiest to fix, because the ceiling tiles generally just rest on the suspended framework. A damaged or stained tile can be lifted out and replaced. You may find that large tiles (2' × 6', for example) can bow or sag, especially if they're exposed to moist conditions, such as in a bathroom. Bowed tiles can easily be replaced, but pay attention to the underlying problem. If the bathroom doesn't have an exhaust fan, have one installed and use it. You can also add additional supports to the framework, which will allow you to use smaller tiles whose lighter weight is less likely to cause sagging.

Tongue-and-Groove Ceiling Tiles

For damaged tiles that are attached directly to the ceiling or to furring strips, keep in mind that they're probably a tongue-and-groove design. To remove a tile, cut through its center and take it out in pieces so that you'll be able to remove its edges from the seams without cutting through them and damaging the tongues or grooves that the new tile will attach to. Remove any pieces of the old tile's tongue-and-groove design remaining in the seams, along with the nails or staples that may be holding its edges in place. Scrape off any adhesive. If the tile was glued directly to the ceiling, you'll need to pry or scrape it off using a putty knife.

To fit a new tongue-and-groove ceiling tile into the old tile's space, cut off the underside of the new tile's grooves along its edges (and, if necessary, one of its tongues). This will allow you to slip the new tile's tongue edge into the groove of an existing tile and lever the new tile into place.

Before you place the tile, run a strip of glue around its edges, on its reverse side (for attachment to furring strips) or in several lines across its back (for attachment directly to the ceiling). You can determine the appropriate glue and usage directions by checking with tile installation displays and staff at home centers. If the glue takes several minutes to set properly, support the tile with a T-brace for the required time.

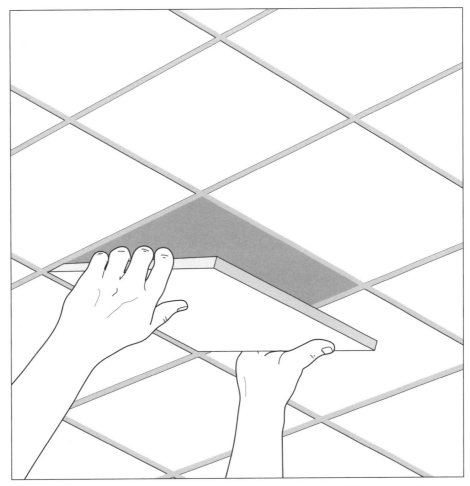

▲ A new tongue-and-groove ceiling tile will slip into place if you cut off the underside of its groove edges.

ALERT!

Some older ceiling tiles were made out of asbestos, for its insulating properties. While asbestos isn't a problem if the tiles are still in good shape, it will release harmful fibers when it's deteriorating or if it's cut (see Chapter 4). If you suspect your tiles could be asbestos, seek expert help to remove or seal them.

Ceiling Fans

Ceiling fans can be very useful to help condition the air in a large room. During the summer, a fan rotating counterclockwise will create a breeze that makes the room feel cooler. In winter, a fan rotating clockwise will help to redistribute warm air that has risen to the ceiling. While some newer ceiling fans have remote control devices that switch their direction, older fans have a switch on their housing that you'll need to operate manually. Simply watch the way the blades are rotating to determine whether the switch needs changing. If it does, wait until the blades stop, climb up a sturdy ladder that's high enough for you to comfortably reach the fan, and push the fan's switch in the opposite direction.

If your fan ever comes down for cleaning, check that it has a safety strap or chain firmly securing it through the ceiling. The strap is designed to hold the fan in case the support for the fan housing ever gives way—so the strap should, of course, be secured to something other than the fan housing's support!

Ceiling Fan Blades

Although they can be a hassle to clean, it's important to keep ceiling fan blades free of dirt and grease. A dirt buildup can actually create wobbling blades, because it throws off the blade's balance. (Don't worry if you notice that the blades aren't sitting flat; they're designed to sit at a slight angle, to help push the air.)

To fix wobbling blades, first check that the screws that hold them to the supporting arms on the fan housing, and the screws holding the supporting arms to the housing, are snug. If they're not, tighten them to see if that solves the problem. You should also clean the blades, using a tall mop, or by climbing a ladder so that you can tackle them by hand using regular household cleaners (formulated for grease removal if the fan is near a kitchen). Check the cleaning solution's label, however, to ensure that it can be used on your particular blade surface.

If this doesn't fix the problem, you might want to call in an expert, who can likely figure out what's wrong quickly and efficiently, and recommend replacing the fan if that's the easiest and most appropriate fix.

Installing a Ceiling Fan

If you have a light fixture in the center of a room, it's a fairly easy job for an expert to replace it with a unit that combines both a light and a ceiling fan, as long as there's sufficient clearance for the fan blades (usually 7 feet between the floor and the blades, but check your local building codes). It's not exactly a fix-it task, however, because of the issues that you might encounter: ladder heights, awkward ceiling angles, insufficient support within the ceiling for the fan's heavy motor, and the electrical wiring knowledge that you'll need.

Call in an expert to handle the installation, but stick around, especially if he or she is working alone. The light fixtures that need to be removed, and the fan/light fixture that needs to be installed, can be heavy and/or awkward. Having two people to carry or position them can be helpful.

To determine the size of fan you need, find the room's area by multiplying its width by its length. A 36-inch fan will suit a 100-square-foot area; a 42-inch fan will generally handle a room up to 168 square feet; and a 48-inch fan will handle up to 216 square feet. To make the electrical wiring easier, choose a fan/light combination with a remote control and a light fixture that plugs into the fan housing (instead of having to be wired to it).

Be aware that dimmer switches for lights aren't designed to handle fan motors. To adjust the fan's speed from a wall switch, choose a variable speed control switch that's labeled for ceiling fans. Also, match the switch to the fan's brand—using different brands can cause the fan motor to hum, or to speed dangerously fast.

Ceilings may often be forgotten when you're inspecting and maintaining your house, but as you've seen in this chapter, you should look up every once in a while to check their condition. A leak investigated or a few screws replaced in a wallboard ceiling at the first sign of a sag is a far better alternative than replacing entire sheets of wallboard after the leak has caused a collapse or the wallboard's nails have pulled away entirely. Ⓔ

Chapter 15
Up in the Attic

Your attic may be a repository for all manner of storage items, from trunks to old clothes, or it may be nothing more than roof trusses and insulation. However it's used, there are some common fix-it tasks to keep on top of up there. Perhaps more importantly, your attic can provide significant signs and symptoms of problems that may be affecting your whole house—so it's a good idea to pay it a little attention.

Identifying Attic Problems

The two biggest problems that an attic faces are interrelated: insulation and ventilation. In cold climates, attics represent one of the biggest sources of heat loss, so adequately insulating the space is essential. In hot climates, insulating the attic properly can reduce the amount of heat transmitted into the house from the roof surface, again significantly reducing energy costs.

An attic with inadequate ventilation, meanwhile, can fall prey to condensation, which dampens insulation (making it much less effective), and soaks into wood (causing rot and molds). In the summer, a poorly ventilated attic will allow heat to build up that can also damage wood surfaces.

Water is a major attic problem, whether it's coming from condensation or from roof or chimney leaks. Your attic might be the first place a roof leak becomes noticeable; catching it before it heads through the ceiling can save you a lot of cleanup and fix-it time.

FACT

To find out whether a water stain is old or new, trace around the stain's outline with a pencil. If the stain continues to grow beyond the outline over weeks or months, you know that you're dealing with an active leak. If it stays put, the leak may have occurred, and been sealed, in the past.

Inspecting Your Attic

While some roomlike attics have a proper stairway up to them, many attics have only an access panel. For the latter style, determine whether you have a safe way of climbing up through the panel. Some might incorporate a pull-down stairway. If this is the case, is it sturdy, and is the pull-down mechanism working smoothly? If not, call in an expert to either repair or replace it. Most people end up climbing up to the attic on a ladder. If you have to use a ladder, make sure that the ladder reaches all the way up to the access panel. A shorter ladder will force you to balance on its upper steps while reaching up to open or close an attic hatch panel—which is *not* a good idea.

Once you've opened the access panel, check it out. If the attic is simply a place under the rafters with some insulation installed, does the panel have a covering of insulation on its attic-facing side? If not, it's causing a heat loss that's easily rectified.

Looking for Water Damage

Take a look at all the wood surfaces, whether they're rafters, trusses, a plywood floor, or the boards or plywood that form the roof surface over which the shingles are applied. There shouldn't be any gaps in the attic floor, walls, or ceiling surfaces. Are water stains, mold, mildew, or rotten areas showing anywhere? Test the wood by pressing an awl or screwdriver against it. If the wood is soft and gives way easily, it's rotten, which indicates a moisture problem.

If you find water stains, try to trace them back to a leak, perhaps by following water tracks up a rafter or by checking for signs of water penetration around brick chimneys (often visible as white powdery efflorescence, which is what's left behind as water evaporates out of a masonry surface). For information on fixing roof leaks, check Chapter 7.

E ALERT!

If your attic doesn't have a floor surface (just joists, for example), step *only* on the joists. Stepping between them puts your weight on the wallboard or plaster ceiling of the room below, which can easily give way. If you're working in the attic, a sheet of plywood (cut down to fit through the access panel) that you can lay over the joists will make things easier.

Check Out the Attic Structures

You may have plumbing vent stacks, electrical wiring, chimney flues, and exhaust ducts running through the attic. Check to make sure that they're in good shape: rust-free, adequately supported, and the right materials (electrical wiring shouldn't rely on extension cords, for example; it should be permanent).

Exhaust ducts from bathrooms and kitchens in cold-climate attics should be insulated to prevent condensation from forming inside the ducts and dripping back down into the bathroom or kitchen. It's especially important that these ducts exhaust to the outside, rather than simply ending in the attic. They're designed to remove moist air from the house; pumping that air into the attic will cause condensation problems.

Your attic may have a combination of vents, including soffit vents in the underside of the area where the roof overhangs the house walls, gable vents that are up in the peak of the house wall just under the roof, ridge vents that run along the peak of the roof, or roof vents cut into the roof itself. All of these vents should be kept clear (insulation, for example, shouldn't cover soffit vents) and should be screened off so that insects, birds, and animals can't get through them. You also need to make sure that you have adequate ventilation. There should be about 1 square foot of venting for every 300 square feet of attic floor space, assuming that there's a vapor barrier in place; if there's no vapor barrier, aim for 1 square foot of ventilation for every 150 square feet of attic space, but keep in mind that power- or wind-assisted roof vents will reduce the ventilation square footage needed.

In cold climates, vapor barriers—usually sturdy 6-millimeter plastic films—should be placed against the warm side of the house (the attic floor, for example). The insulation itself should be adequate for your climate; check local building codes, but look for a total attic R-value of about 38 for most areas. It should also be dry and evenly distributed. Insulation should be kept at least 3 inches away from any heat-producing item, such as electrical or light fixtures (unless they're rated IC, which means that insulation can be placed near them), or chimneys.

Beware of Attic Contents

Although attics can seem like a great place to store unused items, they're not. Especially if they're unfinished and unheated/uncooled, they're exposed to temperature extremes and to water damage from roof leaks, all of which can prematurely deteriorate paper and wood items. Stacks or boxes of paper and clothes are perfect homes for unwelcome guests such as mice. Flammable or explosive items such as pressurized cans or paint thinners may be a fire risk when exposed to extreme heat; they should never be stored in the attic.

If you have an attic that has sufficient overhead clearance to be turned into usable space, such as a playroom, talk to your county or municipality about your building codes. These will provide guidelines for insulating the attic and for providing safe access to and from it (which is essential to ensure that people, especially children, can evacuate the attic in case of a fire). Get help from a qualified contractor for the renovation itself—one who's done attic work before—to ensure that the renovation doesn't create any additional insulating or ventilating problems.

Ventilation Issues

The attic's need for ventilation is why you won't find insulation packed right up to the roof or applied between the rafters (unless it's a heat-blocking rigid board that's applied directly under the roof surface in hot climates). If your attic has insulation actually attached to the roof surface, you may need to remove it and replace it with insulation on the attic floor.

If you're looking at an attic that doesn't appear to have enough vents (it's hot and "stuffy," and there's no air movement within it), call in an expert. They'll be able to tell you where to add vents, and the type of vents to add, to solve your problems in the most effective way. One popular method is the stainless-steel mushroom-shaped "whirlybird" vents that you often see rotating on their "stems" on the back sides of roofs. These turbines require no power, but do an excellent job of pulling air out of attic spaces when there's even the smallest breeze blowing.

Installing Soffit Vents

If you have wooden soffits without vents, you can add soffit vents—usually two to three along the longest sides of the house. Locate the vent position in the attic, between two rafters, and drill a hole or hammer a nail through the soffit to mark it. Head outside, and use the hole or nail to help position the vent. Cut a hole through the wooden soffit to match the vent opening that's required, and then screw the vent into place over the opening. The vent should have a screen incorporated into it to prevent animals or birds from entering the attic.

Installing Attic Baffle Vents

It can be difficult to keep attic insulation away from soffit vents, especially if you have the type of soffit that is self-venting (with slitlike holes running all along it). To solve this, use plastic baffles that fit between the rafters against the roof surface, and guide the air from the soffits up toward the roof.

▲ Baffle vents prevent insulation from covering or falling into soffit vents, ensuring that airflow is maintained.

Depending on the style, install the baffles by nailing or stapling them to either the rafters or the roof surface between the rafters over the soffit vents, making sure that their bottom edge is against the attic floor, between the joists. The plastic can be cut to fit the required length; the baffles need to be high enough to prevent insulation from falling over or into the vents.

Installing a Roof Vent

If you're comfortable working on your roof, and the roof is a standard asphalt shingle style without a high pitch, you can install a roof vent yourself. Otherwise, get expert help; it's not an expensive job, and it can make a big difference to the health of your house.

First, determine how many vents you need, depending on how large your attic is and how much air the vent can move (home center staff can help you with this). The vent should be placed fairly close to the ridgeline of the roof, between roof rafters (so that you're not cutting through the rafters to install the vent). It should be spaced away from vents in the gables or the eaves so that the attic will be ventilated evenly, without "dead spaces."

Whether you're installing a flat roof vent or a whirlybird vent, the kit will come with instructions and, often, a template for the hole you need to cut. Read through the entire instruction list before you do anything else, and ensure that you have all the pieces that should be in the kit, including the vent itself, the template, and the flashing that will create a waterproof seal between the vent and the shingles surrounding it (the vent and flashing are often an all-in-one style).

FACT

Avoid climbing on the roof on hot days. Not only will it become uncomfortably hot, but you can also damage the asphalt shingles. Their surface becomes soft as they heat up, and stepping on them can loosen the surface granules.

To figure out where to place the vent on the roof, head into the attic. Determine the right location (as detailed previously), and hammer a nail up through the roof. When you climb up to the roof, this nail will become the center of your template. Position the template and mark the vent/flashing outline and the hole that needs to be cut for the vent opening. If there's no template, use the vent itself to mark the outline of it on the roof, and measure from the edge of the flashing back to the vent opening to figure out where the vent hole needs to be cut.

▲ The top of the vent flashing will slide under one to two horizontal runs of shingles, while the bottom of the vent flashing will sit on top of one to two runs of shingles, so that water can't penetrate the area around the vent.

Use a utility knife to cut through the shingles where the vent hole needs to be, and discard those that would cover the hole. Drill a hole, or several holes close together, through the roof to give you a place to insert a jigsaw that can cut the opening for the vent hole through the roof.

Pull out any nails that are holding the shingles in place within the space between the vent's opening and its outer perimeter. To install the vent, slide the vent into place below the upper shingles and on top of the lower shingles, so that the vent's opening sits over the hole in the roof. Nail the vent to secure it to the roof as per the vent kit's instructions. Using a caulking gun, seal all the vent seams and the nail heads with roofing cement to ensure a watertight seal.

Insulating Ductwork

You can calculate the R-value of your attic insulation by measuring its depth. Fiberglass batts, for example, have a value of about 3 per inch, while loose insulation rates between 3.1 and 3.7 per inch, depending on the type. You may be surprised to learn just how little insulation your attic contains, especially if your house is more than 30 years old.

The good news is that it's relatively easy to add insulation such as fiberglass batts to the unheated attic spaces that are common in cold areas of the country. Even if you choose to have loose-fill insulation blown into the space by a qualified contractor, the savings on your winter heating bills will pay for the job quite quickly.

One option for insulating exhaust ducts that run through unheated attic areas from kitchen and bathroom fans in cold climates is to wrap them with fiberglass insulation batts; cut the batts down to size and duct tape them in place. This is messy and a bit of a hassle, but it does work.

Another option is to replace the exhaust ducts with insulated ducts. These come wrapped in an insulating material, usually covered by a plastic sleeve. To replace the duct, remove it from the vent in the roof or wall and from the metal ductwork that comes up from the fan. This is usually done by cutting or removing the duct tape, or by cutting or unscrewing the plastic or metal clamps that fasten the exhaust duct over the vent and the fan's ductwork.

You can seal the new exhaust duct to the vent or fan by wrapping the joint with duct tape or by securing hose-type clamps over the exhaust duct to hold it in place. The exhaust duct often comes with either tape or clamps; check the box before you leave the home center to see if you need to buy additional supplies.

To work with fiberglass insulation, wear coveralls that seal at the wrists and ankles (wrap cuffs with duct tape for a tighter fit), a breathing mask, safety goggles, gloves, and a hood or tight-fitting hat. You'll feel hot and slightly ridiculous, but it's far better than the itchy eyes and skin and the breathing difficulties that you'll otherwise encounter.

Installing Attic Insulation

If you have an unheated, unfinished attic (without a floor; it's just joists and the ceiling from the room below) that you want to insulate, first check to see what you're working with. Although the attic needs ventilation, you want it coming from vents, not from gaps around wiring or chimneys. Before you add insulation, check for such gaps, and caulk around them to cut drafts and prevent insects, birds, and animals from entering through them.

If there's already some insulation in place between the ceiling joists, you'll need to choose unfaced insulation (some insulation batts come with a facing on one side that provides a vapor barrier). If there's faced insulation in place already, check that the vapor barrier is facing the right way (down, toward the heated house). If it's not, you'll need to flip it over so that the vapor barrier is installed correctly, or run a utility knife through it to break its seal.

If there's no insulation, either choose faced insulation (the facing goes toward the heated area, so against the attic floor) or install a vapor barrier (available in rolls of plastic from the home center) before laying the insulation in place. Lay the 6-millimeter plastic vapor barrier between the joists, adding a couple of staples at each end of the plastic to tack it while you're laying the insulation. Don't worry about stapling it down really thoroughly, because gravity and the weight of the insulation will hold it in place.

For the insulation itself, choose bags of loose-fill insulation that you can pour between and over the joists (a rake will help to spread loose-fill insulation evenly), or fiberglass batts.

▲ Fiberglass batts just need to be unrolled into place. Don't pack them too tightly, as the air between their layers is an essential part of their insulating ability.

If you'll be laying insulation batts between the joists, measure the space between the joists so that you purchase the correct batt width. This will save you from having to cut the batts to fit between the joists and will help you avoid squeezing the batts too tightly between the joists (which will reduce their insulating ability).

Carry the bags of batt insulation up into the attic intact. Do *not* attempt to open them beforehand; they're tightly compressed, so they're much easier to handle when they're still closed. Open them one at a time, as needed, once they're in the attic.

To lay your insulation, work from the walls toward the center of the attic, and start at the spot furthest away from the attic hatch (like painting a room, you want to work your way toward the exit). Lay the batts in place by unrolling them between the joists, pressing them down without compressing them too tightly. If you lay one batt on one side of the attic and another batt on the other side, you'll likely have a space in the middle that you'll need to cut a batt to fit. Because you're working from the walls in, you'll be measuring and cutting in the area with the highest roof clearance, which should make things easier. To cut fiberglass insulation batts, compress the bat with a straightedge. Cut through the compressed material against the straightedge with a utility knife. Join the ends of batts by butting them up against each other firmly, so that there's no space between them.

ESSENTIAL

Don't forget to weather-strip the attic hatch. Running a length of self-adhesive foam weather stripping around the top of the attic opening will create a good seal when the hatch is placed over the opening.

If you're laying insulation over the top of a layer of batts filling the joists, lay the new batts (which must not have a vapor barrier) perpendicular to the old ones. Insulation can be cut around cross bracing between joists, but remember to keep it 3 inches away from any source of heat, such as electrical fixtures (unless they're clearly rated IC, which means that insulation can be installed near them), or metal chimney flues. And remember not to block venting. If you're using loose-fill insulation, you can nail wooden frames together to fit around vents or heat-producing elements, to keep the insulation away from these items.

Increasing your attic insulation (while making sure that the attic is ventilated properly) can be very gratifying when you start noticing savings on your utility bills, particularly if you've started with an insulation value that's well below what's recommended for your area. You've now walked through your house interior, from the basement to the attic—skipping, however, two important elements: doors and windows. In Chapter 16, you'll find out how to solve the most common problems with doors and their hardware, from hinges to locks.

Chapter 16

Durable Doors

A number of things can go wrong with doors: hinges, handles, doorbells, and even the doors themselves (hollow-core interior doors are particularly vulnerable to having holes knocked through them). Most of these problems have straightforward repairs that can easily be managed in half a day or less. They don't even require expensive or extensive tool lists. Screwdrivers will be your main ally, with a chisel, hammer, and putty knife useful as reinforcements.

Door Handles and Locks

Door handles and locks take a lot of wear and tear over time, especially in high-traffic rooms such as bathrooms. You'll often be able to fix the problem by tightening screws or lubricating the handle or lock mechanism. When this won't work, however, it's still a straightforward task to replace the handle or lock, as long as you choose a replacement that fits the door.

Replacing a Door Handle

To remove the handle, unscrew the screws from the faceplate. This is easier if you hold the handle still on the opposite side of the door. If you can't see the faceplate screws, you'll need to remove the setscrew or release the spring catch (by inserting a small screwdriver into the slot or hole) that's located on the stem of the door handle. Pull the handle away from the door. You'll see the long spindle or the latch assembly that threads through the bolt mechanism and connects the two sides of the handle.

Remove any screws still holding the handle in place. You'll then be able to pull apart the two sides of the handle, leaving the bolt mechanism in place (notice the hole in the bolt mechanism through which the spindle passes).

To remove the bolt mechanism, unscrew the metal latch plate that surrounds it in the edge of the door. You should be able to pull it out, but if the door has been painted, you may need to first break the seal by running a utility knife around the edge of the plate.

Replace the bolt mechanism, sliding the new bolt into place in the old hole. Screw the latch plate into place. (If the old screw holes are stripped, you'll need to repair them as you would for door hinge screws in Chapter 3).

To install the new handle, follow the instructions included with it. Essentially, you'll be reversing the process you followed to remove the old one. Pass the spindle or the latch assembly back through the bolt mechanism so that the two halves of the door handle attach to each other (usually via long screws on one half of the handle that fit into screw housings on the other half). Replace the faceplate and screws as required.

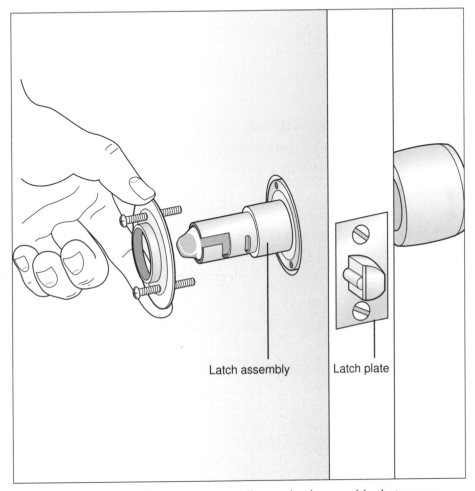

Latch assembly   Latch plate

▲ Door handles use either a square spindle or a latch assembly that passes through the bolt mechanism to connect the two sides of the handles and to operate the bolt.

Loose Door Handles

The most common cause of loose handles is when the screws in one side of the handle work loose from the screw housing in the other half of the handle. Tighten the screws with a screwdriver while holding on to the handle on the opposite side of the door.

If the screws are secure and the door handle is still loose, remove the door handle. If the inner workings are broken, you'll need to replace it. If not, make sure that the spindle or latch assembly that runs between the two halves of the door handle is centered evenly in the door, with the same amount extending toward both halves; then reattach the door handle.

FACT

When you're reattaching a lockable door handle on an interior door, remember that the room's occupants need to be able to lock the door—reattach the door handle so that the lock side faces into the room.

Keeping Handles and Locks Moving Freely

Door handles that aren't moving freely need lubrication. Remove the door handle, and spray penetrating oil on all the moving parts. If the handle has a keyhole for the lock, do *not* spray the oil into the keyhole. Reattach the door handle. Keep locks in good working order with an annual application of graphite powder. Buy squeezable tubes or bottles that will spray the powder into the keyhole, or run a pencil over the teeth of a key and work the lock several times with the key.

To handle a bolt that's sticking, try removing and lubricating the handle. Also loosen the screws that hold the handle's faceplate to the door a little to see if that solves the problem. Check the latch plate, to make sure that it hasn't shifted into the bolt's path.

Freeing Stuck Keys

Having a key break off in a lock can be a major inconvenience. If you can see the key, you may be able to wiggle it free by grasping it with a pair of long-nose pliers. You may also be able to pull out the pieces using a straightened paper clip or a tool called a key extractor.

If this doesn't work, try unscrewing the lock from the door, taking it apart, and pushing the key pieces out. Unfortunately, this is your last resort before calling in a locksmith or replacing the lock (which is also necessary if the key is moving in the lock, but no longer operating it).

Solving Door Problems

If a binding or sticking door doesn't respond to the quick fixes in Chapter 3, you'll likely have to reseat or shim its hinges. First, check whether or not the door is warped. Although you can try straightening it by removing it, laying it down, and weighting the warped area with heavy objects such as concrete blocks for a time, it may be easier and more effective to replace the door. If you are able to straighten the warp, be sure to seal all the door's surfaces, including the edges, to prevent moisture from seeping into the door and causing the warp to reoccur.

ESSENTIAL

If a closed door bangs back and forth in its frame (such as when the wind blows), you can quiet it with self-adhesive foam weather stripping. Just run it along the surface of the door frame that the door closes against.

Reseating/Shimming Hinges

Ideally, a hinge plate should fit level with the surface into which its mortise has been cut. You can make adjustments to the hinge plates, however, to free up a binding door, as follows (in each case, you should be able to see which hinge would be the easiest and most effective fix):

- If the latch side of the door is too high, add depth to the bottom hinge, shims to the top hinge, or both.
- If the latch side is too low, add shims to the bottom hinge, depth to the top hinge, or both.
- If the frame side of the door is binding fairly evenly, shim out both hinges.
- If it's the latch side that's binding evenly, add depth to both hinges.

To add shims or depth to a hinge, first gauge the thickness of the shim or cut that you'll need to make. Push the door until it touches the frame, but don't force it closed. Measure the amount that the door is overlapping the frame; this is how thick your shim or how deep your cut needs to be.

ALERT!

Take out the bottom hinge pin first when you're removing a door. Taking off the top hinge first can cause the door's weight to twist on the bottom hinge, tearing the wood around the hinge's screws. Alternatively, insert a wedge under the door to support it while you're working on one hinge at a time.

To create a shim, unscrew the hinge plate. Cut a thin piece of wood, cardboard, or sheet brass to fit under the hinge plate, using the hinge plate as a pattern. Mark the screw holes on the shim, and use an awl to punch holes in them (or use a drill on the sheet brass). Reattach the hinge plate, placing the shim between it and the door frame.

To add depth to a hinge, unscrew the hinge plate, and use a wood chisel to cut pieces of the mortise away. Hold the chisel almost parallel to the mortise so that you're making very shallow cuts. When you get to the required depth, replace the hinge plate.

Silencing Squeaky Hinges

Squeaky hinges can often be fixed with a quick spray of penetrating oil into their tops. Move the door back and forth to work in the oil, and use a paper towel to sop up any excess oil. If that doesn't work, remove the hinge pin and clean it (sanding it down if it's rusty), then oil and replace it.

Misaligned Strike Plates

If a door is not latching properly, the strike plate (the metal plate on the door frame that the bolt goes into) may need to be realigned. First, tighten the door's hinge screws (Chapter 3) or reseat/shim any hinges (see the previous section) as required. If that doesn't solve the problem, look for scratches or damaged surfaces on the strike plate, to see where the bolt is actually meeting it.

For small misalignments (less than $1/8$-inch), use a metal file to widen or lengthen the hole in the strike plate so that it will accept the bolt (it's easier to do this if you unscrew the strike plate first and clamp it in a vise while you file it). Then, use a chisel to widen or lengthen the hole in the door frame by the same amount.

For larger misalignments, remove the strike plate, and recut the mortise (the depression in which the strike plate sits) in the direction that the strike plate needs to be moved in order to meet the door properly. Use a wood chisel to cut pieces of the mortise away. Hold the chisel almost parallel to the mortise so that you're making very shallow cuts (it's better to make the cuts too shallow, rather than too deep). Then,

cut or chisel out the bolt hole in the door frame to match the new strike plate position. Screw the strike plate into place, and use stainable wood putty to fill the piece of mortise that's now exposed.

A third option—if the strike plate is in the right location but is too far away from the bolt—is to remove the strike plate and use it as a pattern to cut out a shim from sheet brass, cardboard or thin wood. Replace the strike plate, with the shim placed between the door frame and the strike plate.

Trimming Door Bottoms

Occasionally, you'll need to trim the bottom of the door—for example, if you've changed the flooring, and the new surface is higher than the old one.

For a solid wooden door, measure how much material to remove, and transfer that measurement to the door by drawing a line across the door (run your pencil along a level or straightedge to create a straight line). Cut off the extra material using a power saw or a jigsaw. Sand the edges smooth, and refinish the cut edge to match the rest of the door (so that moisture can't enter the cut edge and cause the door to swell or warp).

A hollow wooden door is a little trickier. There's a piece of wood framing in the bottom of the door. If you need to trim just a little, you can handle it as though the door were solid wood. (To prevent the veneer from splintering, cut through it on both sides of the door with a utility knife before you make the saw cut.) If, however, you need to cut above where the wood framing is, save that framing once you've measured, marked the door, and cut off the excess. Rip or chisel off the veneer from the cut-off piece of framing, and run wood glue all around the framing. Reinsert it into the cut edge of the door, so that the framing supports the bottom edge of the door, and clamp it tightly while the glue dries. Seal all raw edges.

Interior doors should sit about ½ inch above the floor surface to allow air to circulate through the rooms. The exception is interior doors that lead to unheated or uncooled areas such as crawlspaces or garages; these should seal tightly and be weather-stripped to prevent air leaks.

Keeping Doorbells Ringing

Doorbells exposed to weather extremes and frequent use may corrode under their decorative covers and eventually stop working. If your doorbell isn't ringing, check your circuit breakers or fuse box first to make sure that the circuit is operating. A transformer steps the electrical current down to a low voltage, so you can usually work safely around the doorbell without having to turn off the current to that circuit (check that this is the case).

Take off the decorative cover, either by removing its visible screws or by prying it off with a flat screwdriver blade (which sometimes reveals screws that must then be removed). You'll be able to see two wires, each leading to a screw terminal. First, try tightening the screw terminals to see if the wires are loose. Test the button's operation.

If it doesn't work, undo the wires, clean off any corrosion with sandpaper, and touch the bare ends together, being careful to hold the insulated part of the wire. If the doorbell sounds, it means there's a problem at the doorbell's button. You need to buy a new button and connect the old wires to the new button's screw terminals; then screw or snap the button housing back on to the door frame, and/or snap the new decorative cover into place.

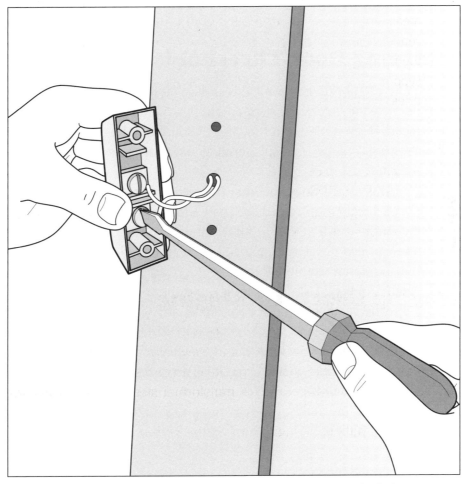

▲ Tightening the screw terminals can be a quick fix for a doorbell that's not working because its wires have come loose.

If the button doesn't sound when you touch the wires together, the problem is in the transformer or in the wiring between the transformer and the bell, or between the electrical panel and the transformer. Shut off the electrical power to the transformer, snap off its cover, and tighten the screw terminals in case one or more of the wires have worked loose. Turn the power back on, and test the doorbell.

If it still doesn't work, you'll need to have either the transformer replaced or the wiring checked and fixed. In either case, it's a good time to call in an expert to find the problem.

Replacing Door Thresholds

Many exterior doors have a threshold that the door closes against. Because they often get stepped on, thresholds (which can be wood, metal, or even plastic in the case of some that incorporate weather stripping) can become splintered, gouged, or broken. Luckily, this is a relatively easy fix.

Measure the threshold that's currently in place, and check to see how it meets the door frame (its edges might be cut straight across, or they may have a cutout to allow the threshold to fit around the door frame). Also measure the height of the threshold. Choose a replacement threshold that can be adjusted or cut to fit, or is already the correct width and height. To test the fit, hold the threshold in place and have someone gently close the door. Make any width or height adjustments as needed.

Follow the instructions that came with your threshold, if applicable, to insert it in place. Generally, you'll be screwing the threshold to the underlying door frame. Metal and plastic thresholds have predrilled holes; with wood thresholds, you may need to drill the holes yourself, to avoid splitting the wood.

Hollow-Core Doors

Many houses have hollow-core interior doors—thin pieces of wood veneer mounted on either side of a wood-strip frame. They're inexpensive, which is why they're so common, but if you have the chance to replace them with solid-core doors, go for it. Solid doors are much sturdier, and they also offer better sound, heat, and fire resistance.

In the meantime, however, the most common problem with hollow-core doors is that they're vulnerable to getting holes knocked through them. You can repair this similarly to a hole in a wallboard wall (see Chapter 13). In this case, however, you'd create a backing for the layers of joint compound by spraying expanding-foam insulation into the hole or by gluing a mesh screen against the inside of the door (a sturdy thread woven into the mesh on two sides of the screen allows you to hold the screen in place while the glue dries).

However, you'll then have to completely refinish the door in order to hide the repair, and even after refinishing, you'll probably be able to tell where the repair was made. It may actually be faster to replace the door. Measure the existing door's height, width, and depth, and the locations of the hinge plates and the door handle. If you buy a new door slab you may have to cut mortises for the hinge plates and the latch plate, and two holes—one for the door handle mechanism that goes through the door and the other for the bolt that goes through the door edge. (Check the sections on installing deadbolts in Chapter 10.)

Alternatively, check out reclamation or second-hand building material stores to find a door that will fit your frame, which has hinge mortises and the door handle in the right locations. You might well get lucky, because many doors have the hinges and handle in the same place.

FACT

To fix a scratch, buy a wood repair pencil that matches the door's finish; run it along the scratch, blending it with the existing finish. For deep scratches or large areas of damage, you may need to use paintable wood putty or an epoxy wood filler that you can finish to match the existing surface.

Sliding Doors

Sliding doors are supported either at the top by rollers on which they hang, or at the bottom on rollers or tracks on which they slide. To remove either type, you generally lift them up, and then angle them out toward you. For some top-hanging doors, you may need to match the position of their rollers with a notch on the track before you can remove them.

Keep the tracks of sliding doors clean by periodically scrubbing them out (a toothbrush works well). A quick vacuum with a nozzle attachment can help prevent dirt from building up in the tracks. While you're cleaning the tracks, tighten any loose screws that are holding the tracks to the floor or wall frame. Spray penetrating oil on the rollers to keep them moving freely. A very light coat of oil on the tracks can also help.

Tracks, particularly those attached to the floor, can become bent. To fix this, take a piece of wood that's long enough to extend past the bent area on both sides, and narrow enough to fit snugly into the track. Place it in the track against the bent portion of track, and hammer the track back into place against it. (To avoid damaging the surface of the track, hammer against a piece of wood or carpet scrap placed against the track, rather than directly on the track itself.)

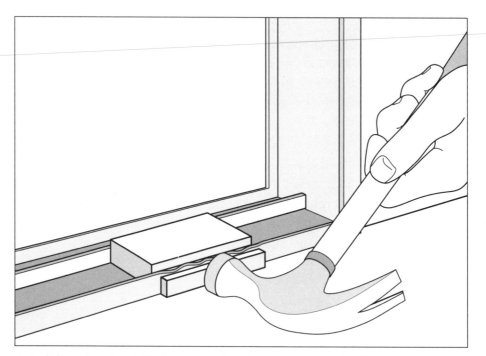

▲ A sliding door track that has been bent can sometimes be fixed by hammering it back into place against a block of wood.

Doors that hang unevenly can often be adjusted using the mounting screw that's designed to hold the door level. It's probably located below a top-mounted roller or above a bottom-mounted roller. Some adjust the door's level when you turn the screw, while others are mounted in a slot. For these, it's good to have a helper. Loosen the screw so that the screw moves within the slot, and move the door up or down until it's level. Have your helper hold the door in place while you retighten the screw.

If the door isn't moving at all, again, check the mounting screws. You may need to adjust them so that they lift both edges of the door up so that they're within the bottom track, but not dragging along its surface. For a top-hanging door that doesn't have bottom tracks, check the guides that are attached to the floor with screws, usually at the center of the doorway and often on each edge of the door frame. If they've shifted, they may be impeding the door. Just loosen the screw, adjust their direction, and tighten the screw.

ALERT!

If none of these fixes work, have a look at the frame around the door. If it has warped to the point of moving or bending the tracks, which are now impeding the doors, you may have to replace the tracks.

Bi-Fold Doors

Clean the tracks in which bi-fold doors operate using a damp rag. If the dirt buildup is substantial, a toothbrush will help scrub it off. A shot of penetrating oil will help lubricate both the track and the pins or rollers that move along the track.

When you look at the closed doors, the gap between them should be straight and even. If it's not, adjust the pivot blocks (which could be located at the top and/or bottom of the door frame). You may be able to reposition how the door sits on the pivot, or raise or lower the door on the pivot. Try to avoid repositioning the door so close to the door frame that the door edge rubs on the frame every time it's opened.

Storm Doors

Most storm doors have a hydraulic closing mechanism that prevents them from slamming and also controls the speed at which they close. To adjust the speed, turn the screw that you'll usually find on the end of the closing mechanism. Turning it clockwise should slow the door down.

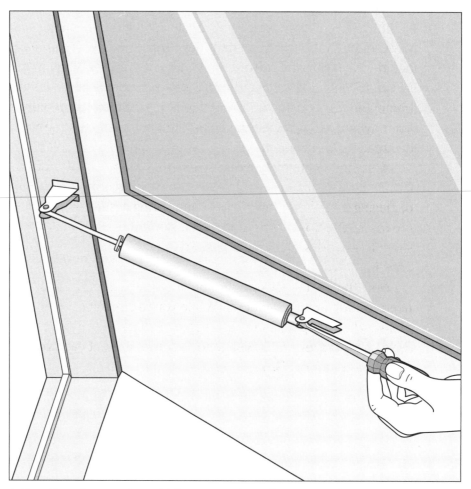

▲ To adjust the speed at which a storm door closes, turn the screw at the end of its hydraulic closer (which might be attached to the top, middle, or bottom of the door).

If the screw on the hydraulic closer isn't changing the speed of the door, replace the closer. You may not need to take the brackets off the door frame and the door; just undo the closer from the bracket on the door frame and on the door (often by pulling out a pin from the brackets), and replace it with a new one of the same size. Then, adjust the closing mechanism screw so that it closes as fast or slowly as required.

If you need to replace the brackets, fill the old screw holes in the door frame and a wooden storm door with wood putty and let it dry before drilling holes for the new brackets. (You may be able to reuse the screw holes in a metal storm door.) Attach the brackets to the door frame and the door; then connect the hydraulic closer (the end with the adjusting screw will face out toward the latch edge of the door). Adjust the screw as necessary.

A strong wind can blow an open storm door out of your hands, forcing it beyond where the closer would ordinarily operate, and damaging it. You can buy a chain and spring assembly that attaches to the top of the door frame and to the storm door (usually with hooks that slip into eye-bolts) to prevent this. Predrill holes for the eye-bolts in the door frame and the door.

Now that you've tackled the major types of doors in your home, you need to look at your windows. While you've already handled caulking and weather-stripping them (in Chapter 6), there's still plenty to fix, from replacing a broken windowpane to making sure that each pane is operating smoothly.

Chapter 17

Ways with Windows

The various types of windows—sash, casement/awning, and sliding—all have their quirks, but it's older wooden sash windows that are most likely to cause problems. The wood can swell, the sash cords can break, and the glazing putty that holds the glass in place can fail. Fix-it solutions for these and other window problems are fairly straightforward.

Freeing a Stuck Window

Wooden sash windows (two windows that slide up and down, sometimes called double-hung windows) and casement/awning windows (windows that swing outward on hinges) are the most likely types to become stuck. They're especially vulnerable to having the wood swell during humid weather or to being painted shut.

If you've just moved into the house, check that the windows haven't been nailed shut. If they have, use pliers or a small pry bar with a nail puller to remove them. Work gently, using a piece of scrap wood or cardboard under the leverage point of the pry bar to avoid damaging the window sash (the frame around the glass) or the stop (the piece of wood trim that runs up the window frame on the wall, forming a neat seal against the sash).

FACT

Newer sash windows use springs for smooth operation. Examine the channel that runs up and down beside the sash (called a track insert) to find the adjusting screw. Turning the screw will change the spring tension, allowing you to choose the best setting.

Breaking Through Paint

To break a paint seal, carefully run a utility or putty knife through the paint where the window sash meets the stop and the windowsill. (Tap the knife with a hammer to penetrate the seal.) Repeat this on the house exterior if needed. If that doesn't work, place a piece of wood against the sash to protect it, and tap the wood lightly with a hammer, or, working from outside, try to insert a thin pry bar between the window sash and the sill to break the seal.

Keeping Windows Moving Freely

Windows that are sticky, rather than completely stuck, may need to be removed so that you can clean the channels in which the sashes slide up and down. Excess paint can be removed with paint thinner, steel wool, or sandpaper, and rough wood can be sanded smooth.

If the problem is high humidity that's a persistent characteristic of your weather, try sanding the window sashes and the channels/trims wherever the two surfaces meet until they move freely. Follow up by sealing the raw edges with paint or varnish to prevent the wood from absorbing any more moisture. If the humidity's temporary, wait until the window operates freely again, and then seal the window sash edges and channels or frame with paint or varnish. Rubbing a wax candle along the channels or trim and the window edges can also help.

When the Stop's the Problem

Sometimes, the window stops can bind against the sashes. If this is happening in one isolated spot, you may be able to move the stop by placing a block of wood against it and tapping the wood with a hammer in the direction you need the stop to move.

Otherwise, remove the stop completely, and reposition it. (Scrape off paint edges as needed to ensure that the stop sits flush in its new position.) Place a thin strip of cardboard between the window sash and the stop, to ensure that you're giving the window room to move, and nail the stop into place.

Sash Windows

Older sash, or double-hung, windows slide up and down in their channels courtesy of a system of cords, pulleys, and weights that is hidden inside cavities in the walls beside the window. If the window won't move properly (but isn't stuck), won't stay up, or hangs crooked, it's the cord and weight system that needs attention.

Fixing Cords and Weights

Access the cord and pulley system by using a small pry bar or stiff putty knife to pry up the stops on either side of the window. Remove the lower window, noting how the cords are attached to the tops or sides of the window. If you can, have someone hold the window for you so that you don't have to remove the cords. With the lower window removed, you should be able to see a removable panel that accesses the cords and weights inside each wall cavity. Remove the panel's screws or nails.

Once you've removed the access panels, check that the weights are still tied to the cords. If not, check that the cords are in good shape. If they're okay, tie the weights back onto the cords, put the lower window back in, and check the window operation; this may be all that's necessary.

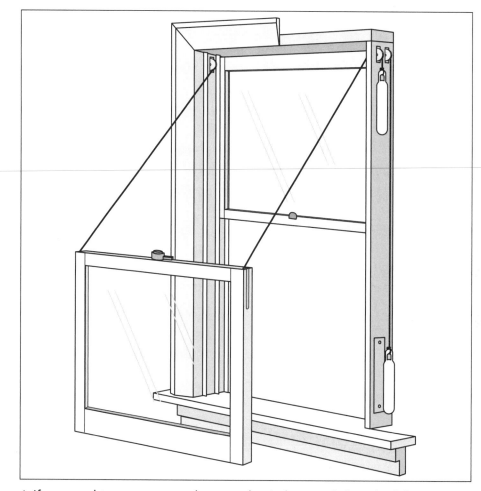

▲ If you need to remove or replace a sash window cord, first check how it runs from the window, through the pulley, and into the wall cavity.

If that doesn't do the trick, or the cord is frayed or worn, remove the cord from the lower window, and take the old sash cord to your home center to ensure that you buy new sash cord that has the same thickness (buy more length than you need). Before you remove the cord, however, note how it hangs in the pulley so that you'll know how to thread the new cord into place. Also check that the pulleys are operating freely. Clean them if necessary, and apply penetrating oil to them to keep them lubricated.

If you're replacing the cords for both upper and lower sashes, work with the upper (exterior) window first. To install the new cord, feed it through the pulley, let it drop down inside the cavity (a nail tied to the end of it makes this easier), and tie the weight on to the end of it. Using the old cord as a guide, cut the new cord and knot it or nail it into position on the sash.

Check the window operation. Adjust the cord length to make sure the window opens all the way, but since it's much easier to make the cord shorter if necessary, go longer at first. Once you're satisfied, replace the cords on the other side of the upper window and the lower window as necessary, close the access panels, and reattach the window stop.

New cords can stretch, so you may need to adjust the cord length after the window has been in operation for a little while. If your windows feature chains instead of cords, replacing the chains with nylon cord can eliminate the noise made by the chain.

Repairing Sashes

Sash windows are formed by four pieces of wood that create a frame around the glass. The corner joints between the wood pieces can come loose, allowing the sashes to work apart. You can reglue these by cleaning the joint with a stiff brush, injecting wood glue into the joint, and clamping the corner while the glue dries. Another option is to screw L-shaped corner brackets over the joint. (Drill pilot holes for the screws, and place them carefully so that you don't drill into the glass.) These can also reinforce a reglued joint.

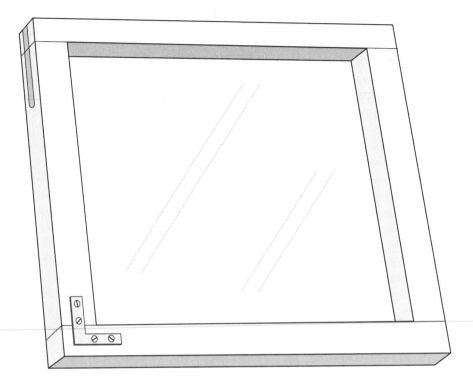

▲ Corner brackets will help to secure joints in window frames.

Replacing Sash Window Glass

Windowpanes can often be replaced without removing the windows, working on the exterior side of the window. If you've never replaced glass before, however, or the window is in an awkward location, it may be easier to remove the window and lay it on a flat surface (with the exterior of the window facing up).

The glass in wooden sash windows is usually held against the sash with putty and glazing points (triangular pieces of metal inserted into the sash about every 4 to 6 inches), with a sealing layer of putty or caulking that runs all along the edge of the glass. Use a chisel, scraper, or putty knife to carefully remove the old putty and glazing points from the glass. You may need long-nose pliers to pull out the points. You can soften stubborn putty by coating it with linseed oil or warming it with a hair dryer.

If you're working with a broken window, try to remove the pieces of glass as you go, so that they don't fall, to make cleanup safer. For a full pane of glass or any remaining glass pieces, apply gentle pressure to the glass from the interior side of the window (a helper is useful here) to pop it out of the frame.

Use a chisel to scrape out any remaining putty or rough areas where the glass has been removed, and sand the surface so that the new glass has a smooth, clean surface against which to sit. Seal this surface with wood sealer such as linseed oil. If the sash corners are loose, repair them as detailed previously.

ALERT!

Window glass is easy to break, and it can cause deep, serious cuts. Always wear gloves designed for working around glass; they should be tight fitting and flexible, to give you dexterity, but thick, for protection. Safety glasses are also important.

For the glass dimensions you need to buy or have cut, measure the height and width of the opening, less $1/8$-inch. Also check the opening to see if it's square; the diagonal measurements from corner to corner should be the same. If they're not, check your height and width measurements in several different places, in case the glass needs to be cut to allow for the out-of-square frame. Take a piece of the glass with you so that you buy the right kind to replace it.

To seal the glass against the window sash, buy latex glazing compound that can be applied with a caulking gun. Apply a line of it about $1/4$-inch wide on the surface of the window sash against which the glass will sit. Press the edges of the glass gently into place, and use a putty knife to scrape away any excess compound. Gently tap or press new glazing points into the sash every 4 to 6 inches so the glass is held snugly in place. Avoid pressing down hard on the glass, because it could break.

Apply another $1/4$-inch bead of compound, this time on top of the glass where it meets the window sash, and smooth it out using a putty knife held at a 45-degree angle against the compound to create a neat seal. (You can also use a moistened finger, but wear latex or similar gloves to make cleanup easier.) Glazing compound can be painted to match the color of the frame, but check the package directions to ensure that you let it cure sufficiently first.

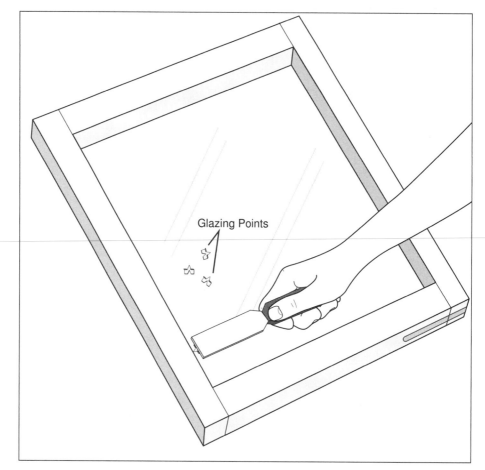

▲ Glazing points help keep the glass firmly in place against the window frame.

Casement/Awning Windows

Many older casement or awning windows simply have an arm with several holes along its length. As the window swings out, the holes fit over a peg in the window frame, allowing you to prop open the window at various positions. Newer casement windows replace this arm with a rod on a pivot mount, or with a crank mechanism.

With arm-type windows, the screws can work loose over time. To fix them, see the fix for loose door hinge screws in Chapter 3. Regular maintenance includes cleaning the rod of any grease that might accumulate on it and applying a few drops of lubricating oil to the pivot.

For crank-type windows, the crank mechanism can break or wear down. In this case, it's best to buy a replacement crank, removing the screws from the old crank and taking it with you to your home center to choose a replacement. Occasionally lubricating the crank with a machine oil spray can also smooth its operation (operate the crank several times after you spray to spread the oil throughout the mechanism, keeping a rag handy in case any oil drips out), as can keeping the extension arm free of dirt or grease.

To replace the glass in a wooden casement window, follow the same steps as for a wooden sash window, detailed previously. If you need to remove the window, first remove the crank mechanism, then the window hinges, making sure that you remove the bottom hinge first so that the weight of the window doesn't twist the bottom hinge screws. (It's helpful to have a second pair of hands here.) For newer metal or vinyl casement windows, you probably need to call a glass professional. These windows tend to have weather stripping and energy-efficient gases built into their design, putting them beyond a fix-it solution.

Sliding Windows

The most useful thing you can do for sliding windows is to keep the tracks in which they slide clean. Depending on their width, try using a toothbrush or a larger stiff brush to loosen the dirt and use a handheld vacuum to remove it. Wrapping a cleaning rag over a flat-bladed screwdriver also works well. To help the windows slide more easily, rub a wax candle in the tracks.

Large sliding windows sometimes have rollers on the top and/or bottom of the sashes. They can gum up with dirt or grease over time, so a shot of silicon spray can help keep them clean. If they're broken, take the window out of the frame, and have it repaired by a professional.

To replace the glass in a wooden sliding window, or to repair loose or broken corner joints, follow the directions for wooden sash windows. For metal windows that have loose corner joints, look for a corner screw that can be tightened gently (overtightening it could bring the window out of square enough to break the glass). Some weather stripping can also be replaced by removing a corner screw that holds a metal channel in place. For other repairs, seek out a glass professional who has the tools and expertise to deal with the ways these windows are put together.

FACT

Whenever you're cleaning the tracks, check that the small holes through the window frame aren't clogged (use a paper clip to poke out any dirt). These weep holes are designed to let water such as condensation escape, so they need to be kept free of debris.

The catches that hold sliding windows closed can wear out, no longer locking the window securely, and in some cases, not engaging the window at all. If it's a metal catch that's bent, try using pliers to bend it back into place. Bent plastic catches need to be replaced. Consider buying metal catches, which last longer and are more secure. Just make sure that the replacement catch will fit over and hold the window properly.

The screws that hold catches in place can loosen. Use the quick fix for door hinge screws in Chapter 3 to solve this problem.

Window Screens

Repairing or replacing the mesh in window screens is a quick way to stop insects such as mosquitoes from invading your home and to keep your house looking well cared for. To start, it's a good idea to clean the screens annually. For a quick clean, brush them to remove dirt and dust. For a more thorough cleaning, remove them from the window, spray them gently with a garden hose, and then brush or sponge them down with a solution of hot water and all-purpose detergent.

Small gaps in the screen can result from the mesh weave becoming uneven or stretched. That's easily fixed with a toothpick or straightened paper clip; just move the individual strands of mesh back into place.

Mesh screen comes in a variety of materials and colors. Buy replacement mesh screen that matches your existing screen, to avoid having one window that looks significantly different from the rest.

Patching Screens

There are several ways to patch holes in mesh screens, but they all result in a fairly visible repair. They are, however, good temporary fixes until you have time to replace the entire screen.

Very small holes in mesh screen can be sealed with several coats of clear nail polish or clear-drying glue (allow each coat to dry between applications, and poke a toothpick through the individual mesh holes before each coat dries). For rips, realign the individual mesh wires as closely as possible with a toothpick or awl; then run a piece of wire or low-visibility cord (such as fishing line) back and forth across the rip, as if you're sewing or weaving it back up, to close it.

You can buy mesh patches that are designed to cover holes, or you can create a patch from a piece of spare screen. The patch should be slightly larger than the hole. First, trim any loose wires from the edge of the hole, and flatten any protruding wires to create an even surface for the patch. Glue the patch to the screen around the hole using clear-drying glue or caulking, or sew the patch into place with wire or low-visibility cord (use a curved upholstery-type needle so that you can make the repair from just one side of the screen).

Replacing Aluminum-Frame Screen Mesh

You'll need a splining tool for this repair; it has a handle with a roller on either end. Several spring-loaded clamps are also useful for keeping the mesh straight in the frame.

Remove the window screen, in its frame, from the window or door. A narrow channel runs around the frame, holding a length of spline (cord) that secures the screen. Pop out the old spline with an awl or flat-bladed screwdriver.

Cut the new mesh to fit the frame, plus 2 inches extra on all sides. Lay the new mesh over the frame, ensuring that it's straight, and clamp it into place on each corner of the frame (or have someone hold the mesh).

Now insert the new mesh and spline into the spline channel. For aluminum mesh, you'll first need to use the convex (outward curving) roller on the splining tool to gently crease the mesh into the spline channel, taking care not to cut or tear it. If you're using clamps, you may need to release them on the opposite side in order to do this, but be sure to reattach them as you make your way around the window.

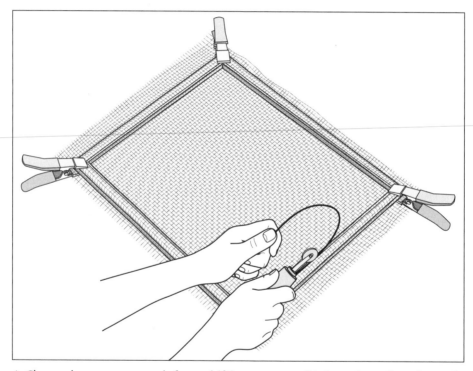

▲ Clamps keep screen mesh from shifting as you roll it into the spline channel.

For all types of mesh, use the concave (inward curving) roller on the splining tool to roll the spline into the channel, taking the screen with it. Remove the clamps as needed, pulling the screen snug on the opposite side to eliminate wrinkles or bunching, but not so snug that you pull the window frame out of alignment. Cutting away excess mesh at each corner at a 45-degree angle will help avoid bunching.

The splining tool will have a tough time fully seating the spline at the corners of the frame; use a flat-bladed screwdriver to push the spline into place there. Carefully trim the excess screen with a utility knife, angling the knife away from the newly installed mesh to avoid accidentally cutting it.

Replacing Wood-Frame Screen Mesh

Remove the wooden frame from the window, and use a flat-bladed screwdriver or small pry bar to pop off the molding that's covering the edges of the screen. Run a utility knife blade through the paint around the molding, if necessary, to free the molding from the frame.

Cut new mesh to fit the frame, plus 2 inches excess on all sides. Lay the mesh over the frame so that it's straight, and clamp it to the frame or have someone hold it in place, pulling it snug. Staple the mesh to the window frame on all sides, making sure that it doesn't wrinkle or bunch.

Reapply the molding with small nails, and then carefully trim the excess screen by running a utility knife around the window frame, with the blade cutting between the molding and the frame so that you're not cutting against a wood surface that can be seen.

Window Film

Window films that block heat and ultraviolet rays can be applied to east-, west-, and south-facing windows to keep the heat in during the winter and out during the summer, and to protect upholstery and fabric against premature fading. The film is usually applied to the inside surface of the outermost windowpane, and it can pay for itself in terms of energy efficiency within a year or so. You can expect most films to last for ten to fifteen years, possibly longer if you choose a film that's professionally installed.

The kits that home centers sell tend to have highly detailed directions, but in general, you need to thoroughly clean the window, cut the film to the window size (or slightly larger, allowing you to trim the film to size once it's on the window), and then wet the window with the kit's special soapy solution. Apply the film as directed (there may be a backing to the film that you have to remove first) to the window, spray the soapy solution over the film, and squeegee out any air bubbles.

QUESTION?

How do you remove window film that's damaged or cracking?
Home centers that sell window film also sell a product that removes old window film. Spray the product on the film, and use a plastic putty knife to scrape off the film. Or, try spraying on a solution of water and liquid dish detergent.

These films are much easier to install if you have a helper, especially if you're dealing with large windows. Working alone can be a recipe for creased or wrinkled film, and once the film is creased, it's always creased.

At this point, you've fixed all manner of problems throughout—and around—your house, including doors and windows. Except for a few quick fixes in Chapter 3, however, the house's operating systems, including the plumbing and waste system, have yet to be tackled. In Chapter 18, then, you'll learn all about plumbing fixes.

Chapter 18

Practical Plumbing

Plumbing. Just the word can strike fear into a homeowner's heart. It's a mysterious system, full of pipes and fittings that cause problems ranging from odd noises to catastrophic failures. Touring the plumbing aisles at your home center won't exactly help your anxiety, considering their confusing array of connections and valves. This chapter guides you through the confusion to help you solve some of the most common plumbing fix-it problems.

Introduction to Plumbing

Depending on your home's age, a combination of cast iron, galvanized steel, copper, or various types of plastic piping may form your plumbing system. Although copper's durability still makes it a popular choice, plastic pipe is gaining ground. It's flexible, easy to cut and work with, and doesn't require soldering. Be sure to check local building codes to ensure they allow plastic piping.

Copper pipe can be cut with a hacksaw (use a blade with 18 to 24 teeth per inch) or with a pipe cutter (which makes cleaner cuts and is relatively inexpensive). When measuring pipe for cutting, go from the bottom of each fitting that the pipe will slide into so that you include the length of pipe that will slide inside the fitting.

Soldering copper joints goes beyond a fix-it job, so repairs in this chapter focus on joining copper pipe without soldering (compression joints), or using plastic pipe. A variety of fittings is available to join various types of pipes together. The best way to determine what you need is to take a sketch or photo of your setup along with your pipe diameter measurements to the home or plumbing center, and find a good staff person. They should be familiar with local building codes and will let you know what will work within those codes. One thing that you should never do, however, is join two different types of metal pipe together—unless you use a dielectric fitting between the two. Otherwise, the metals will react, corroding the joint and resulting in leaks.

Compression Fittings

Compression fittings join two pieces of pipe by squeezing a union fitting against rings that are slipped over the pipe. First, make sure that the ends of the pipe are cut square, and clean (debur) the ends by running a pipe reamer or file around the inside of each end of pipe. When you cut the pipe, remember to take into account the ½ inch needed for the pipe length that will slide into each side of the compression fitting. Slip a compression nut and then a compression ring over both ends of the copper pipes you wish to join. The nut's threads need to face the cut end of the pipe. The ring should be located so that the union fitting will fit onto the pipe over it.

Rub a small amount of pipe joint compound over the ring, and slip the union fitting over the pipe so it meets the compression ring. Loosely screw the nut over the fitting's threads. Repeat for the other piece of pipe. To tighten the nuts, hold the fitting in place with a wrench while you tighten each nut with another wrench. Check for leaks by slowly turning on the water.

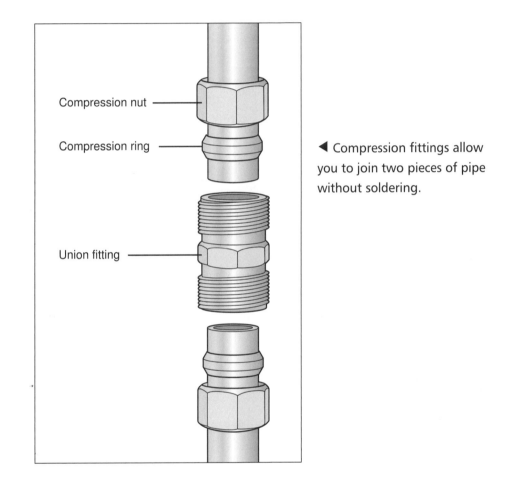

Compression nut

Compression ring

Union fitting

◀ Compression fittings allow you to join two pieces of pipe without soldering.

Plastic Pipe

There are three types of rigid plastic pipe: PVC, used for drain and vent pipes; ABS, used for drainpipe; and CPVC, used for both hot and cold water. The main difference in working with these is that ABS doesn't need a primer prior to gluing it, while PVC and CPVC do.

Plastic pipe can be cut with a hacksaw or pipe cutter. To clean up the edges, run a utility knife around the end of the pipe. Once you've measured (twice!) and cut the pieces of pipe you need, it's essential to test fit them together without using any glue. Once they're all together, mark the joints with a felt-tip pen so that you'll know how to put the pieces together when you're gluing them. Take them apart, laying them out in the order in which you'll put them together. Rub the contact surfaces of the pipes and fittings that will be glued together with an emery cloth.

For CPVC and PVC pipe, prime the surfaces of the pipes and fittings that will be glued together, and allow the primer to work (usually just fifteen seconds) according to its instructions. (Primer isn't necessary for ABS pipe.) Coat the surfaces with pipe glue to match your pipe type. Firmly press together the two pieces of pipe with the alignment marks offset by about 2 inches, twisting the pipe pieces as necessary to match up the marks. Hold them in place for thirty to sixty seconds. You should wait about five minutes before gluing the next joint onto either piece that you've just glued.

ESSENTIAL

You *must* be prepared to work quickly once you've applied the glue; it sets up within a minute, and if the pipe pieces aren't in alignment by then, you'll have to start again. If you've never worked with this before, practice on a few scrap pieces of plastic and some extra fittings (they're not expensive).

Installing Shutoff Valves

Shutoff valves installed on individual fixtures, such as sinks and toilets, allow you to shut off the water flow while you work on that fixture without having to shut off the water to the entire house. If you're working on a fixture without shutoff valves, your first job should be to install them, usually where the water supply comes through the wall. If you buy the type that work as compression fittings, they're easy to install.

Buy a flexible water supply tube that will fit between the shutoff valve location and the fixture itself (whether it's a hot or cold supply for a faucet, or a cold supply for a toilet). Flexible braided steel or nylon pipes are excellent but must be bought to fit, because they can't be cut.

Once you've shut off the water supply to the house, removed the existing water supply tube(s) between the wall and the fixture, and bought replacements and shutoff valves to fit, you're ready to go. Slip a compression nut (threads facing the pipe's cut end) and a ring over the pipe where it comes through the wall. Add pipe joint compound over the ring, slide the shutoff valve over the ring, and tighten the nut.

Braided water supply pipes incorporate a threaded end that can be screwed directly onto the shutoff valve. If so, go ahead and tighten it over the valve. Otherwise, slip a nut and ring over the water supply tube, apply pipe joint compound to the ring, and slide the tube down into the shutoff valve. Tighten the nut over the valve first by hand, and then by holding the valve in place with a wrench and turning the nuts with another wrench. With the valve closed (remember that you haven't connected the water supply tube to the fixture yet), check for leaks by turning on the water. Tighten the nut further if necessary, but avoid overtightening.

FACT

These instructions apply where you're working with copper pipe coming through the wall and a metal shutoff valve. For joining other materials, it's the same theory, but check with home center staff for the correct shutoff valve.

Repairing Leaky Faucets

The biggest problem with fixing leaky faucets is identifying which type of faucet you're working with. There are four basic types—compression, ball, cartridge, and disk—but endless variations. Even if you think you've figured yours out, it's best to take the faucet apart before heading to the home center for the replacement part. Take the old parts with you so that finding the exact replacement won't be a guessing game.

For *all* faucet repairs, *first shut off the water supply to the faucet,* either at the shutoff valve or at the house supply. Open the faucet to drain the water. Put the plug in the sink, and line the sink with a towel to protect it. Wrap pliers with masking tape to avoid scratching faucet surfaces. As you remove faucet parts, examine them to see how they're seated within the faucet, and lay them out on a paper towel in the order you removed them.

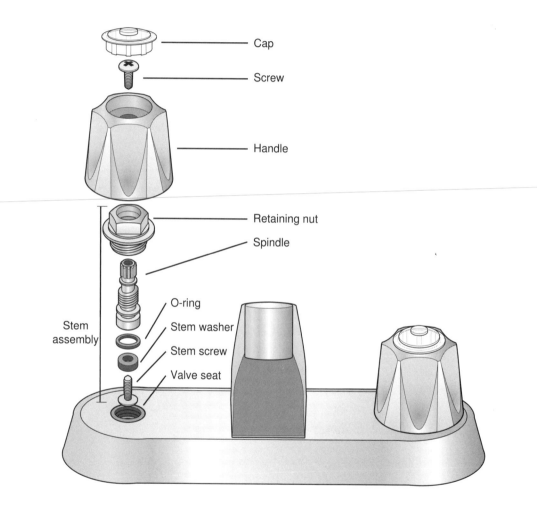

▲ Compression faucets have two handles that twist on and off to control the flow of water. These older-style faucets, which include valve-type faucets often found in utility rooms, contain washers that often need to be replaced.

Compression Faucet

Remove the cap from the handle so that you can undo the screw holding the handle in place. The handle should lift off, but it's often seized. If so, use a tool called a handle puller that fits over the handle and applies pressure using a screw-down handle.

Use groove-joint pliers to remove the stem assembly from the faucet. To access the O-ring and the stem washer for replacement, take the stem assembly apart: Remove the stem screw, and unscrew the retaining nut from the spindle. Replace the O-ring (the old one can be cut off with a utility knife), stem washer, and stem screw, coating the new items with plumber's heatproof grease. Sometimes, you'll find packing string instead of an O-ring; in that case, wind new packing string in its place.

Before reassembling the faucet, check the valve seat. If it feels rough, use a seat wrench to remove it and replace it with a new one. If it can't be removed (some can't), smooth it instead by rotating a valve seat cutter (available at home centers) clockwise within the seat for several turns.

Ball Faucets

For a dripping faucet, try a quick fix by tightening the faucet cap with groove-joint pliers. If this doesn't work, the culprit is probably the ball, valve seats, or springs. For leaks around the base, replace the O-rings. Frankly, once you have the faucet apart, it's easy (and not expensive) to replace all of these items at once.

Use an Allen wrench to undo the setscrew on the handle, and take off the handle. Use groove-joint pliers to unscrew the faucet cap. You'll see the stem of the ball sticking up through the cam and cam washer. Remove the cam and washer, and then the ball. If the ball is worn, buy a new metal one (longer lasting than plastic). With the ball removed, the valve seats and springs are accessible. Pry them out with a small screwdriver or awl.

Lift off the spout (you may need to twist it while pulling up). Cut off the old O-rings with a utility knife and install new ones, first coating the new ones with plumber's heatproof grease. Reassemble the faucet with new valve seats, springs, and cam washer. When you're placing the cam in position, look for the slot on the faucet that matches the tab on the cam. Turn the faucet on, and then restore the water supply slowly to check for leaks. If leaks occur, reseat the ball and tighten the faucet cap and screw as needed (don't overtighten).

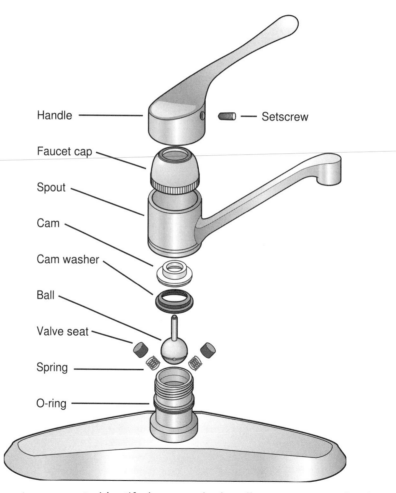

▲ Ball faucets are easy to identify, because the handle rotates around a dome-shaped faucet cap to control both water flow and temperature.

Cartridge Faucets

Replace the O-rings to fix leaks at the base of a cartridge faucet; replace the cartridge to fix dripping spouts. First, pry up the access cap so that you can remove the screw in the handle, and then the handle. If there's no access cap, look for a clip and an Allen screw on the handle; remove both.

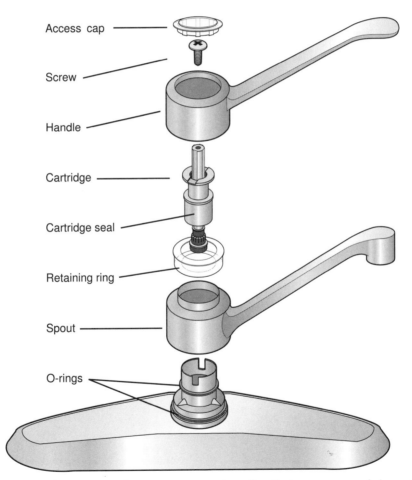

▲ Cartridge faucets may have one or two handles that move up and down to control the water flow.

Use groove-joint pliers to remove the retaining nut or ring combination, holding steady the assembly below it with an adjustable wrench. Look for a retaining clip, which may or may not be holding the cartridge in place, and note the position of the cartridge. Carefully pull the cartridge straight up and out, using groove-joint pliers. Buy a replacement cartridge to match, and insert it in the same position.

At this point, to replace the O-rings at the base of the faucet, lift the spout up and off. Cut off the old O-rings with a utility knife. Replace them, first coating the new O-rings with plumber's heatproof grease. Replace each piece of the faucet, and turn on the water slowly to check for leaks. If leaks occur, go back and tighten the nuts and screws slightly (don't overtighten).

Disk Faucets

Disk faucets rarely need repair, and when they do, it's usually to clean or replace their neoprene seals or to clean the openings in their ceramic disks. First, remove the setscrew in the handle so that you can lift off the handle and the escutcheon cap. This allows you to unscrew the mounting screws and lift out the cylinder that contains the ceramic disks; make sure to note the cylinder position so that you can replace it the same way. Pry out the neoprene seals from the openings in the disks, being careful not to scratch the disks.

Clean the seals, the disk openings, and the water inlets in the faucet body with a dish scrubber that's safe for ceramic surfaces (i.e., not steel wool). Reassemble the faucet, and turn it to its "on" position. Because the disks can crack if water surges against them too suddenly, turn on the water supply *very* slowly. If the faucet's still leaking, install a new cylinder, again noting the position of the old cylinder so that you can match it.

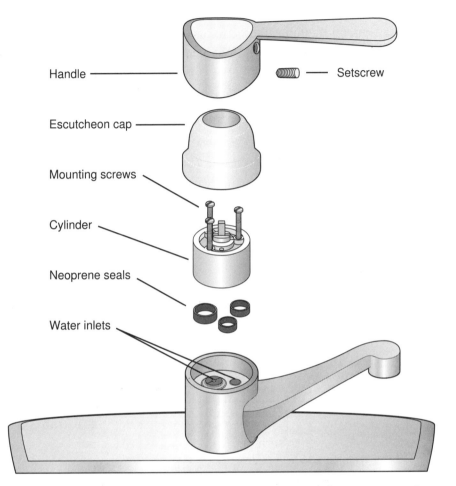

Handle — Setscrew

Escutcheon cap

Mounting screws

Cylinder

Neoprene seals

Water inlets

▲ Disk faucets have a single handle that moves up and down to control water flow.

Replacing Faucets

Sometimes—especially if the faucet is older—it's easier and faster to replace the faucet rather than repair it. To choose a replacement faucet, first measure the distance between the centers of the two holes where the faucet pipes (the tailpieces) come down through the counter below the sink, and the diameter of the two holes. You'll need to buy a faucet that matches these measurements.

Check to see if the new faucet comes with supply tubes; if not, buy them. Also check for shutoff valves on the old supply tubes—if there aren't any, now's the right time to install them (see the previous section).

Removing the Old Faucet

Label the water supply so that you'll know which pipe carries hot and cold later on (identify the hot-water supply by running hot water—the pipe will warm up); then shut off the water supply to the faucets, either at the individual shutoff valves or the house supply.

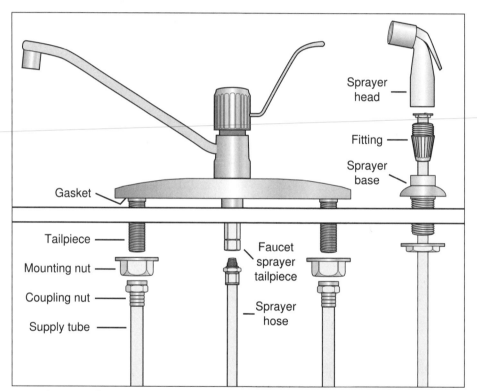

▲ Replacing a faucet is a fairly easy fix-it task. Adjustable wrenches and a putty knife will be your most important tools, along with penetrating oil and possibly a hacksaw or pipe cutter if you need to cut the old supply tubes away.

The toughest part of the installation will likely be removing the old supply tubes, which will have mounting and coupling nuts that are often corroded. A shot of penetrating oil should help loosen them, but you can also cut them off. Pull up the old faucet, sliding a putty knife between the faucet and the sink to loosen the old sealing putty if necessary. Clean the sink of any remaining putty.

Installing the New Faucet

Read the installation instructions for the new faucet, and test-fit the faucet and supply tubes by holding them in the existing holes. If all is okay, remove them, and put the gasket (contained in most new faucet kits) on the bottom of the faucet so that it will sit between the faucet and the sink. If there's no gasket, or the sink is uneven, line the bottom edge of the new faucet or gasket with silicone caulking. Insert the faucet so that the tailpieces go through the holes and the faucet is lined up in position on the sink, and press firmly. Clean up any caulking that squeezes out from under the faucet.

If the faucet has supply tubes attached, the faucet is held against the sink with a gasket, retainer ring, and a locknut that you need to place over the threaded tailpiece. Then, attach the supply tubes to the shutoff valves, matching the hot and cold water tap supply tubes to the pipes that you labeled as hot and cold.

If the faucet doesn't have supply tubes attached, it's held against the sink with a friction washer that's placed over each tailpiece, followed by a mounting nut. The supply tubes are then attached to the tailpieces with their preinstalled coupling nuts, and to the shutoff valves, matching hot tap to hot supply, and cold tap to cold supply.

Drain Stoppers and Strainers

The kindest thing you can do for drain stoppers—and for your drains—is to clean them regularly. It's amazing how quickly hair and soap scum can clog them, causing slow-draining sinks and tubs, and contributing to drain clogs down the pipes. Adjusting and replacing the stoppers is also an easy fix-it job.

Strainers

If a strainer that's sealed to the sink with caulking is leaking, first unscrew the slip nut on the drainpipe, and then the locknut, that connects the drainpipe to the strainer. This will expose any gaskets that may need to be replaced and will also allow you to remove the strainer from the sink (use a utility knife to break the strainer's seal if necessary).

Clean off any old putty or caulking where the strainer met the sink, dry the area, and lay a new bead of silicone caulking. Press the strainer into place, and then replace the gaskets (use new ones) and the nuts in the reverse order from how you removed them.

Shower and tub drain strainers can often be removed using long-nose pliers. Open the pliers so that the arms grip the strainer, and twist counterclockwise. Clean out the strainer and the drain, and reinsert the strainer, turning clockwise to seal it tightly.

Pull-Up/Push-Down Stoppers

To remove a pull-up stopper in a sink or tub drain, turn the knob on the stopper counterclockwise to remove it. This will reveal a screw on the stopper itself, which you can then turn to remove the entire stopper. A small screwdriver will help you remove any debris in the drain.

If the stopper is no longer sealing, the gasket that sits between the stopper and the drain may be failing, or the stopper mechanism may be wearing. Take the stopper to your home center, and—especially if you can't buy a new gasket for it—buy a replacement to match. Screw the stopper back into the drain, and then attach the knob to the stopper.

Pop-Up Sink Stoppers

A sink stopper operated at the faucet is often referred to as a pop-up sink stopper. Take a look at the mechanism under the sink that connects the pop-up handle at the faucet with the stopper under the sink. Basically, you're looking at a perforated strap (the clevis strap) that runs down from the handle and connects to a rod (the pivot rod) that operates the stopper.

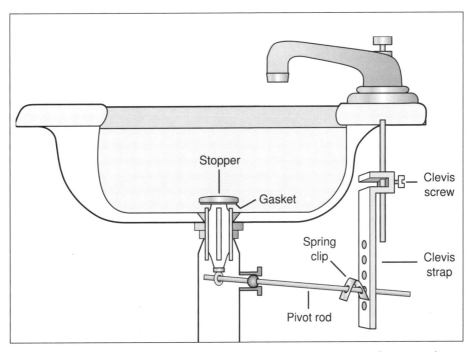

Stopper

Gasket

Clevis screw

Spring clip

Clevis strap

Pivot rod

▲ The names of a pop-up sink stopper's components may sound strange, but once you see how they connect to each other, solving stopper problems becomes much easier.

To remove the stopper to clean it out, pull the stopper handle up to raise the stopper. Feel for the retaining nut on the pivot rod where the rod enters the drainpipe. Unscrew it, and pull the rod out of the drainpipe. Pull the stopper up out of the drain, and clean the stopper and the drain (depending on how the stopper connects to the pivot rod, you may need to twist the stopper counterclockwise as you lift it).

Check the stopper's gasket, and replace it if it's worn or damaged. Replace the stopper in the drain, lining it up so that the pivot rod will reinsert into it. Tighten the retaining nut.

To fix a pop-up sink stopper:

- If the stopper won't stay up when you pull up on the handle, or there's water leaking from the retaining nut, tighten or replace the retaining nut.
- If the stopper isn't seating correctly in the drain, undo the clevis

screw, push the stopper into the right position in the drain, and tighten the clevis screw in a higher position on the lift rod.

- To raise the stopper so that it allows water to drain more quickly, adjust the clevis screw so that it's in a lower position on the lift rod.
- If adjusting the clevis screw doesn't work, adjust the pivot rod position: Pinch the spring clip that holds the rod in place so that you can remove it from its existing hole in the clevis strap and place it in either a higher or lower hole.

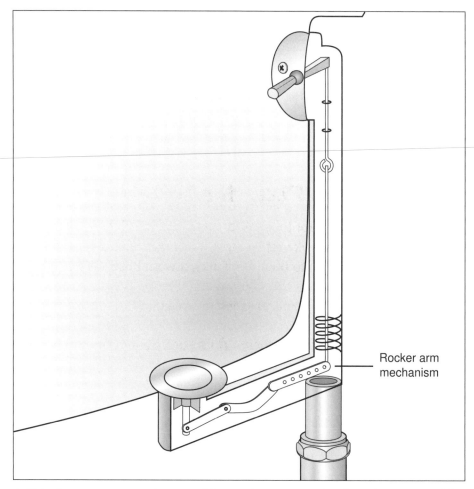

Rocker arm mechanism

▲ This shows a pop-up stopper with a rocker arm mechanism. A stopper with a plunger would connect to a plunger instead of the rocker arm spring.

Pop-Up Tub Stoppers

Pop-up tub stoppers (that usually have the stopper handle on the tub overflow plate) work by dropping either a plunger mechanism down behind the overflow plate that prevents the water from draining out, or a rocker arm mechanism that operates a stopper in the tub drain. Both mechanisms can be cleaned and adjusted in a similar way.

First, unscrew the overflow plate. Carefully pull the plate away from the tub; the stopper mechanism will come with it. Remove any debris from the mechanism, and scrub it clean with a toothbrush. For a rocker arm mechanism, carefully pull the stopper out of the drain, and clean it, too.

If the stopper or plunger isn't sealing the drain properly, adjust the mechanism by unscrewing the adjusting nut on the lift rod and sliding the link up so that the mechanism is shorter. Alternatively, if the stopper or plunger doesn't reach high enough to let the water drain properly, slide the link down so that the mechanism becomes longer.

Not-So-Quick Fixes for Toilets

If the quick fixes for toilet problems in Chapter 3 didn't work, you'll need not-so-quick fixes, like replacing a worn inlet valve assembly (which brings the water into the toilet tank), a worn flush valve assembly (which takes the water from the tank into the bowl), or—to fix a leak between the floor and the toilet—reseating the toilet.

Replacing an Inlet Valve Assembly

Shut off the water supply to the toilet, and drain the tank by flushing it and soaking up any remaining water with towels or rags. Have rags handy for mopping up the water that will spill out when you remove the supply tube from the toilet tank.

Undo the supply tube mounting nut, which is found on the water supply tube close to the tank (see the toilet illustration on page 30). Hold the old inlet valve assembly, and use pliers or an adjustable wrench to loosen the locknut directly under the toilet tank. Remove the nut and pull out the assembly.

It's a good idea to replace the old assembly with the same kind—either float arm or float cup—to ensure there'll be sufficient room in the tank for the new assembly. You basically insert the new assembly by reversing the process, but first read the new assembly's instructions, and place any required seals or washers on the bottom of the inlet assembly where it meets the toilet tank and the water supply tube.

Hand-tighten the locknut that holds the inlet assembly in place, holding the inlet assembly as you do so. Place the bowl-refill tube in the overflow pipe. Reconnect the supply tube and the mounting nut, tighten the nuts just past hand-strength, and restore the water supply, checking for leaks and for the tank water level. Gently tighten the nuts to stop leaks. To adjust the water level, see Chapter 3.

Replacing a Flush Valve Assembly

If you need to replace the flush valve assembly (to stop a toilet from running continuously, for example, when quick fixes to the flapper haven't worked), remove the supply tube from the toilet tank, as described in the previous section, and disconnect the toilet handle from the flush assembly. Unscrew the mounting bolts that hold the toilet tank to the bowl, and remove the tank. You need to access the spud nut that connects to the flush valve assembly on the bottom of the tank. To do this, turn the tank over, or rest it securely on a raised platform so that you can reach under it to unscrew the spud nut (you may need to hold the old flush assembly in place while you turn the spud nut), and remove the old flush assembly.

If the new flush assembly came with a cone washer that fits over the threads on the bottom of the assembly, insert it so that the washer's beveled edge faces the bottom of the assembly (so that it fits against the toilet tank). Place the flush assembly in the tank so that its threaded bottom sits in the hole in the tank. Screw the spud nut over the washer from under the tank. You should also place a new spud washer, or soft seal, over the bottom of the assembly to line the surfaces where the toilet tank and toilet bowl meet.

Reconnect the inlet valve assembly, overflow pipe, toilet handle, and flapper as required, restore the water supply, and check for leaks.

Reseating a Toilet

If the toilet is leaking where the base meets the floor, you need to replace the wax seal on the bottom of the toilet bowl. Shut off the water supply, remove the water from the tank by flushing several times and mopping up any remaining water, and then disconnect the supply tube from the toilet tank (as detailed previously). Remove water from the toilet bowl by bailing and sponging.

Unscrew the bolts that connect the toilet tank to the bowl, and remove the tank. Set it somewhere safe, where it can't be damaged. Remove the toilet seat. Look for the bolts that fasten the toilet to the floor. Their plastic covers can be pried up with a flat-bladed screwdriver, but be careful not to scratch the toilet base. Undo the nuts and washers from the bolts.

ESSENTIAL

Have rags handy so that you can mop up any water that spills. Water spilling from the toilet drain may not be clean; use rubber gloves when you're mopping it up, and throw out the rags afterward. A rag stuffed in the drain will help block any odors or gases from escaping into the bathroom.

Stand over the toilet bowl and gently rock it back and forth to loosen it until you can lift it up from the bolts and lay it upside down or on its side so that you can work on it easily (have a helper nearby, as toilets are heavy and easily cracked).

You'll now be able to see the old wax seal on the toilet base. Use a putty knife to remove it, and place a new wax seal over the opening in the toilet base. Many seals come with a sleeve that holds them in place; it needs to face away from the toilet. Run silicone caulking around the bottom edge of the toilet.

With your helper, lift the toilet back into place over the bolts and press it down, rocking it back and forth a little to seat the seal properly. Reinstall the washers and nuts over the toilet base bolts and replace the decorative covers.

Place a new spud washer, or soft seal, over the assembly where the toilet tank connects with the toilet bowl, place the tank on the bowl, and tighten the tank mounting screws. Reconnect the supply tube, restore the water supply, and check for leaks. Replace the toilet seat.

Now that basic plumbing, from faucets through to toilets, is taken care of, there's another major house system to tackle: electricity. Although most electrical wiring should be handled by a licensed electrician (and in some areas, must be done that way by code), there are some simple electrical tasks that you can handle yourself, revealed in Chapter 19.

Chapter 19

Easy Electricity

In this chapter, you'll learn how to recognize signs that there's a problem with your home's electrical system, how to test outlets and switches, and how to handle very basic electrical fix-it jobs. Because of the risk of electrical shock and fire, everything else should be referred to an electrician. You also need to check local building codes before attempting any electrical fix-its, because some areas require all electrical work to be done by a qualified professional.

Problem Signs

Although the electrical system won't always warn you when there's a problem with it, there are some easily recognizable warning signals. If you notice any of them, call in a licensed electrician to trace and solve the problem(s).

Warning signs at the house's main electrical panel include moisture, rust, frayed wiring, scorch marks, hot fuses or circuit breakers, melted or damaged insulation, or other damage. They also include aluminum wiring (the cables may be marked with an "AL"), which was used in the 1960s and 1970s but no longer meets building codes because of its fire risk. Old knob-and-tube wiring, and older main service panels that no longer meet code requirements, should also be replaced.

Other problem signs include dimming lights, switch or outlet cover plates that are warm to the touch, outlets or switches that spark, arc, smoke, or sizzle, black sootlike marks on cover plates, circuits that trip or fuses that blow frequently, plugs that are loose in outlets, and main electrical panels that have fuses or circuit breakers with higher amperages than the circuits should support.

ALERT!

The safest way to handle an outlet, appliance, or switch that starts to smoke is to shut off the power to that circuit on the house's main electrical panel. If there's any doubt as to which circuit, shut off the power to the entire house (see Chapter 2). Evacuate the house and call the fire department.

Safety Reminders

When you're working at the house's main electrical panel, protect yourself from receiving a shock:

*   Stand on a dry surface.
*   Wear rubber-soled shoes.
*   Don't touch anything metal, including plumbing pipes or appliances, while touching the electrical panel.

- Use one hand to operate the panel; keep the other hand by your side.
- Use wooden or plastic ladders, not metal ones.

Extension cords can be handy, but handle them with care. They carry a maximum capacity in watts that's printed on the cable. Electrical appliances such as lawnmowers are also marked with the wattage that they need to draw. If the wattage exceeds the cord's capacity, buy a heavier-duty cord. Do not use extension cords as a substitute for permanent wiring, don't run them under rugs (they could overheat), and don't secure them with metal staples or nails. Replace them if they're frayed or cracked.

Electrical outlets are designed to fit specific plugs: two-prong polarized (with one blade larger than the other); or three-prong, for example. Never alter a plug to fit an outlet that it's not designed for.

Lamps should have maximum wattages clearly marked on them; never use a bulb that exceeds the maximum. Since halogen lamps in particular can become very hot, keep them three feet away from soft furnishings such as curtains or beds.

When buying electrical components—from extension cords to appliances—ensure that they carry the UL sign, showing that they've met safety standards.

Wire Tips

Although you can't guarantee which wires will be live, black or red wires generally are. White wires are often neutral, but not always, especially if they're marked with black or red paint or tape. Green or bare copper wires are ground wires.

When you're replacing a switch or outlet, the insulation that covers the wires will need to be trimmed to reveal about a ½ to ¾ inch of bare, clean wire at the end. Although you can use long-nose pliers to strip the insulation off the wire, a "multipurpose" or "combination" tool that clamps together to form holes to fit various wire diameters (gauges) is designed for this. Close the tool over the wire in the appropriate wire-gauge hole, twist the tool around to cut the insulation, and pull the tool toward the end of the wire to strip off the insulation.

Most switches and outlets come with two options for connecting the wires: screws around which you bend the wire (trim ¾ inch of insulation from the wire's end, and bend the end into a hook that fits over the screw; then tighten the screw down around the wire); or holes into which you push the wire (trim ½ inch of insulation from the wire's end, and push the wire into the hole). Although the push-in wire holes are acceptable by most codes, the Consumer Product Safety Commission suggests that these can loosen and overheat. Check the cover plates on these switches and outlets regularly to see if they're warm to the touch (if they are, replace them, and use the screws instead of the push-in holes). Better yet, use the screws in the first place.

If you need to remove wires from push-in holes, use a small flat-bladed screwdriver to press the metal tab down in the slot beside the hole. This should release the wire. If it doesn't, you'll have to cut off the wire as close as possible to the outlet or switch.

When replacing outlets and switches, buy replacements with the same voltage and amp markings as the old ones. If in doubt, remove the old outlet or switch, and take it to your home center.

Your Home's Electrical Circuits

The electrical circuits that serve your home are controlled from the main control panel (see Chapter 2). The panel uses some version of fuses, cartridges, or circuit breakers to sense a problem on the individual circuits. When a problem is detected, the fuse will blow or the breaker will trip, shutting down the electricity to the circuit.

Testing Circuits

The first switch that you need to test is the main circuit shutoff. Not all electrical panels have a shutoff for the entire house, but if they do, it will be either a large switch (for circuit breakers) or a lever (for fuses) on the main electrical panel. Turn on the lights throughout the house, and flip the switch or lever to the "off" position. If the lights don't go out, call an electrician to repair the panel. To test individual electrical components, such as outlets, switches, fuses, and appliances, you'll need several fairly inexpensive electrical testers.

Continuity Testers

A continuity tester looks like a pen, with a long metal probe on one end and a wire with a metal clip on the other end, and can be used to test switches to make sure that they form a complete circuit. It should be used only on circuits with the power turned off, *not* on live circuits. Once you've shut off the power, remove the switch and place the probe on one screw terminal and the clip on the other. If the tester illuminates, it means that the switch's internal circuit is complete and working.

Neon Circuit Testers

A neon circuit tester has a narrow body containing a light that is connected to two wires with short metal probes at their ends, protected by two insulated grips. To check to see if an outlet is working, hold the tester by its grips, and place the probes into the vertical slots in one of the outlets (the power to the outlet needs to be on). The light on the neon tester will light up if all is well. To check whether a three-pronged outlet is properly grounded, place one probe into the third slot on the outlet and one probe into either of the vertical slots. If one of the vertical slots lights up the neon tester, the circuit is properly grounded.

To test a switch with a neon tester, turn off the power supply to the switch, remove the cover plate screw and the screws that hold the switch to the wall, and gently pull the switch out of its metal box. Once the switch is free of the metal box, turn the circuit back on. Hold the neon tester only by its insulated grips, and touch one probe to the live (black or red) wire or screw terminal and one probe to a neutral (white) wire or screw terminal, or, if the box is grounded with a third (copper or green) wire, to the metal box itself. The light on the neon tester will light up if power is flowing through the switch.

Multimeter

A multimeter has two wires with insulated grips and short metal probes, just like a neon tester, but it has a meter with a readout attached that allows you to check circuits within appliances and batteries. The multimeter's instructions will give you specific readings to look for, but as a rule, you can test the plug on an appliance by unplugging the appliance, turning it to "on," setting the meter to its lowest range, and touching a probe to each of the plug's blades. A multimeter reading of zero signals a problem with the circuit.

Mapping Your Home's Circuits

Mapping which circuit operates which switches and outlets in your home is a time-consuming and tedious task, but it's necessary. Find a helper and a couple of hours, and get to work.

First, switch on all the lights in the house, and plug radios or lamps into all the electrical outlets that don't already have something plugged into them, and turn them on, too. Then, switch off the first circuit breaker or remove the first fuse or cartridge. Whatever appliance or light shuts off is operated on that circuit. Label the electrical panel with what it operates, and draw a map of the house with that circuit's operation clearly marked.

Keep in mind that the two outlets on a single electrical outlet box could be on two different circuits, and that circuits often run into different rooms. Heavy electricity users such as stoves and clothes dryers will usually have their own dedicated circuit.

Resetting Circuit Breakers

When they trip, circuit breaker switches may move all the way to "off" or only part of the way. To reset them, push the circuit breaker switch all the way to "off" before moving it back to "on." To make sure that circuit breakers remain operational, switch them to "off" and back to "on" at least once a year. (This helps prevent the switches from seizing up.)

Replacing Fuses

If your house has fuses, a blown fuse will give you a clue as to the reason it blew. If its glass window is cloudy, the problem was a short circuit. If the glass is clear and you can see a break in the metal filament inside it, the problem was an overloaded circuit. Either way, a blown fuse must be replaced.

Check the electrical panel to verify that the old fuse was the correct amperage, and replace it with a fuse of the same amperage. Although a variety of fuses is available, the old fuse can usually be screwed out, and the new fuse screwed in. Hold the fuse by its bottom only. If you have any doubt, ask an electrician or your home center staff.

For cartridge-type fuses, you may need to first remove the block that contains the cartridges by pulling it out by its handle. Use a tool called a cartridge puller to remove the individual fuses from within the block, or— if there's no block—from within the electrical panel itself. To determine which fuse needs to be replaced, touch the clip and the probe of a continuity tester to opposite ends of the fuse. If the tester lights up, the fuse is fine; if not, it needs to be replaced.

ALERT!

Never install a fuse with a higher amperage than is recommended for the circuit. The whole point of the fuse is to trip the circuit when too much electricity is being drawn. A higher amperage will allow a dangerous electricity draw that could lead to a fire.

Frequently Tripped or Blown Circuits

If a fuse or circuit breaker needs to be replaced or reset frequently, you need to find out why. It may be as simple as using too many appliances on one circuit. Move some of the appliances to a different circuit to see if that solves the problem, or turn on the switches and appliances one by one until the circuit trips again.

If this doesn't solve the problem, there may be a fault with the electrical panel or the wiring, in which case you should call an electrician. If, however, you find that the circuit to which you moved some of the appliances is now tripping, faulty wiring within one of the appliances or a cord could be the problem. Narrow it down by using the appliances one by one. Once you identify the culprit, have it fixed or replaced.

Replacing Light Switches

Frequently used switches may wear out, or their connections may loosen over time. It's easy and inexpensive to replace the switch, but you need to know what you're replacing. The most common switches are single pole, where an outlet light fixture is operated by a single switch, and three-way, which allow an outlet or fixture to be operated from two different switches.

Single-Pole Switches

Shut off the circuit breaker or remove the fuse that operates the circuit that the switch is on. Put a sign on the panel to let people know that you're working on the circuit and that they must not restore power to it.

Remove the switch cover plate and the two mounting screws that hold the switch itself to the wall. Carefully pull out the switch. Use a neon circuit tester (place one probe against the metal wall box, and the other probe against each of the switch's screw terminals in turn) to ensure that the power is in fact off (the light should not illuminate). If the power is still flowing to the circuit, shut it off at the main electrical panel (you may have switched off the wrong circuit).

Examine how the switch is wired. There should be two wires connected to the switch, both of which will be live when the switch is on, regardless of their color. You may also have a third wire—a "ground" (green or bare copper wire). Depending on where the switch is located on the circuit, you may see other wires connected together with plastic marrettes, or connectors. Of the wires that are connected to the switch itself, one wire will be connected to the brass screw or the push-in hole closest to the brass screw. The other wire will be connected to the silver screw or the push-in hole closest to it. If there's a ground wire, it should be connected to a green ground screw on the metal wall box or on the switch.

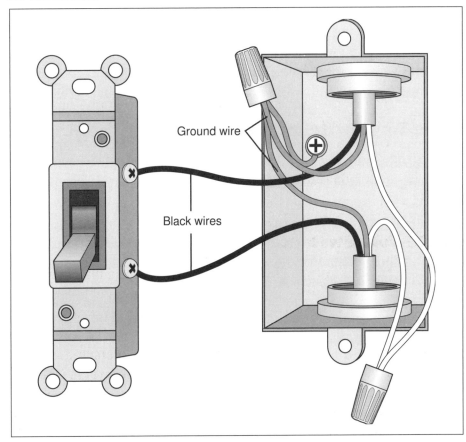

Ground wire

Black wires

▲ This single-pole switch has two wires (both live) and a ground wire.

Remove the wires from either the screws or the push-in holes of the old switch. (If the ground wire is connected to the metal wall box, it doesn't need to be removed.) Reconnect the wires to the new switch: First, cut as little as possible off the end of the wires to provide you with clean, undamaged wires for the connection. Then, strip the insulation from the last ½ to ¾ inch of the wire and connect the wires to the screw terminals or the push-in holes. The two live wires can be connected to either of the screw terminals, but a ground wire must be connected to the green screw (on the switch or the metal box). Tighten the screw terminals down even if you're not using them to connect the wires—there's less chance of them accidentally touching the metal wall box if they're screwed down.

Ensure the switch is the right way up, and push it gently into the box. Snug up the mounting screws, and replace the cover plate so that it's flush against the switch. Turn the power back on, and check the switch's operation.

Three-Way Switches

Shut off the circuit breaker or remove the fuse that operates the circuit that the switch is on. Put a sign on the panel to let people know that you're working on the circuit, and that they must not restore power to it.

Three-way switches are replaced in the same way as single-pole switches, except that there will be more wires and more screw terminals. There'll be a dark-colored common screw terminal, which holds the black wire; two traveler screw terminals, which hold one each of the red or white wires; and possibly a ground (green) wire connected to the green screw on the switch or the box.

FACT

If at any point you encounter complicated wiring or you're unsure how to proceed, stop what you're doing and call in an electrician. Electricity isn't worth taking risks over.

To install the new switch, first label the black wire that's attached to the old switch's common screw terminal before removing the wires from the switch. Reconnect the black wire to the new switch's common screw terminal. The other two wires can be removed and attached to either of the traveler screw terminals. The green (ground) wire is attached to the green screw on the switch or the metal wall box.

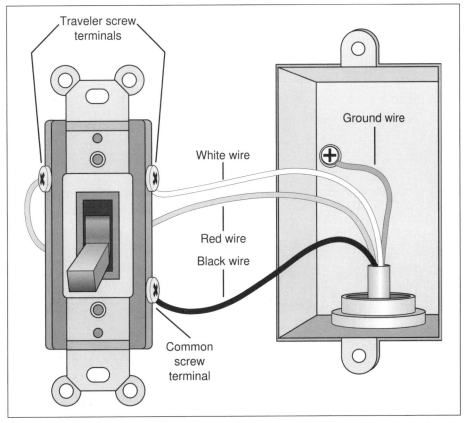

▲ This three-way switch has wires attached to its common screw terminal and to its two traveler screw terminals, plus a ground wire.

Replacing Electrical Outlets

Shut off the circuit breaker or remove the fuse that operates the circuit that the outlet is on. (Remember that one outlet box could be on two different circuits; shut off both.) Put a sign on the panel to let people know that you're working on the circuit(s), and that they must not restore power to them. Plug in a lamp or radio to both of the plug-ins. If it still operates in either of the plug-ins, return to the main electrical panel to shut off the right circuit.

Once the power is off, remove the outlet cover plate and the two mounting screws that hold the outlet to the wall. Carefully pull out the outlet, and label the wires that lead to the screw terminals or push-in holes. The live (black) wire goes to the brass screw; the neutral (white) wire goes to the silver screw; and the bare copper or green (ground) wire goes to the green screw either on the outlet or in the metal wall box. Once you've labeled the wires, remove the wires from the outlet.

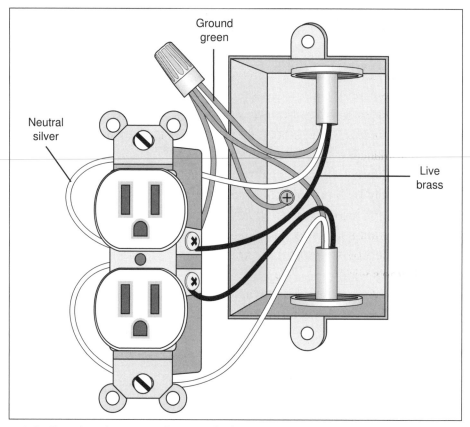

Ground green

Neutral silver

Live brass

▲ Labeling the wires according to which screws they attach to on the old outlet is a more reliable guide for connecting them to the new outlet than relying on the color of the wires.

Using a new outlet that matches the old outlet's amp and voltage rating (take the old outlet to the home center if you need help identifying these), reconnect the wires. Tighten down the screw terminals. Gently push the outlet back into the box. Screw the outlet to the wall with the two mounting screws, and screw the cover plate over the outlet so that the two sit flush together. Restore the power, and use a neon circuit tester in both of the plug-ins, in turn, to check that both are working and properly grounded.

Ground Fault Circuit Interrupters

A ground fault circuit interrupter (GFCI) outlet offers additional antishock protection wherever water is present: in bathrooms, kitchens, utility rooms, and exterior outlets. They work by detecting the electrical current flowing into and out of the switch. The flow should be the same. If it's not, the current has been somehow diverted unsafely, and the outlet automatically shuts off the power.

Although they're relatively straightforward to install, you may run into difficulty because of your house's wiring—there may not, for example, be a ground wire in the box. For this reason, and since GFCI outlets are an important safety measure that need to be installed correctly, have them installed by a licensed electrician who can deal with the specifics of your home's wiring.

Test your GFCI outlets at least monthly by plugging a radio or lamp into the outlet and turning them on. Press the test button (often red, or marked with a "T"); the radio or lamp should turn off. It should turn on again when you press the reset button (often black, or marked with an "R"). Call an electrician if the buttons aren't working properly.

Replacing Plugs

When plugs become cracked or loose, or their prongs are damaged, it's time to replace them. Choose a replacement plug that's similar to the old one: round-cord plugs for heavier-duty round cords, and flat-cord plugs for (you guessed it) lighter-duty flat cords.

Flat-Cord Plugs

There's a quick fix for flat-cord plugs, called a quick-connect plug. Cut the old plug off the cord. Squeeze the new quick-connect plug's prongs together, and pull out its inner portion. Thread the old cord through the back of the new plug. Spread the prongs on the inner portion of the plug apart so that you can push the cord into the back of it. Squeeze the prongs together again, and push the inner portion of the plug back into the plug itself. You're done!

Round-Cord Plugs

These are a little more difficult than quick-connect plugs, but still an easy fix. Cut the old plug off the cord, and strip about 1 inch of the outer insulation and ¾ inch of the insulation that covers the two or three individual wires within the outer insulation. Pry off the new plug's cover plate to expose the screw terminals inside the plug. (Some plugs come in two pieces that screw together. If this is the case, you'll need to take the two pieces apart to expose the screw terminals.) Thread the old cord through the back of the new plug.

Tie the black and white wires together using an Underwriters' knot. An Underwriters' knot is a looped knot tied in two wires that helps prevent them from slipping apart and is a safety measure. Make a loop in each wire, pass the other wire through that loop, and pull to tighten, as illustrated.

Use long-nose pliers to form hooks in the exposed copper ends of the wires. Then, connect the wires: black wire to brass screw; white wire to silver screw; and green wire (if present) to the green, or ground, screw. The copper parts of the wires must not touch each other. Tighten down the screws and put the plug's cover plate back on. Tighten the screws on the cord clamp that many round-cord plugs have at their back.

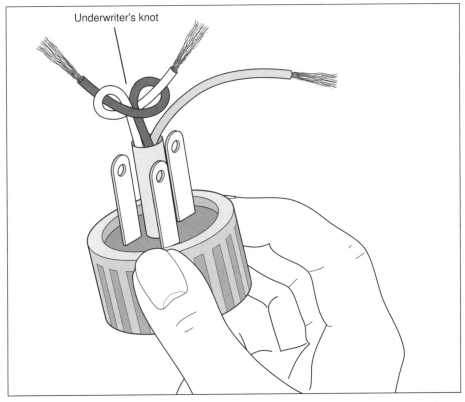

▲ An Underwriters' knot is a safety technique used when wiring lamps and plugs to help the wires stay in place.

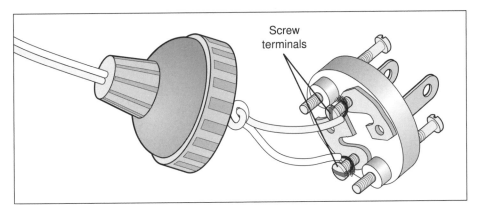

▲ Although plug design may vary, connecting the plug to the cord is simply a matter of attaching each wire to the plug's screw terminals.

Lamps and Lights

Replacing a wall or ceiling light is usually a cosmetic choice. Rewiring a table or standing lamp, on the other hand, means that you can reuse a favorite lamp while replacing its worn components. Both fix-it tasks are relatively straightforward.

Rewiring a Lamp

Unplug the lamp. Take off the shade, the bulb, and the framework that holds the shade in place. The bulb socket is protected with an outer casing and an insulating sleeve. Remove the outer casing by either pressing it (where it says "press") or undoing the screws that are holding it in place, and lifting it off. Slide off the insulating sleeve.

You'll now be able to see the screw terminals that hold the wires to the socket. Loosen them enough that you can remove the wires and take off the socket. Untie or cut off the Underwriters' knot that sits below the socket (or remove whatever mechanism is holding the wires in place there). Remove any hardware, such as the base of the shade framework, that's held in place under the socket.

Cut the plug off the old cord that leads through the base of the lamp. Twist the ends of the old cord securely to the ends of the new cord, and pull the old cord up through the lamp. Untwist the cords.

ESSENTIAL

If a new bulb doesn't work in an old lamp, try cleaning the socket. Unplug the lamp, and use a flat-bladed screwdriver to rub off any dirt that has accumulated in the socket. Also pry up the tab in the bottom of the socket so that it meets the bulb's base more firmly.

You'll need to work with about 3 inches of the new cord. Split it apart, and remove the insulation from the last ¾ inch of each wire. Replace any hardware that sits under the socket. Tie an Underwriters' knot in the wire, and hook the ends of the wire under the screw terminals of a new socket (the silver wire goes onto the silver screw). Slide the new insulating sleeve and outer casing back over the socket, and reattach the lamp's shade framework, bulb, and shade. Plug the lamp in, and test its operation.

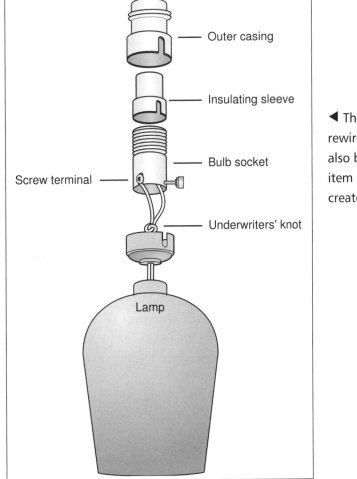

Outer casing

Insulating sleeve

Bulb socket

Screw terminal

Underwriters' knot

Lamp

◀ The method used to rewire an old lamp can also be used to wire an item such as a vase to create a new lamp.

Replacing a Light Fixture

First, shut off the power to the circuit that operates the wall or ceiling light. Check that it's off by trying the switch. (If the light comes on, shut off the correct circuit.) Leave the switch in the "off" position.

Remove the light shade so that you can see how the fixture is screwed to the ceiling or wall. Unscrew the fixture as needed. When you pull it away from the ceiling or wall, you'll be able to see the wires connecting to it. There's usually a black wire and a white wire, either leading directly from the ceiling to the fixture or connected along that path with a plastic marrette, or connector. There may also be a ground, or green, wire attached to a ground screw in the metal box or on the metal mounting strap. If you need to remove it to take off the light, be sure to reattach it when you install the new light.

If there are connectors involved, unscrew them without touching any part of the bare wires that are twisted together inside the connector. If not, remove the wires from the light fixture. Use a neon tester to double-check that the circuit isn't live: Holding the tester's insulated grips, hold one probe against the exposed black wire and the other probe against the exposed white wire. Repeat, holding the probes against the bare black wire and the metal box inside the wall or ceiling that the wires come through. If the tester illuminates, there's still power going through the wires, and you need to find a way to shut if off (possibly by shutting off the entire house's power supply).

Once you know the power is off, untwist the wires so that you can take off the light completely, if you haven't already done so. To install the new light using connectors, reverse the process. Twist the wires from the fixture and the ceiling together (black to black, and white to white), and cover them with a marrette, or connector. If the new light doesn't have wires leading from it, it will have screw terminals, much like a switch or outlet. Hook the black wire over the brass screw, and the white wire over the silver screw. Screw the new light's base to the wall or ceiling, pushing the wires into the metal box as you do so, and install the glass or shade.

You now know how to recognize when all is not well with your electrical system, and how to handle simple repairs to switches, outlets, and lamps. The subject of Chapter 20, your heating, ventilating, and cooling system, covers similar ground: basic maintenance tasks. These will extend the operating life of your systems, but won't cross the line into territory that only qualified professionals should be working in. Ⓔ

Chapter 20

HVAC Systems

Aside from some essential maintenance techniques, heating, ventilating, and air-conditioning systems are not
fix-it territory. In fact, you should have them
cleaned and serviced annually by qualified
professionals not just to keep them in top
working order, but as a safety measure as
well. Good technicians will be able to tell
you if you need to oil any motors regularly,
what other routine maintenance tasks you
need and how to do them, and when it's
time to replace a system.

Forced-Air Furnace Maintenance

If you're not familiar with your furnace's operation, your best course of action is to find the owner's manual and read it—but don't stop there. During its annual servicing (done either at the end of or just before the heating or cooling season), have the technician explain the furnace's operation to you, any regular maintenance (such as changing filters and cleaning humidifiers) that you need to perform, and emergency procedures (how to recognize when something's wrong, how to shut off the furnace, and how to restart it).

FACT

If you don't have an owner's manual for the furnace, contact the manufacturer or installation company (usually marked on a label on the furnace) to obtain one for your model. Furnace repair services may also be able to help you out.

Forced-air furnaces can be fueled by gas, oil, or electricity, and often have an electrical supply even when the main fuel is gas or oil. Older furnaces will have a pilot light that stays lit all the time, while newer (higher efficiency) furnaces will have an electronic pilot light igniter that lights only when needed (thus saving the fuel that would otherwise be burned to keep the pilot light lit).

Signs that something's not right with the furnace include:

- Unusual noises such as rumbling, clunking, or squeaking
- A gas pilot light that's not burning blue with a few yellow streaks
- An oil pilot light that's not burning yellow
- More frequent operation cycles than usual
- Inadequate heating or cooling
- Unusual odors (although a dusty smell when the furnace is switched on after sitting idle for several months isn't unusual)
- Rust on the exterior of furnaces, ductwork, oil tanks, or boilers
- Smoky marks around the furnace exhaust

Call a qualified repair professional immediately to deal with these problems. Otherwise, your regular maintenance includes changing or cleaning furnace filters, making sure you have sufficient oil in your oil system's tank, and keeping humidifiers and ductwork clean.

Replacing and Cleaning Furnace Filters

Furnace filters clean the air flowing into the furnace. This makes the air flowing through the ducts and into the house cleaner and reduces the load on the furnace motor. It also increases furnace efficiency, thus decreasing utility bills.

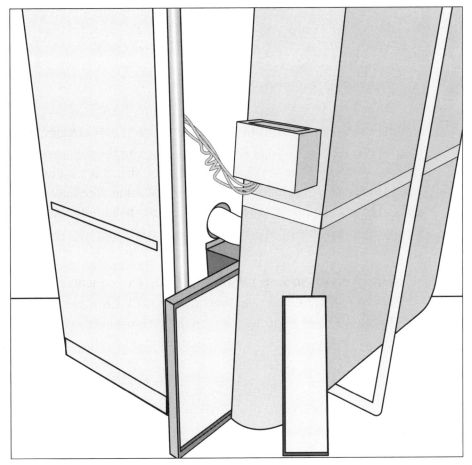

▲ Cleaning or replacing the furnace filter regularly is one of the easiest and most effective fix-it jobs around the house.

To replace the filter, first shut off electrical power to the furnace, either at the furnace's switch or at the house's main electrical panel. If you can't do this, turn the thermostat right down to prevent the furnace from coming on.

Look for a filter pocket located on the ductwork leading to the furnace. These allow you to slide the filter in and out easily (some furnaces may have two pockets and two filters, so don't worry if you find more than one—you need to replace both). If the filter is stuck in the pocket, use a screwdriver or small pry bar to pull it out far enough that you can then grip it with your hand to remove it.

If there's no filter pocket on the ductwork, the filter is located within the furnace. Remove the furnace panels so that you can look inside. The filter is probably held in place against the side of the furnace with a metal clip. Undo the clip and remove the filter, being careful not to knock it against any of the furnace components.

If your filter is a permanent style, you can clean it and replace it. Although running a gentle spray from a garden hose through the filter works well, it's not practical to do that outside in the middle of winter. Instead, wash the filter out in a utility sink (if you use a bathtub, lay down towels or blankets to protect the tub surface, because the filter will scratch it). Let the filter dry, and then reinstall it. Pay attention to the directional arrow on the filter; it points the same way as the air flows.

ESSENTIAL

Have disposable furnace filters on hand, even if your filter is a permanent style. That way, you can install a disposable filter in the furnace, allowing you to operate the furnace while the permanent filter is drying.

If your furnace uses disposable filters, buy high-quality replacements such as electrostatic types that work more efficiently and need replacing less often. Always check the filter size before heading to the home center, as there'll be an entire aisle of different sizes to choose from. Remember to install the filter with the arrow pointing in the direction that the air is flowing.

Filters should be changed or cleaned every one to three months, depending on the filter type, how dusty your outside environment is, and whether you have furry pets. Start by checking the filter every month. If it looks dirty, clean or replace it. If it doesn't, you may be able to extend the period between cleanings.

When you remove or replace the filter, check how it's fitting within its pocket. There shouldn't be any air spaces between the filter and the housing against which it sits that would allow air to flow past, instead of through, the filter. You may need to call in a repair expert if the filter isn't sealing properly, but in the short term, sealing the gap with duct tape will work.

Ductwork Maintenance

The ducts leading from the furnace to individual rooms in the house will accumulate dust and dirt over time. While it's good practice to regularly remove the individual room registers and vacuum inside the duct as far as you can, that won't clean out all the dirt. Every five years or so, have a professional duct-cleaning company clean the ducts (do this more or less frequently depending on how sensitive house occupants are to dust, how dusty your outside environment is, and whether you have furry pets).

You can also buy filters that fit behind the individual registers that will help to reduce the dust particles coming into the room from the ducts. Replace them as soon as they start looking dirty, to maintain an efficient airflow into the room.

Inspect your ducts regularly for holes, rusty areas, or loose connections between ducts. Seal these by cleaning the surface, installing metal screws where necessary to tighten joints, and covering them with duct tape designed for warm surfaces.

Cleaning Forced-Air Furnace Humidifiers

By adding moisture to the air, the humidifier on your furnace can make your indoor environment feel much more comfortable. It's important, however, to keep the humidifier clean and free of molds and mineral deposits that would otherwise spread throughout the house on the furnace's airflow or reduce the humidifier's efficiency. Plan on cleaning your humidifier monthly.

A humidifier will likely be one of two types: a drum, which rotates a circular pad through a water tray; or a drip, in which water drips through a pad. Both work by transferring the moisture from the pad to the air flowing through the humidifier and into the house through the ductwork.

Cleaning a Drum Humidifier

First, shut off electrical power to the furnace, either at the furnace's switch or at the house's main electrical panel. If you can't do this, turn the thermostat right down to prevent the furnace from coming on. Remove any screws holding the humidifier's cover in place so that you can take off the cover. You'll be able to see how the circular pad runs through the water that sits in the tray beneath the pad. Ensure that the water is, in fact, soaking the pad.

QUESTION?

How do I know if the water level in the humidifier tray is high enough?
Check your furnace owner's manual or the humidifier instructions (if it was an add-on). They often specify a depth for the water. They'll also specify how to adjust the water level to either increase or decrease it as needed, but look for an adjusting screw on the float that sits in the water tray.

With one hand on either side of the circular pad (the drum), lift it out. The pad is held in place by a plastic framework on either end that's secured either by a nut or a clip. Undo it so that you can inspect the pad. If it's especially dirty or stiff (which often happens if the humidifier hasn't been cleaned for a while), it's best to replace it. Otherwise, you can dip the pad in a bucket that contains 3 parts white vinegar to 1 part water. Also remove the water tray and clean it out using the same vinegar-water solution.

Put the circular pad back on its framework, and carefully replace the drum in the humidifier. Replace the cover, and turn the furnace electrical supply back on or return the thermostat to its normal setting.

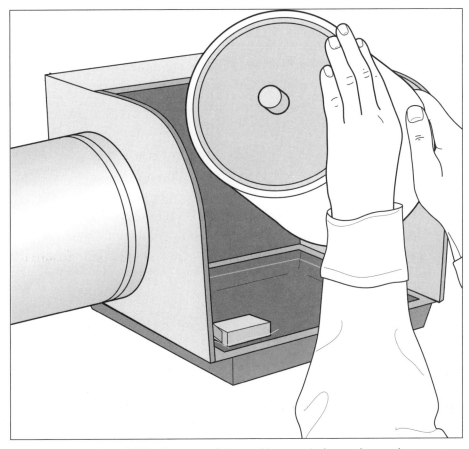

▲ A drum-type humidifier has a pad shaped into a circle, or drum, that rotates through water contained in a tray and then releases the moisture into the air.

Cleaning a Drip Humidifier

First shut off electrical power to the furnace, either at the furnace's switch or at the house's main electrical panel. If you can't do this, turn the thermostat down to prevent the furnace from coming on. Remove any screws holding the humidifier's cover in place so that you can take off the cover. You should see a tube that carries water into a tray that sits above the pad; disconnect the tube from the tray. This will allow you to pull out the tray, and then the flat pad.

The holes in the tray can clog up with mineral deposits; carefully scrape these away with an awl or screwdriver. If the pad is especially dirty or stiff (which often happens if the humidifier hasn't been cleaned for a while), or it's starting to disintegrate, replace it. Otherwise, you can dip the pad in a bucket that contains 3 parts white vinegar to 1 part water, twisting the pad to help loosen mineral deposits.

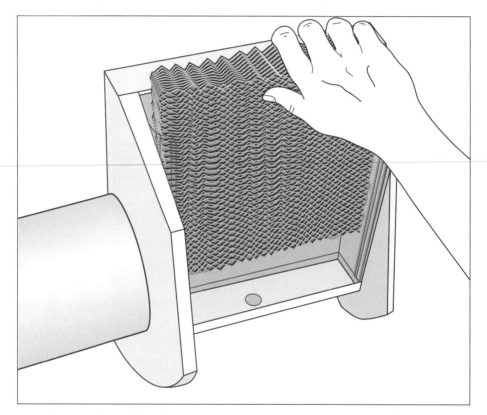

▲ A drip-type humidifier features a tray that lets water drip through a flat pad, which then releases the moisture into the air.

Look at the humidifier to see where the drain hose connects to it to take excess water away from the unit. Remove the hose from the unit, and run cold water through it to get rid of mineral deposits that could build up and block the hose. Put the hose back on the unit and replace the pad, tray, and cover. Turn on the furnace's electrical supply or return the thermostat to its normal setting.

FACT

The only maintenance that electric heat registers need is to be kept free of dust and dirt. If a heat register is damaged or dented, the fins inside the register will need to be straightened—but the register's wiring should also be checked for damage if this is the case, so call in a qualified service technician who's familiar with wiring and repairing these.

Water-Based Heating Systems

Instead of heating air, hot-water heating systems use a boiler for heating water and pipes through which hot water or steam flows to radiators or convectors in individual rooms. The most common maintenance task for radiators is to release the air that can become trapped inside the radiator. The radiator won't feel as hot as it should in this case, especially near the top. This is especially common after the system has been sitting unused during the nonheating season. Check all the radiators to determine how many are a problem.

To release the air, begin with the radiator nearest the boiler (with the heating system on). Look for the air vent, bleeder valve, or vent screw, usually located on the top of one side of the radiator unit. You can use a tool called a radiator key to open the vent, but a flat-bladed screwdriver may also work. Hold a small bucket under the air vent, open the vent, and hold it open until water begins to flow out of the vent. (Wear rubber gloves to protect your hands, because the water from the vent will be hot and may splash.) Then, close the vent quickly.

Repeat the process with the other radiators that you suspect have air trapped inside them. When you're checking your radiators, also make sure that the valves are sealing properly, as leaking valves can damage flooring. Keep your radiator surfaces clean and dust-free, and make sure that the heat radiating from them isn't blocked by furniture or other obstacles.

If you have convectors (with thin fins) instead of radiators, they may or may not have air vents. If not, call in a professional to bleed the system.

There are several maintenance tasks involved with steam systems. First, keep an eye on the system's water-level gauge. This should be located near the boiler, and it should have the required water level marked. If it doesn't, ask your service professional to mark it for you. If the water level is below the mark, open the water supply valve until the water reaches the required level.

Steam-based systems often have noisy radiators. To eliminate knocking, first open the radiator's valve; then raise the opposite end of the radiator slightly, either with shims or by adjusting the bolts in the radiator legs. This should stop water inside the radiator from blocking the steam.

One of the problems with water-based systems is that water contains minerals that can leach out and be deposited on boiler interiors, reducing their lifespan. You may be able to prolong the lives of steam-based systems by opening the drain valve monthly. Place a bucket under the drain valve, and turn the valve so that water begins to drain. (Wear rubber gloves to protect you, as this water is hot.) Keep the valve open until the water looks clean.

Hot-Water Heater Maintenance

Much like water-based home heating systems, the boiler or tank that heats water for your plumbing system needs maintenance—primarily flushing the bottom of the tank monthly to prevent minerals in the water from being deposited in tank. If your hot-water tank is electric, shut off its power supply first. If it's gas, turn the thermostat setting down to switch the heater off, or to the pilot or vacation settings. Your hot-water tank should have a drain valve near the base to which you can attach a garden hose. With the opposite end of the hose draining into a floor drain or a bucket, open the valve. When the water starts to run clear, close the valve.

The pressure relief valve that sits on top of a hot-water tank is an important safety feature that will open in case of a dangerous buildup of steam pressure inside the tank. It's connected to an overflow pipe that runs down the exterior of the tank, and it should be checked annually (ideally, by the service technician when the rest of the system is being checked). To do it yourself, put a bucket under the overflow pipe and open the valve. It should release water into the bucket. Close it immediately.

If you've never opened the pressure relief or drain valves before, have a qualified service technician open them for the first time. Just like valves in hot-water heating systems, these valves can seize or become blocked with mineral deposits. Start your own maintenance routine only after you know the valves are operating properly.

FACT

Signs that a hot-water heater needs professional attention include water puddling under the tank and rust on the bottom of the tank. Rusty or disconnected flues also need quick attention, because they could leak noxious gases into your house.

Fireplace, Wood Stove, and Chimney Maintenance

Fireplaces, wood stoves, and chimneys should be professionally inspected once a year and professionally cleaned as necessary. In the meantime, you can check the chimney by opening the damper and looking up. If you can't see daylight, don't light a fire until you've had the chimney inspected. Either the chimney is blocked or the damper isn't operating correctly.

By holding a light up into the chimney, you should also be able to see how much creosote (a product of burning wood that is deposited in chimneys and can build up to become a fire risk) is accumulating. Also check the condition of the chimney interior (look for crumbling bricks). If you have any doubts as to the health of your chimney, call in a professional before lighting a fire.

Ventilation System Maintenance

From bathroom and kitchen exhaust fans to house air exchangers, the most important tip for ventilation systems is to keep them as clean as possible. Periodically remove the covers from bathroom exhaust fans, and vacuum the accumulated dust from inside the fan housing. A damp cloth will help clean the fan blades.

For kitchen exhaust fans, you should be able to remove the filter (usually by unclipping it and sliding it away from the fan housing) that collects cooking grease. Clean it by immersing it in hot water with a grease-cutting dish detergent added. Clean the fan blades with a cloth soaked in the same solution. If the filter is starting to deteriorate, replace it with a new one. Similarly, if your fan unit has two filters (a metal one for grease and a charcoal one for odors), the charcoal filter will have to be replaced periodically, as it can't be cleaned.

For air exchangers, first shut off the power supply to the exchanger. Open the cover that protects the filter, and remove and clean the filter (for the filter location, check your owner's manual). Replace the filter and cover, and restore the power supply.

Air Conditioner Maintenance

Air-conditioning systems and heat pumps (which pump cooled air in summer and heated air in winter) share similar maintenance procedures, which focus on keeping them clean.

ALERT!

Always wait five to ten minutes after you've shut off the power to an air-conditioning unit before removing its cover or cleaning around it. These units contain capacitors that store electricity, so you need to let the electricity discharge first.

Room Air Conditioners

Shut off the power supply to the unit, and wait five to ten minutes to let the capacitor discharge. Take off the unit's front grill. This should reveal the filter that sits on the cover. Remove the filter, and either vacuum it or wash it to clean it. Let it dry before reinstalling it. This should be done every two to four weeks.

If you can access the rear of the unit fairly easily, you can remove its back grill so that you can see its fins. Use a vacuum or soft brush to gently clean them, and use a fin comb of the appropriate size to straighten any bent fins. You should also be able to reach into the drain pan to clean any deposits or dirt that have accumulated in it.

Replace the grills and the filter. If the grills are dirty, you can vacuum them, wipe them with a damp rag, or brush away the dirt with a soft brush.

Central Air Conditioners/Heat Pumps

Shut off the power supply to the unit, and wait five to ten minutes to let the capacitor discharge. Clear any brush or plants that are blocking airflow immediately around the unit. Undo the screws holding the top grill to the unit so that you can remove the grill—carefully, because in some models, the motor and the fan are attached to the top grill. Use a soft brush or vacuum to remove any dirt inside the unit.

ESSENTIAL

If your air-conditioning unit has a removable or replaceable filter, replace or clean it just as you would for a forced-air furnace filter (see the previous section, and check your owner's manual for its location). Check it monthly at first, to gauge how often it needs cleaning or replacing.

Take off the grill that circles the unit if necessary, and gently clean the fins and the coil with a cloth or a soft brush, or the spray from a garden hose. Check the fins and straighten them if necessary with a fin comb of the appropriate size. Replace the grills.

Use a level on the top grill to make sure that the unit is level. Either install shims under the unit's feet to bring it into level or adjust the threaded feet if the unit has them.

You've now learned how to maintain—or at least where to go to learn how to maintain—your home's major heating, ventilating, and cooling systems. Remember, however, that maintenance is no substitute for annual servicing by a qualified professional. If in doubt, call in a pro. Ⓔ

Chapter 21

E When You Can't Do It Yourself

There will inevitably come a time when you can't do it yourself—when you need to call a professional. So, how do you find the right qualified tradesperson for your particular job? Most importantly, how do you avoid the not-so-reliable contractors out there who are in the game to make a quick profit? In this case, a little knowledge goes a long way.

Knowing When to Say No

An essential skill for your personal list of fix-it techniques is knowing when you can't—or shouldn't—fix it. This will be obvious if a fix-it job covers potentially dangerous situations where your own knowledge is sketchy, such as electrical, heating, and refrigeration systems. The risks here are obvious—electricity, if not respected, can kill; a malfunctioning heating system can be lethal as well; and some of the chemicals used in refrigeration are, at the very least, toxic to the environment.

The risks in other situations, such as fixing a second-story windowpane, are less obvious. In these cases, you need to assess a worst-case scenario before you start the job. Ask yourself the following questions:

- What is the worst possible thing that could happen (e.g., falling off a ladder, breaking the window glass, cutting yourself)?
- Do local building codes require a licensed tradesperson for this job (e.g., electrical systems)?
- Do you have all the right tools for this job (e.g., a sturdy ladder that will safely reach the window)?
- Are you comfortable in this working environment (e.g., no fear of heights)?
- Are you familiar with the necessary materials, tools, and techniques?
- Do you have backup available in case you need extra materials or expert advice?
- Do you have someone who can help you or call for help if you run into trouble?

FACT

If potential risks involve you or your family's health and safety, or the structural integrity of your house or its operating systems, think before you start. If you're unsure, always choose the route of caution (i.e., calling in an expert), even if it's more expensive.

Essentially, you're conducting a risk-benefit analysis. What are the potential risks involved in the fix-it-yourself job—to yourself, to your family, and to your house? What are the benefits of fixing it yourself? Are the risks worth it? Most of the time, such as when you're fixing a damaged piece of siding on the exterior ground floor of the house, the risks will be minor. The worst-case scenario here might be having the repair be more noticeable than it should be. At worst, you may need to ask an expert to fix your fix-it job (it won't be the first or last time they've been called in for this reason).

Finding Qualified Contractors

Whether you need a new electrical outlet wired or your entire basement refinished, you need to select a contractor with a style, size, and skill range that suits the job. Some contractors prefer to handle exterior work; others are equipped for kitchen specialties; still others are happy to take on a full range of work.

When you're searching for a contractor, start by asking friends, coworkers, neighbors, and other contacts for recommendations. It's a fact of life within the renovation industry that advertising, while useful, isn't nearly as effective as word-of-mouth recommendations from satisfied customers. Ask what type of job the contractor worked on (someone who did a great job on your neighbor's garage might not be the ideal choice to refit your kitchen).

Other sources of qualified contractors include local homebuilders or renovators associations, material suppliers (vinyl siding retailers, for example, may have a list of licensed installers), home renovation expos, and home centers. You can even drive around residential areas, looking for similar work being done (many contractors put up a sign with their name and phone number).

QUESTION?

How do I find a contractor for small around-the-house jobs?
Check your phone book for "handyman" services. Several companies feature experienced, often semiretired, tradespeople, including plumbers, electricians, and carpenters, who specialize in small jobs that larger contractors often aren't interested in.

Once you have a draft list of potential contractors, start narrowing it down. Do they take on your type of job? How long have they been in business? Are they registered with your local building department? Are they licensed by local or state authorities? Do they post a performance bond (a sum of money that's returned to them at the successful completion of the job, which protects your financial investment in case of the contractor's bankruptcy or nonperformance)? Do they carry workers compensation, liability, and property damage insurance coverage?

Other questions include whether they use employees or subcontractors (either is fine, but you'll need to make sure that the subcontractors are being paid on time by the contractor). Ask how they handle cleanup; ideally, it should be at the end of every day on site.

You can also ask for references. Check them out, touring the job site and asking questions about the customer's level of satisfaction with both the finished job and the whole process, but keep in mind that contractors are unlikely to provide the names of dissatisfied customers. You can, however, check with local Better Business Bureaus to find out if the company has had any complaints registered against them, and whether those complaints were handled to the customer's satisfaction. You can find the Better Business Bureau online at ✍ *www.bbb.org*.

Avoiding the Wrong Contractor

Pay attention to the warning signs that indicate a contractor may not be operating honestly or providing adequate quality. A salesperson who arrives unannounced at your door with news of a safety issue requiring your immediate attention should raise a red flag. Reputable contractors don't use scare tactics or high-pressure sales techniques, such as telling you that the price for the job is on special but must be committed to right away.

Contractors offering lower prices for cash payments should also be viewed with suspicion. Cash payments are designed to avoid paying taxes, and so don't include proper contracts and invoices. If you're unhappy with the job, you'll have nothing in writing to back up your side of the situation.

Also avoid a particularly low bid. The contractor may not have factored in extra costs, or may be bidding on the basis of poor quality materials or labor. A contractor also shouldn't be asking for job payment up front.

Check out business licenses, association memberships, references, and insurance coverages. If they're invalid, stay away from the contractor.

Selecting the Right Contractor

A job tender is all about defining the job as specifically as possible. This allows the contractors to bid for the job on the same basis—using the same measurements and the same materials—which makes it much easier for you to compare their bids and select the right one.

Writing a Job Tender

First, a picture really is worth a thousand words. Taking several photographs of the work area may identify problems to the contractor that you hadn't considered. You'll also need a sketch of the work area, with measurements. If you want to replace the vinyl siding on your home's exterior, for example, a sketch of all four walls, with window and door placement and measurements, will enable the contractors to easily calculate the material required.

ESSENTIAL

For major renovations, such as additions and kitchen or basement refits, you may need properly drafted drawings that detail your plans not only in your job tender but also in the building permit application. You can pay one of the potential contractors to handle the drawings, or hire a draftsperson, designer, or architect.

When it comes to both the design and materials, be specific. If you're replacing a kitchen countertop, include the new countertop's dimensions (shape, width, depth, length, and height) and its materials (granite, laminate, etc.). Specify whether you or the contractor are providing the materials. If you want to use specific brands and nonstandard colors, include these in the details. Where you don't specify materials, leave it open to the contractor to provide an allowance, with the understanding that the material you eventually choose may be more (or less) expensive than that allowance.

The job tender should require the contractor to specify what guarantees are offered on materials and labor, what liability and workers compensation coverage they cover, and their business license numbers. The contractors also need to specify the length of time their bids remain valid.

Making Your Choice

Some of the bids submitted on the basis of your job tender may be clearly unsatisfactory to you—prices that are too high or suspiciously low, for example, or contractors who haven't followed the materials and specifications that you laid out, and haven't offered explanations for the differences.

The contractor will most likely return a total quote to you, rather than quoting on each individual item in the tender. If you're concerned that the job will cost more than you can afford, call the contractors and ask what you and they can remove from the contract to reduce it to your budget level. They should be happy to negotiate with you and make suggestions.

Investigate the bids that look acceptable. Call to check that insurance coverage, license numbers, and workers compensation coverage are all valid. Call your local building inspection department to find out if the contractor has a good track record with them.

Making a choice also comes down to gut instinct. Can you talk to and work with this contractor? Is the contractor listening to your needs and concerns, and making helpful suggestions? Do you trust them?

The Job Contract

Your job tender, and the contractor's bid on it, will provide the basis for the contract, which basically specifies what you and the contractor are each responsible for. Make sure that all of the following elements are contained in the contract, and don't sign a document that you're not fully satisfied with. You and the contractor will sign two copies of the contract, and you'll each keep one. If you sign the contract but then reconsider, check your state or local "cooling off" period to see if you can cancel the contract without penalty (usually within three days of signing the contract).

FACT

Many homebuilders or renovators associations offer brochures or even contract templates to use when drawing up your own contract or job tender, or to guide you in reading the contract that the contractor offers you.

- The basics. The contract needs to include your name and address, and the contractor's name, address, and phone number. License and taxation identification numbers, membership in builders or renovation associations, and proof of insurance and workers compensation coverage should be included.
- Building permits. Specify who is responsible to apply for and obtain any required building permits. Include who is responsible for supplying any drawings that the application requires.
- Job description. The contract needs to describe what work will be performed and which materials and designs will be used. This includes drawings. You also need a form for handling changes to the work. These "change orders" will act as amendments to the contract, specifying the change, addition, or deletion of the work described in the contract, and the resulting change in price.
- Payments. Lay out a payment schedule that relies on the amount of the job that has been completed to your satisfaction. Never sign a contract that requires payments on specific dates; those dates could come and go without any work being done
- Schedules. Estimated start and completion dates should be included, but remember that weather and material delivery delays may be beyond the contractor's control.
- Guarantees. The contract needs to specify what guarantees are offered on the various materials, and on the job itself. How long do the guarantees last, what exactly do they cover, and who is responsible

(i.e., you or the contractor) for following up if the materials or job quality fails?

- Dispute resolution. You may never need to put this clause into action, but if you can't resolve a problem with the contractor informally, having a dispute resolution clause to rely on will provide important backup.
- Contract termination. The contract also needs a termination clause, so that either you or the contractor can pull out if necessary. This clause can include valid reasons for termination, and the cost to terminate.

ALERT!

Always obtain written receipts for payments that you make to the contractor, and keep them handy in a file folder, along with copies of canceled checks or bank statements showing that your payment was cashed.

Working with the Contractor

Good communication with your contractor is essential. Find out what the contractor needs and expects from you. At the very least, you must provide access to the job site, be available to the contractor and the tradespeople, and respond to questions with reasonably quick decisions. Make sure you have an after-hours or emergency number to call in case of urgent problems.

You also need to know what to expect from the contractor. They should keep in touch about progress and next steps, let you know what measures they'll be taking for cleanup and protecting areas outside the immediate job site (by sealing off doorways with plastic sheets, for example), and tell you when to expect various tradespeople.

Determine who on the contractor's staff you should be dealing with. Your job may have a specific person who's in charge, and that is the person you need to talk to if you run into trouble with subcontractors or workers not showing up when scheduled or with the quality of the job. Check on daily progress, visit the job site regularly (if you can't be there all the time), and make sure that the materials and design specified in the contract are the ones that are actually being installed or created.

If you notice problems, or have questions, voice them to your contact immediately. If you delay, the problem or mistake may become permanent, or at least a serious hassle to reverse. It's good practice to write the questions down and plan a time with the contractor to talk about them either by phone or in person. That way, you'll be less likely to forget an issue or be rushed for time.

FACT

Use common sense when preparing the job site for the contractor. Remove valuables that could be broken, clear the area so that there's lots of room to work, and take measures to protect walls, flooring, and furniture. Talk to the contractor about the need to take paintings off walls, for example, and dishes out of cabinets.

Expect that a renovation or even a fix-it job can escalate. It's impossible to anticipate every contingency, and when you're working on an older home, one job can quickly reveal new problems. Be available to the contractor to deal with these, and enlist the contractor's help in finding a solution that's within your budget (they've often run into similar difficulties before, and should have good ideas to share).

Anticipate that the quoted price for the contract will increase as you deal with unexpected problems, or if you change your mind about materials or design. Making changes after the contractor has started the job is one sure way to inflate the price.

Keep in mind, too, that the contractor is likely working on jobs other than yours. This is just the way that the industry works. The contractor's task is to keep the momentum going on your job, but it helps if you can be understanding of the contractor's position, too.

Never underestimate the effect of a friendly conversation with the contractor or tradespeople on site, or the arrival of coffee and donuts, or soda on a hot day. It's one of the oldest rules in the book, and it still works: Treat your contractor as you yourself would want to be treated.

Resolving Problems

Early identification of problems is key to resolving them successfully, but it won't always help. If you're unhappy with the job's progress or quality, call your contractor right away and express your concerns. Have a list of specific problems handy, and tell the contractor when you expect to hear back on how the problems will be resolved. Approach the problem from the perspective of a negotiation. Remain pleasant, but firm, about the need for resolution.

If you're not satisfied with the contractor's response, put your concerns in writing, and send them to the contractor via a registered letter. Include a reasonable time frame for the contractor's response. At this point, you can also bring in a home inspector or qualified expert as a second opinion.

In a situation where you're still not receiving an adequate response, send another registered letter to the contractor, with a copy of the first one attached, but this time also send copies to your lawyer, local building department and builders/renovators associations, and the Better Business Bureau. Check whether an association that the contractor belongs to has a dispute resolution process that you can use.

ALERT!

Don't sign a certificate of completion (which contractors often ask for) or make the final payment due at the end of the job unless the job has been fully completed (no punch list tasks left), and you're satisfied with the quality of the job.

This book has walked you through recognizing and fixing a wide variety of problems around and inside your house, from leaky pipes to cracked sidewalks. Whether you choose to fix the problems yourself or hire a qualified professional instead, knowing how your house works, what problems you're likely to encounter, and how to solve those problems will save you both time and money. It will also protect the financial and emotional investment that you have in your house, helping to make it a home for you and your family. Enjoy it: You deserve it!

Appendix A

Resources

**American Architectural
Manufacturers Association**
☎ 1-888-323-5664
✍ *www.aamanet.org*

**American Association of Poison
Control Centers**
☎ 1-800-222-1222
✍ *www.aapcc.org*

**American Homeowners
Foundation**
☎ 1-800-489-7776
✍ *www.americanhomeowners.org*

American Institute of Architects
☎ 1-800-242-3837
✍ *www.aia.org*

**American Society of Home
Inspectors**
☎ 1-800-743-2744
✍ *www.ashi.com*

**American Society for the
Prevention of Cruelty to Animals**
☎ 1-888-426-4435 (Animal Poison
Control Center)
✍ *www.aspca.org*

**Association of Home Appliance
Manufacturers**
☎ 1-202-872-5955
✍ *www.aham.org*

**Canada Mortgage and Housing
Corporation**
☎ 1-613-748-2000
✍ *www.cmhc-schl.gc.ca*

Ceramic Tile Institute of America, Inc.
☎ 1-310-574-7800
✍ *www.ctioa.org*

Chimney Safety Institute of America
☎ 1-317-837-5362
✍ *www.csia.org*

**Electrical Safety Foundation
International**
☎ 1-703-841-3229
✍ *www.nesf.org*

**Federal Emergency Management
Agency**
☎ 1-800-480-2520 (publications)
✍ *www.fema.gov*

**Gas Appliance Manufacturers
Association**
☎ 1-703-525-7060
✍ *www.gamanet.org*

Living with Wildlife (MSPCA)
☎ 1-617-522-7400
🖂 *www.livingwithwildlife.org*

**National Association of
Home Builders**
☎ 1-800-368-5242
🖂 *www.nahb.org*

**National Association of the
Remodeling Industry**
☎ 1-800-611-6274
🖂 *www.nari.org*

National Fire Protection Association
☎ 1-617-770-3000
🖂 *www.nfpa.org*

National Glass Association
☎ 1-866-342-5642
🖂 *www.glass.org*

National Lead Information Center
☎ 1-800-424-5323
🖂 *www.epa.gov*

**National Park Service (Architecture
and Heritage Conservation)**
🖂 *www.cr.nps.gov*

National Safety Council
☎ 1-630-285-1121
🖂 *www.nsc.org*

National Wood Flooring Association
☎ 1-800-422-4556
🖂 *www.woodfloors.org*

Organization for Bat Conservation
☎ 1-800-276-7074
🖂 *www.batconservation.org*

**Plumbing-Heating-Cooling Contractors
Association**
🖂 *www.phccweb.org*

Poison Prevention
☎ 1-301-504-7058
🖂 *www.poisonprevention.org*

**U.S. Consumer Product Safety
Commission**
S1-800-638-2772
🖂 *www.cpsc.gov*

**U.S. Environmental Protection
Agency**
☎ 1-202-272-0167
🖂 *www.epa.gov*

U.S. Fire Administration
☎ 1-301-447-1000
🖂 *www.usfa.fema.gov*

Water Quality Association
☎ 1-630-505-0160
🖂 *www.wqa.org*

Window Covering Safety Council
☎ 1-800-506-4636
🖂 *www.windowcoverings.org*

Wood Floor Covering Association
☎ 1-800-624-6880
🖂 *www.wfca.org*

Maintenance Schedule

This list will help you keep track of the things you should do on a regular basis to keep your house problem-free.

Monthly

✓ Test smoke and carbon monoxide detectors

✓ Test GFCI outlets

✓ Check fire extinguisher pressure gauges

✓ Check automatic garage door safety

✓ Clean or replace forced-air heating/cooling system filters

✓ Keep leaves/shrubs/debris away from central air-conditioning unit

✓ Partially drain hot water tank

✓ Pour water into floor drains to keep traps full

✓ Check for water leaks under plumbing and hot water heater fixtures

✓ Clean stove exhaust filters

✓ Inspect for signs of insects

Semiannually

✓ Inspect your home (see Chapter 1)

✓ Hold family fire drills

✓ Install/remove storm windows

✓ Install/remove window air conditioners

- ✓ Check and clean gutters and downspouts
- ✓ Check exterior vents for operation and screening
- ✓ Service outdoor tools
- ✓ Adjust forced-air system dampers for heating/cooling seasons
- ✓ Check sump pump systems

Annually

- ✓ Inspect, test, and maintain water well
- ✓ Have fuel-burning systems and appliances serviced
- ✓ Operate circuit breaker switches on main electrical panel
- ✓ Test seldom-used valves, such as the water shutoff
- ✓ Replace smoke and carbon monoxide detector batteries
- ✓ Test smoke alarms with a blown-out candle
- ✓ Lubricate locks with graphite powder
- ✓ Clean and repair window screens
- ✓ Pressure-wash roof, exterior walls, and garage floor
- ✓ Winterize exterior faucets
- ✓ Protect shrubs and trees for winter
- ✓ Weather-strip and caulk exterior
- ✓ Weather-strip interior windows and doors
- ✓ Replace programmable thermostat batteries
- ✓ Inspect septic system
- ✓ Prune trees to keep branches away from roof

Index